THE OSTRICH WAKES

For Judy —
Great working with you
on AI.

With warmth & peace,
Jean Davison

ALSO by Jean Davison

Agriculture, Women and Land: The African Experience (Edited)

Voices From Murtira: Lives of Rural Gikuyu Women (First Edition)

Voices From Mutira: Change in the Lives of Rural Gikuyu Women:
1910-1995
(Second Edition)

Gender, Lineage and Ethnicity in Southern Africa

THE
OSTRICH WAKES

Struggles for Change in Highland Kenya

Jean Davison

KIRINYAGA
PUBLISHERS

All photographs by Jean Davison
Maps and cover design by Rebecca Bretz
Family diagrams modified from diagrams produced by Jean Davison & Lesli
Brooks in Voices From Mutira by Jean Davison, with permission of Lynne
Rienner Publishers.

Published in the United States of America by
Kirinyaga Publishers
9333 Notches Drive
Austin, Texas 78748
www.kirinyagapublishers.com

Library of Congress Cataloging in Publication Data
Davison, Jean
        The Ostrich Wakes: Struggles for Change in Highland Kenya
        / by Jean Davison
        210 pp.   Cm.
        Includes endnote references
ISBN 0-9785150-0-5   (pbk.)
    1. Social/Political change--Kenya‹Kirinyaga District--Kikuyu
2. Women‹youth‹Narratives‹Changing conditions‹HIVAIDS
3. Kikuyu tea farmers‹Kirinyaga District‹Social issues.

CONTENTS

PREFACE

Africa is like an aphrodisiac. Each time I think, "That's it, my last trip," something else pops up calling me back. The first time I ventured there in 1977, it was to explore how Kenya's independence in 1963 had changed villagers' lives. I could have gone to Ghana (and later did), but a Gikuyu connection in Kenya prompted me to head for East Africa. I took my kids along to share in the adventure and got hooked on the coming-of-age rites that were still a prerequisite for adulthood in many African groups. I ended up producing a documentary comparing rites of passage in Maasai herding camps with those in Gikuyu farming villages to share with my teenage students back home.

I found the means to go back to Kenya the following two summers, traveling from the central highlands to the Rift Valley, visiting African friends. One of those summers I lived for a month in Eastern province, helping Kamba villagers make bricks for a rural secondary school. In 1980, I was part of a university research team. We interviewed Maasai herders and Elgeo farmers on the impact of Kenya's run-away inflation. Each time I returned thereafter, some magnetic force drew me back to Kenya's highest point, *Kirinyaga,* the mist-shrouded mountain that gave the country its name.

In the early '80s, I lived with an extended Gikuyu family in Mt. Kenya's lush tea-growing foothills, picking tea and coffee with women as they shared their life stories, hopes and frustrations. To talk with them about the more intimate details of their lives, I had to learn their mother tongue, Kikuyu (the name of the language begins with a *K* and that of the people with a *G*). My fieldwork in Kirinyaga took the better part of two years.

Seven Gikuyu mothers, some young and others middle-aged, became the heart of my book *Voices From Mutira: Lives of Rural Gikuyu Women* (Lynne Rienner, 1989; Second Edition, 1996). I've kept track of these women, returning in 1985 and then every other year through 1994. Four of them—now long-time friends—are still alive.

This time round, I want to learn how they've been doing since I last visited in 1994, and what they think of the tumultuous elections that changed Kenya's political landscape at the end of 2002. I'm eager to talk with their twenty-something daughters, sons and granddaughters, who were infants when I first lived in the highlands. How does the quality of their lives differ from their parents? What local and global shifts over the past decade have most influenced them? As tea and coffee producers do they see their lives altered by the expansion of a global economy? With the dramatic change in Kenya's leadership, what are their fears and hopes for the future?

Nagging me are the villagers' attitudes toward the AIDS pandemic. Have their views changed since they told me in 1994, "AIDS is an urban problem, so it doesn't affect us"—as if they were living on high ground. At the time, I was skeptical of their response, having just come from three years at the University of Malawi in southern Africa, where AIDS was beginning to steal the lives of students and faculty I cared about. Its insidious spread horrified me as it swept into rural villages outside Zomba, the university town. Malawians, especially women, knew little about it. Women in Kirinyaga who'd heard of HIV/AIDS in 1994 attributed it to the stress of urban life.

Now, I'm returning to find out.

To honor the need for anonymity, I've changed many people's names.

Jean Davison
January 2006

CHAPTER 1

Election Euphoria

It's the tail end of 2002. Mwai Kibaki has just emerged, like some phoenix from the ashes, to become Kenya's first new president in over two decades. People are celebrating, dancing nonstop in Uhuru (Freedom) Park as I touch down in Nairobi. I've been away for nine years.

Pulling my roll-on suitcases through the double doorway that marks the end of a cursory customs check at the airport, I spy my friend Junet Mithamo and her grown son, Maina. They stand in a tight cluster with other friends from Kirinyaga in the expectant crowd. Junet is a buxom woman with inquisitive brown eyes and skin as smooth as a stretched drumhead despite her 60-plus years. She's wearing a henna-toned pageboy wig that hides her thinning hair. Her son, Maina, is a surprise. He must be visiting her from California where he settled in the late '80s to pursue his studies. He's grown big, like a football player, on an American diet and is casually dressed in a golf T-shirt and jeans.

I wave to them, swinging my whole arm back and forth like a windshield wiper to get their attention. Their faces break into smiles as they surge forward to embrace me.

"*Karibu, Nyina-wa-Stepheni,*" Junet welcomes me. My friends, in keeping with Gikuyu custom, call me "Mother-of-Stephen," recognizing my revered status as a mother.

Maina picks up my suitcases as if they were mere sticks of wood. Karuana Mutiti, my long-time pal and colleague, pushes her way in and hugs me. I don't recognize her for a moment. She has filled out and wears her hair piled on top of her head instead of cropped close as she did when we were working together in the '80s. She's clad in a pale blue suit and black heels, ever stylish. She introduces two men. One is her new "friend" Dr. Mugo; the other,

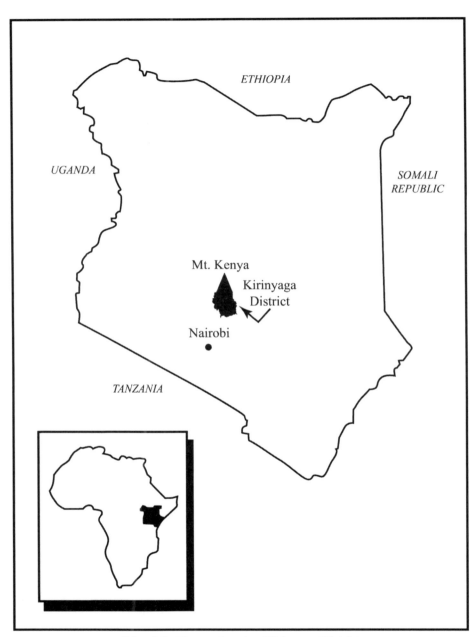

Map 1.1. Kenya showing Kirinyaga District.

his cousin. Mugo is tall and dark-skinned with an engaging smile and warm handshake. His cousin is shorter, lighter-skinned.

"*Tu thii.* Let's go." Karuana takes my canvas tote bag as she walks me out through the crowd to the parking lot. The rest of the welcoming committee trails behind us.

"It's good you didn't want to stay a night in Nairobi," she confides. "It's crazy after the handing-over ceremony yesterday. Can you believe we finally have a new president? After all these years?"

"It's exciting! I can't wait to hear about the election. I've missed you, Karuana."

"You've been gone too long," she teases, steering me towards a bright neon yellow Peugeot. As my luggage disappears into the trunk, I squeeze into the back between Junet and Maina.

Mugo maneuvers out of the airport and onto the Outer Ring Road, bypassing Nairobi streets still crowded with election celebrants. Our destination is Kirinyaga, some three hours north of the capital.

Scrunched between Junet and her son, I feel as if I'm back in a *matatu*. These competitive, grossly overcrowded, undermaintained vehicles (usually minibuses) ferry Kenyans from one place to another, their radios blasting out the latest rap or African highlife to attract customers. Chickens and pedestrians scatter when they see one, lest they become roadkill. Hurtling up the road, a small kernel of excitement begins to grow. I soak up the conversation unfolding around me. It's in Kikuyu. Everyone is talking at once. It sounds like a bebop jam session in high gear. I feel as if I've come home, nestled amongst these ebullient friends. I listen intently trying to make out the words, catch the meaning. The elections are front and center. Kenyans love talking politics. So do I.

"Kibaki trounced Uhuru Kenyatta," Junet says. "But it took three days for them to announce the results! We were waiting and waiting as the district totals came in, showing him way out in front. People started becoming restless when the Electoral Commission didn't announce the outcome. It was waiting for a statement conceding defeat from Uhuru Kenyatta, the KANU candidate."

I nod in understanding. KANU, the Kenya African National Union, had been the entrenched party since independence. Jomo Kenyatta was Kenya's first president. Uhuru is Jomo Kenyatta's son. He was drafted to run, not for any political experience he had, but for his connection with Kenya's revered founding father. Name recognition counts.

"You know he was Moi's handpicked successor," Karuana interjects.

"So I heard."

"When Uhuru wouldn't give up," Junet continues, "the opposition forced the Electoral Commission to meet. It finally declared Kibaki the winner."

I'd been following Kibaki's career and was delighted to learn that a Gikuyu, a member of Kenya's largest ethnic group and the one I knew best through my ties with Gikuyu friends in Kirinyaga district, had won. A veteran politician, Kibaki grew with Kenya's political system in the halcyon days after the country's liberation from British rule in 1963. He served as a vice president under Daniel arap Moi in the 1980s then broke with KANU to launch the Democratic Party in 1991 when Kenya's one-party state drew donor criticism. Known as a shrewd negotiator, Kibaki in 2002 brought together several opposition groups that had squabbled in past elections. These groups coalesced in the National Rainbow Coalition (NARC). Kibaki became their candidate of choice.

"How did NARC pull it off?" I ask now.

"Two things helped," Dr. Mugo offers in English. "First, the coalition groups finally put to rest their differences so they could defeat Uhuru Kenyatta. People feared he'd become Moi's puppet." He pauses for effect. "Another thing, Kenyans, regardless of their tribe or where they come from, were very tired of KANU's obvious corruption under Moi. Twenty-four years is enough!"[*]

"*Ciaigani ni ciaigani.* Enough is enough!" Junet Mithamo exclaims, spitting out the words. We both laugh. It reminds us of a saying that came from a family-planning comedy we once saw together. "This time Moi wasn't able to cheat the people like he did in the last two elections. He's out for good."

It's a defining moment in Kenya's history. I feel the buzz.

"*Nyina-wa-Stepheni,*" Junet continues, "You'll notice changes now. Kibaki has promised to end the corruption. Even the holes you see in this road will be filled." She chortles.

I laugh too, knowing as she does how slowly things move here.

---

[*] As of 2005, the Kenyan government surmised that up to $4 billion may have been embezzled by former officials under Moi with much of it sent to foreign banks.

"Another thing," Karuana picks up the thread. "We're hoping Kibaki will make education free again. That's what he promised. A lot of kids were forced to leave school since you left. With some, their parents don't have means to send them."

"We're tired of being ignored!" Mugo explodes. "Things will get much better now, God willing. Maybe people will even start growing coffee again."

"Why did they stop?" I'm surprised.

"For good reasons," he replies, then turns his attention to a knot of traffic ahead.

"People have been neglecting their coffee for a long time—since you last came," Karuana answers for him. "The coffee board cheats them. It pays the farmers almost nothing while its members line their pockets. People just ignore their coffee now."

What these friends haven't said is that world market prices determined by large multinational commodity traders, such as Cargill, also affect the lives of Kenya's small farmers. To help you understand how the global economy, led by the United States, has come to dominate what my tea-and-coffee-growing friends earn, a little background provides a useful context. If history turns you off, however, leapfrog to the next section.

Kenyan farmers' link with global traders began with its colonization. Before Britain colonized East Africa at the end of the 19th century, the Gikuyu were self-sufficient hunter-gatherers who gradually added horticulture to their survival skills, domesticating wild yams, bananas and millet. Trade with neighboring groups, including cattle herders such as the Maasai, added to their repertoire of foods. There were hungry times, but they were cyclical.

Traders from Portugal introduced maize in the 16th century. By the 20th century, the British colonial government began forcing Gikuyu farmers, both women and men, to grow the crop on marginal tracts of land the administration allocated as "tribal reserves." It fed the British soldiers in World War I. Setting a precedent, the government paid African farmers for their maize in cash. A few Gikuyu men began accumulating wealth by cultivating food crops for a growing army of settlers in and around Nairobi in between the world wars. More often than not these privileged farmers were government-selected headmen rather than traditionally recognized chiefs.

By World War II, most Gikuyu had become accustomed to meeting their basic needs partly through farming and partly through earned income, the latter to purchase key commodities that the British introduced, including kerosene for lanterns, matches, refined sugar, cooking oil and wheat flour. Growing dependency on imported goods forced Africans to seek wage work or produce export crops on their own land. Many Kenyan men (and some women) found employment on European tea, coffee and sisal plantations. However, in Kirinyaga district, coffee and tea production didn't take off until later. The struggle for independence that gripped Gikuyu in the 1950s delayed their growth there.

Coffee, that stimulus of the West, became the primary cash-value crop throughout the '60s and '70s because of growing world market demand, with tea following second. Tea caught up in the mid-'80s, and continued to expand on the slopes of Mt. Kenya and elsewhere as the world's coffee market became saturated. Coffee prices began to fluctuate wildly in the 1990s, finally slumping in 2000. For example, the average price earned by Kenyan growers in 1993 was 48 cents per pound of coffee. It went as high as $1.90 per pound in 1998 and plummeted to 78 cents in 2000.[1] The price has continued to drop even further, with dire consequences for my coffee-growing friends.

Now, on my trip north to Kirinyaga, I've grasped the essence of what Karuana has said about the dilemma of Kenya's small coffee growers.

"I don't blame them for neglecting their coffee. But what are they doing for money?"

"They switched to tea. It's earning good money. And the KTDA, the Kenya Tea Development Authority, isn't so corrupt," Karuana adds in English. In fact, my friends are throwing in English phrases at regular intervals now.

"What happened to your Kikuyu?" Karuana chides me.

"It has suffered because I don't have anyone to practice with at home."

Karuana nods. "Don't worry. It will come back now that you're here."

"You'll be talking like a Mugikuyu[*] by the end of the week," Maina assures me.

I grimace, keeping my doubts to myself.

We've been traveling north on the Thika Road, a divided highway out of Nairobi, for an hour. In the last few minutes, however, the highway has shrunk to two lanes. The traffic is ferocious, with vehicles passing one another as if we were on a NASCAR track. A journey on Kenya's roads is nerve jarring. I'm glad I'm not driving.

It's midmorning, and the car has heated up. "Time for a break," Mugo announces. He pulls off the highway near a pineapple stand.

The piquant smell of pineapple from the nearby fields and the lush prickly fruits lined up on the counter draw me in. Mugo hands me a small carton of juice. I suck it up in three gulps, taking in the neat rows of gray spiky plants marching up the hill behind the stand. Karuana and Junet buy several pineapples, wedging them in the trunk against my luggage. We climb back into the car, our thirst barely slackened. It's stifling inside. We quickly roll down all the windows. There's no air conditioning.

The intense heat that marks December in Kenya beats through the rear window, causing beads of perspiration at the nape of my neck. My legs in jeans are damp with sweat. The conversation around me recedes to the level of humming bees. My concentration wanders away to the landscape.

What I notice most about Kenya after being away for nearly a decade is how lush and green the countryside looks—both from the air and now on our way to Kirinyaga. I'm returning in the same month as I did nine years earlier, but instead of drought-parched brown hills and wilting maize crops, this year the country has been blessed with abundant rains. New green maize crops pucker the brick-hued hills interspersed with ribbons of fecund, dark-leaved banana trees, leafy vegetable crops, and, in Thika, acres of commercially grown pineapple owned by the multinational Dole corporation. It's as if the verdant land echoes the people's election joy.

The startling beauty of Kenya's emerald hillsides always takes my breath away, filling me with exuberance. "New beginnings, a promise of greener times," the hills seem to whisper.

---

[*] Singular of Gikuyu

We cross the broad, muddy Tana River. A few minutes later, we're turning east through the undulating Sagana plains before heading north toward Kerugoya and the shrouded mountain the Gikuyu call *Kirinyaga*. It means "mountain of the ostrich." To early Gikuyu, the mountain's snow-covered twin peak surrounded by icy mist resembled the shape and white plumage of a male ostrich, a misty god-mountain. Early British explorers, taking a cue from Kamba elders who called the mountain *Kinyaa*, labeled it Mt. Kenya on their maps.

People living in Kirinyaga's shadow embody the ostrich spirit. Resourceful and persistent, they cry bloody murder when their God-given resources are plucked from them, as they were under colonial rule.[*] Historically, they resisted domination, retreating into the mountain's primeval forests, only to resurface in different places, twice as strong. Yet, like the ostrich, these highlanders can bury their heads in the sand when something unfathomable, such as AIDS, seeps into their communities.

Kirinyaga is Kenya's heartland. Its iron-rich ridges and hills are in my bones. The mountain's spirit nourishes my soul, brings clarity in moments of doubt. I long for a glimpse of its solid, snow-capped double peak. When I see it shining above the mists, I know I have come home.

As the car climbs north, I begin shifting to get a better look. We're nearing Kerugoya, the district seat. It's where I used to come once a week in the '80s to buy fresh vegetables in the market, collect my mail and drink a cup of tea or glass of Tusker beer with friends in the fading afternoon. We'd end up at the Safari Club, Kerugoya's derelict three-story hotel. It took two *matatu* rides with a transfer in Kagumo to get down from Gatwe, high up on the ridges of the mountain where I lived.

Still, a trip to this bustling town provided a diversion from my stripped-down existence, living in a place without running water (if you don't count a stream at the bottom of the ridge where I collected mine twice daily) or a bathroom. I bathed standing in a plastic bucket barely big enough for my feet. I used the outhouse behind the family compound. There was no electricity for miles. A kerosene lantern got me through the evenings as I read or pecked away on a 1932 portable typewriter inherited from my former mother-in-law. Yes, a trip to Kerugoya with its constant supply of electricity,

---

[*] The Gikuyu believe in a Creator of All, or God, known in their language as *Ngai*.

bustling marketplace and post office that promised letters from home always felt like a holiday.

Mugo slows down, now, as we arrive at the outskirts of Kerugoya town.

I look northward, straining to see *Kirinyaga*, but metallic gray clouds are closing in, and, alas, I cannot find its rugged, snow-frosted peak.

"Are we here?" The town has spread southward like thick glue, clinging to the only tarmac road. I have no idea where I'll be staying, but Karuana had e-mailed that she was taking care of it.

"Aye," she confirms as Mugo makes a turn into a packed, red-clay driveway that is hardly noticeable from the road because of tall grass on either side. "This is home now. I moved in with *Doctari* [the doctor] just before Christmas."

It's a total surprise. I'd envisioned staying with Karuana at the school where she teaches and has a small house. We approach a compound surrounded by high, off-white stucco walls and stop at a pair of sturdy wire gates marking the entrance. A dark-skinned slip of a man on bare feet appears silently. He opens the gates then backs to the side for us to enter. He looks after the compound's yard and doubles as a watchman. Driving through, we cross a large, well-maintained lawn bordered by beds of flowers. The car stops next to a square stone house crowned by a red *mabati*, or corrugated-iron roof.

"The kids are all at home on vacation. Your godson is anxious to see you. It's been too long." Karuana opens the car door.

"I wonder if he'll recognize me. He was only eight when I was last here." There's a hint of nervousness in my voice. Nine years is a long time.

Karuana gets out of the car with a shrug.

Checking out the doctor's house, I see it's divided into two sections. On the right is the main part where Karuana and Mugo, whom everyone calls *Doctari*, live with their daughters. On the left, with a separate entrance, is the boys' quarters, a modern adaptation of the *kithunu*, or bachelor's hut. It still serves to keep boys, once they've been initiated or circumcised, separate from their mothers and sisters. The first time I saw a *kithunu* in the late '70s, my teenage sons were along. We were so impressed with the notion of a separate space for adolescent boys to call their own that when we arrived home we turned our attic into a *kithunu*. It even had an exterior stairway and entrance. My sons loved the arrangement. So did I, especially since one was an enthusiastic drummer in a jazz band—his muffled beats kept my pots moving in the kitchen below.

Now, from the entrance of the *kithunu* attached to Mugo's house spill several guys in their late teens. A girl with carefully plaited braids down her back joins them. She's taller than two of the boys and looks about 16. They eye me from a distance.

"Doctari has two sons and a daughter," Karuana explains. "But the daughter—she's older—usually stays with her mother."

The teenagers amble slowly across the lawn to greet us as Mugo begins unloading the trunk. While I'm waiting, I scope out the rest of the compound.

A straight row of trees and a hedge on one side separate the main compound from several acres of terraced vegetable gardens, maize fields and banana orchards. Dark-leafed mango, avocado and fig trees jut above the fields here and there. A high, dark-green hedge borders the other side. The compound is well landscaped with a generous lawn bordered by tree-sized poinsettias covered with a profusion of bright red blooms at this time of year.

A queenly mango tree holds a central spot in the lawn with two smaller papaya trees in its shadow. Green and blue plastic clotheslines, from which drying shirts and trousers hang, are strung between the mango tree and one of the papayas. In a far corner I notice a rectangular structure with brick walls, covered by a square, bright yellow plastic tarp, open at one end. Large stacks of red bricks stand next to it.

"What's over there? Under the tarp?" I ask Karuana as the welcoming committee of teenagers comes up.

"It's our brick-making project," she explains. "We got together with Mary, my sister—you remember her—and bought a brick-making machine. It's inside. We're making bricks for a larger house we want to build."

The trio of young men and the girl come to shake our hands. I hardly recognize my godson, Wang'oo. He's a bit shorter than the other two boys, with intelligent eyes like his father. The girl, as I've suspected, is Karuana's 13-year old daughter, Wamuyu. Taller than the boys, she's grown, too, and looks older than her years.

All four teenagers wear T-shirts with various messages and logos, faded jeans or slacks, and rubber thongs. The boys' hair is close cropped except for the eldest, Jumbe, who at 20 years wears his slightly longer. He also sports a small mustache. This quartet—along with Karuana, Doctari, and his aged mother, who sleeps out in a small wood-slab house in back but eats her meals with everyone else—become my family.

Karuana shows me where I'll be staying. A carefully made double bed with a solid foam mattress fills most of the room. "I'm glad you can work with me before school starts," I tell her putting my backpack down on the bed. "You've heard my Kikuyu."

She grins. "You do need me this time. Did you bring a tape recorder?"

"Yes. But we'll have to share it."

Karuana was 18 when I first met her in 1983. She's just 40 now, although her exact age is guesswork, as rural Kenyans didn't keep birth records in the early '60s. Still, her mother remembers she was carrying Karuana on her back when "Munyao raised the new flag on Mt. Kenya," when Kenya became independent at the end of 1963. Karuana has settled into middle age. Her jet-black hair is piled up in a knot with a few ringlets spilling onto her smooth forehead. I miss the close-cropped African cut she used to wear that set off her high cheekbones and her large, intelligent eyes that demand respect. Both of us have spread a bit, no longer the slim reeds we were when we hiked up and down the ridges of Kirinyaga, talking with women farmers while we helped them pick coffee and tea. In the 1980s we each had our own tape recorders for transcribing and translating the women's taped life stories. This time we'll have to take turns.

"The toilet is across the hall," Karuana finishes my orientation to the house.

I'm happy about that arrangement. It's a far cry from having to trudge across a cow pasture in the dark, avoiding patties, to a pit latrine.

" I like your Doctari," I tell her. She wrote me that they met in 1998, at a time when she thought she would never remarry. "Where does he practice?"

"He has a clinic in Kerugoya. He calls it 'The People's Clinic' to let *wanachi* know that it's theirs, open to anyone."

"Where did you meet him?"

"We met at the clinic." She giggles. "I'd taken Wamuyu to see him. She had a stomachache or something. We both thought we'd finished with marriage, but then we found our situations were so similar that we began seeing each other. He's a good man, someone I can depend on."

In the mid-'90s, Karuana's former husband had "gotten lost" in another country, abandoning her. She was left with two young children to rear on her own.

"Those days are over," she says, reading my thoughts. "Things are better. After we have tea, we'll drop Doctari off at the clinic and go up to Kagumo. Mrs. Mithamo offered to help contact people you want to meet with."

"I know that Junet is anxious to get home to *mzee*[*] since he just got out of the hospital." Junet's husband is suffering from advanced diabetes.

"When did you learn to drive, Karuana?" In the 1980s when we worked together, Karuana had refused to learn to ride a bicycle— "women don't ride bicycles here"—and the notion of driving a car had been beyond her wildest dreams.

"Two years ago. Doctari arranged for the lessons. "It costs 7,000 shillings [$95]. And a license is hard to get here. They keep telling you to come back after each test, hoping for a little *chai* [payoff]. I've only had the license for six months."

"She drives pretty well now." Mugo gives Karuana a playful grin as he sits down for a cup of milk tea.

"You'll get a chance to see." She looks at me mischievously.

It was Doctari's yellow Peugeot, I learn, that fetched me from the airport. "I need to be at the clinic," he says. "You can drop me there and go on to Kagumo. But don't forget to pick me up on the way back. Actually, I don't use the car once I'm at the clinic. You two can use it for your work while you're here."

After dropping Mugo off, we head north towards Kagumo, slowing down for several mean speed bumps on the outskirts of Kerugoya. What I notice as we ascend the snaking road are rows of spindly anemic-looking coffee plants where robust, dark-green coffee trees once grew on each side. Farmers are indeed abandoning their coffee crops.

Kirinyaga, the ostrich mountain, I note, is still wrapped in a silver mantle.

---

[*] Honorific term meaning elder, or revered one.

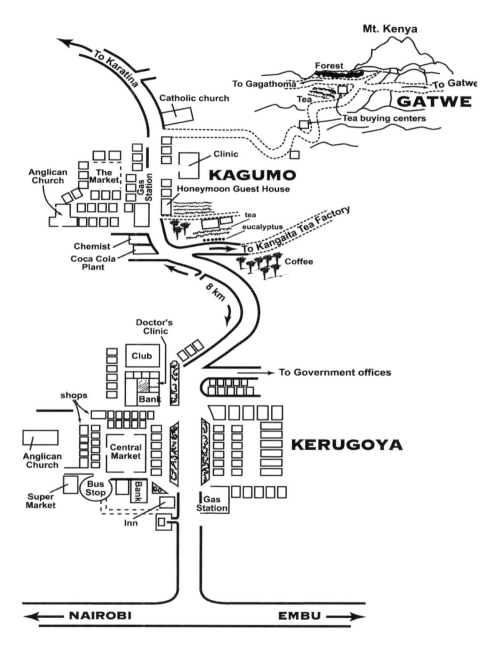

Map 1.2. Diagram of relationship between Kerugoya, Kagumo and Gatwe

CHAPTER 2

Kagumo Village Outgrows Its Bark

Just south of Kagumo, named for a small fig tree that grew into a stately shrine where Gikuyu elders once made their sacrifices, we reach the turnoff to Junet Mithamo's compound. I'm shocked to see a brightly painted, two-story building with a long veranda on the top floor at the corner of her drive. The building faces the main road. On the front of the veranda's solid wood railing is a sign running its length. It is painted flamingo pink with large block letters in ice blue. They read "HONEY MOON GUEST HOUSE" and below, in carefully scripted English, "Self and Single Rooms, Hot Water, Guaranteed Spacious Car Park." I love the sign's entrepreneurial savvy. The whole edifice is painted electric turquoise with a brown geometric border around the bottom. It's outrageous and appears to be emblematic of the changes hitting Kagumo.

"*Niki giki*? What's this?" I turn to Junet, thinking the roadside inn might belong to her.

"Kagumo has grown since you were last here," she gestures toward the main road. "This guest house was put up four years ago. It belongs to a businessman."

In one decade, Kagumo has transformed itself from a sleepy market village to a full-blown, frontier-style town. Visible from the corner of the Mithamo's drive are three- and five-story buildings flanking the tarmac road. Electric lines hang haphazardly across it. Minibuses and ancient station wagons functioning as *matatu* cruise up and down, their horns beeping to get attention while one or two boys, known as "*touts*," hang precariously from their doors with one hand, calling out the *matatu*'s destination at pick-up spots along the road. "Kerugoya? Kerugoya?" "Embu? Embu?" A *matatu* driver won't leave until the boys have filled the *matatu* to the gills with passengers, which can take an hour or more some times. Then the *touts* bang sharply on the side of the vehicle to let the driver know he can go. Kagumo has morphed into a noisy place, bursting with energy.

Two and three story buildings are going up everywhere, but sanitation has become a problem as this once sleepy village grows into a town.

We continue up the Mithamo's long drive, turn into their compound and park the car on the lawn. A small beige dog with full teats and four puppies tumble down an embankment and bark at us as we get out of the car. Junet tries to hush them. The Mithamo's stone house hasn't changed, but the outhouse is gone; plumbing has moved indoors.

"*Karibuni*," Junet welcomes us as she takes off her shoes, leaving them on the covered cement porch. We do likewise. Maina disappears around the side of the house as two young women come from the kitchen to greet us. They are Junet's nieces. One leads us into the spacious sitting room where I've spent many hours in the past. Karuana and I settle down on one of several mottled-yellow couches that line three walls, glad to have a quiet place to plan our work. Junet goes to check on her ailing husband.

After some time Junet returns with mugs and a thermos of tea. A niece follows with two glass plates with fried eggs, sausages and buttered bread. The other niece brings out a bowl of purple passionfruit and finger bananas. The first one returns with a pitcher of warmed water, a small basin and soap. A hand towel hangs over her wrist. She pours water over my extended hands, catching it in the basin while I wash. I take the towel and dry my hands, then pass it to Karuana. Junet tells us that she'd like to offer a small prayer of thanks for my safe arrival before we eat. We bow our heads, and she stands in front of the coffee table, her soft Kikuyu words falling on my ears like petals on a pond. Kikuyu is a tonal Bantu language, very melodious.

"Now you can eat," she says after the "Amen." Junet is habitually in motion, planning new projects, like the rental building she's putting up in Kagumo's center, managing her tea with its constant harvesting demands and caring for an ill, nearly blind husband. As a former community organizer for the Kenya Family Planning Association, Junet knows and is known by everyone. People seek her advice, as I often did in the early '80s.

"I need to see about some matters," she tells us as we begin eating. "Then we can talk about your project." She disappears, leaving us to finish our eggs and sausages. As I think about it, I can't remember Junet ever sitting down to eat with visitors. She always disappears—like many other rural Kenyan women after they've served a meal. Hospitality is something you do *for* people, not with them.

As we finish our lunch, Junet returns and settles into a nearby couch to inquire how she can help me.

"I'd like to have some discussions with small groups of young women and men in their late teens and 20s. I want to find out how they view their lives in comparison with their parents' time. We'll have to do them separately—the girls and the boys."

"I can help with the girls," she responds immediately. "Do you want both Christian and non-Christian girls?"

I hesitate, perplexed. In the early '80s, most women I talked with were Christian converts (largely Anglican or Catholic). Very few were traditionalists who stuck to the old beliefs in *Mwene Nyaga*, the Creator of All (symbolized in the purity of Mt. Kenya) who controlled human destiny, and spirit worship. None were Muslim or Hindu, the other major religions in Kenya. Muslims live mainly in Eastern Province along the coast and in some urban areas. Hindus, who came originally from India to work on the railroad linking Mombasa with Kampala, Uganda, largely live in Nairobi, Nakuru and Mombasa.

"Are there many non-Christian girls in Kagumo now?"

She tells me there are some. "I'll arrange for two groups, one made up of church members and another of non-Christian girls," she says. "I'll let you know when it's organized."

Junet, as a retired community educator, will always be an organizer. I decide to let her carry on, thanking her for her help.

"When are you going up to Gatwe?"

"Tomorrow. Karuana and I are going to spend New Year's Day up there. We should find people at home." I'm thinking about all the people I have to see up in this more remote area where I once lived as I suck the tart seeds and juice out of a passionfruit. Not only are there Nyambura and Wanja, the two women who were in their 20s when they shared their life stories with me in the 1980s, but the families of children I've sponsored for "further studies" in the U.S. over the years. The first one, Mararu, came to live with our family in 1976. His brother and girlfriend followed in 1980. Njoki, pronounced "Jo-key," arrived in 1987. She's like a daughter to me. A diabetic with little hope of securing a constant supply of insulin in rural Kenya, at 16 she left Gatwe, accompanied by my oldest son and his fiancée who were visiting Kirinyaga at the time. Njoki made the long trip to California in hopes of finding a solution to her medical problem and further education. She found both. She's now a nurse. All but one of the Kenyans completed college and found jobs in the U.S. None returned to Kenya to help their country, as I'd hoped they would. Lack of job opportunities deterred them.

"This afternoon," I continue with Junet, "we want to visit Wainoi."

"Who?" Junet asks.

"*Wainoi wa Karani*," Karuana identifies Wainoi with her husband.

"Oh…that midwife," Junet says with barely masked distain. I've always suspected that she and Wainoi don't get along. Junet views herself as a modern woman. She views Wainoi as backward and demanding. But both women are movers and shakers. "You know, the husband died this past year," Junet tells me.

"No, I hadn't heard." The news saddens me. "I'm glad you told me. If you'll let us go now, we'd like to leave the car here and walk over to her place."

"That's a good idea. I'll show you a shortcut to the road through my tea fields. Let me get a headscarf, and I'll meet you outside."

Wainoi, in 1984, was a beautiful woman with sharp, chiseled features and piercing eyes that gave her the slightly haughty look of a medieval queen. She also was an ambitious farmer and midwife. I met her in an adult education class; she was learning to read and write for the first time. She'd just turned 50. The leader of a choir, she also chaired a women's self-help group. Our relationship was not always easy. She was bold in asking me for things, such as my coat and a typewriter that I couldn't part with. Her behavior embarrassed Karuana, who tried to make excuses. Still, as I came to know Wainoi, I found she had a unique set of skills that I admired. She had learned them from her mother, as she explained to me in 1984:

My mother was a circumciser and midwife. She was very good at her job. She was a woman who worked fast, without delay. But nowadays, she no longer is a midwife…She used to circumcise girls during Irua.* And she helped women give birth, even removing the afterbirth by pressing on the ribs of the mother. As I accompanied her everywhere, I saw all that she was doing…she did not wash her hands when she delivered a baby. She just took some migio [stinging neetle fiber] and used the string to tie the umbilical cord. Then she'd wash the baby with cold water in a broken cooking pot…I saw that soon after the child came out, she told the mother to kneel down and hold the child close to her. After the mother knelt, my mother would tie the cord and cut it with a sharp piece of sugar cane or razor and then take the baby and wash it. Then she would wrap it in blankets. The afterbirth was taken outside and buried away from the place. Right after the baby was born, I used to hear the women give the ululations—ariririti—five times if it was a boy-child and four times if a girl-child. So I saw all my mother did and I told myself that someday I would be doing like her.[2]

I was delivering women when we were in the concentration camp [the enforced villages set up by the British beginning in 1953 after the Mau Mau guerrilla fighters launched Kenya's independence movement.] *Later, just before we got our freedom, I was about eight months pregnant with Njeri when a woman and her husband came from Nairobi in the evening to visit our relatives from the same home village. The woman, Kabuchi, was very pregnant, too, and she happened to deliver that evening in the house of our relatives. But the afterbirth got stuck up inside her. My brother's wife came for me.*

---

* The Gikuyu coming-of-age rite. It encompassed lessons in adult behavior, responsibilities and privileges as well as circumcision for both boys and girls.

I went to see if I could help. Kabuchi's stomach had swollen by now as it had been several hours since she gave birth. I asked for a razor blade and cut my sharp nails and removed all the dirt and washed my hands. Then I asked for Sunlight soap to apply on my hands and make them slippery. I slipped my hands up inside the woman's body and pulled out the afterbirth. Everybody got astonished—even my mother when she heard about it. So after that, people started talking about what I'd done and the skill I had, and the news traveled wide. For that skill of removing the afterbirth that way, I learned it on my own—maybe it was God that gave me the knowledge. I left right after and returned straight home. I was feeling angry as Kabuchi had given birth and left me still pregnant. [By this she meant that Kabuchi had beaten her in having a first child.][3]

When somebody comes for me to help with a delivery now, I can't go without those people giving me something in return, as going has made me leave my own work.[4]

Sometimes it was yams, sometimes a goat or a chicken. Later Wainoi was paid in shillings as Kenya's rural economy became more linked to a monetary system.

In the early '80s, at a time when Kenya's national health care system was integrating Western medical practices and the infant mortality rate was dropping, the country's birthrate began to soar. The Ministry of Health launched a training course for TBAs (traditional birth attendants). Wainoi enrolled in it. The purpose was to teach TBAs how to perform deliveries using improved sanitation methods and better instruments than a razor for cutting an umbilical cord. They received scissors, rubber gloves, cotton, and a bottle for keeping their things sterile, a boon for TBAs in impoverished rural areas. Equally important, the trainees learned how to deal with difficult birth scenarios and at what point a mother ought to be sent to a hospital. The women were taught family planning techniques they could disseminate. Wainoi loved the course. It made her realize she needed literacy skills to record births: she joined an adult education class. That's the way Wainoi is—creative and resourceful, with an independent streak. I'm looking forward to seeing her.

"There's the track." Junet points to a muddy path between two sections of nubby emerald tea. Workers, with no wasted motion, pick leaves and throw them into large woven baskets on their backs, suspended from tumplines stretched over their foreheads.

"Give Mama Njeri, Wainoi, my greetings," Junet adds politely.

Karuana and I move carefully between the waist-high tea bushes, trying to avoid the sharp twigs that can poke and scratch the unwary. Branches of what looks like a silver pepper tree have been laid down on the path at intervals to protect walkers from falling on the slippery clay mud. We thread our way along the path. When we emerge on the opposite side of the field, two pickers wave and call to us. I recognize them from years back. After greeting them, Karuana and I walk through a stand of eucalyptus trees, crushing the fallen leaves beneath our feet. They exude a sharp odor reminiscent of Vic's Vapor Rub. Arriving at the main tarmac road between Kagumo and the Kangaita Tea Factory, we head north. At a junction, we turn onto a grass-filled path wide enough to be a road. It has seen more foot travel than cars, by the looks of the worn narrow track up the middle.

"I always remember this spot," I muse aloud to Karuana. "One morning when I came to see Wainoi, I found a group of men clustered together here in the maize field, looking down at someone sprawled on the ground. I went over to see what the problem was. The man on the ground, dressed in a muddied shirt with dried blood on it and worn slacks, was dead. 'He was murdered,' one of the men said. 'He was drinking with money to burn in his pockets from the tea bonus. Somebody knew. They must have followed him here and killed him, then robbed the man.' I remember feeling clammy, scared. I had never seen a murdered man up close, let alone in a maize field."

"It's a good thing they don't give the annual bonus in cash anymore," Karuana says. "All men did was use it for drink and meat. Very little got back to their wives and children."

"At least wives have more control over the money since it goes directly to their bank accounts now," I add.

We move up the path, greeting women and children bent over weeding maize plants, until we get to a bedraggled looking coffee field, its trees thin and neglected.

"Wasn't this where I used to meet with Watoro?"

"Yes," Karuana confirms. "That's her coffee."

"This is where she told me, when I asked her if she saw her life getting any better, 'Poverty is like dust.' That stuck with me." Thinking about Watoro, the most impoverished of the women who entrusted me with their life stories in 1984, I feel tears forming. Her analogy had been so apt as we sat there in the red dust under her coffee bushes. Her situation had improved by the time I visited her a decade later. She'd educated all her sons through eighth grade, a great achievement. And she was satisfied with what she earned from her coffee. I was happy for her. Six months later, she was dead of some "intestinal disease." I recalled watching her use a hand sprayer to apply DDT to her coffee plants to prevent copper fungus in the 1980s. I'd warned her about the pesticide's dangers.

Karuana and I continue up the broad path passing several fenced compounds on the left, until we reach the opening to Wainoi's homestead. Three cows tethered to wooden stakes are munching dried maize stalks. Karuana hangs back, looking nervous. I pass into the compound, stepping carefully around pungent fresh cow pies, wondering what is bothering her. Then I remember; she has always distrusted cows, tethered or not. It has something to do with a childhood incident. I step past one of the cows slowly and begin calling, "Hodi…Hodi?" to see if anyone is about. I can smell woodsmoke.

A man in his 30s appears around a small, wooden slab house. It's Wainoi's oldest son, Mwangi. He greets me, shaking my hand. "Yes, I remember you," he confirms.

"We're looking for your mother. Is she here?"

"She's in the *shamba*, her fields. I'll go fetch her."

He's spoken so rapidly, I'm not sure I've caught his Kikuyu drift. I turn to Karuana, who has braved the cows and come up beside me. "She's here. He's going to get her."

"*Ni wega*," I thank him.

Karuana and I laugh about the cows as he runs off. We enjoy teasing each other about our respective fears. She knows mine relate to large, ferocious-looking dogs.

Mwangi returns with Wainoi. She runs toward me shouting, "*Nyina-wa-Stepheni, Nyina-wa-Stepheni,*" throwing her arms around me as we rock back and forth embracing one another. I'm overcome by her welcome, tears threatening, a lump in my throat.

When she backs away, I can see she has lost weight. She looks terribly thin; her cheeks, marked by tribal slashes, are hollow. And, of course, she has aged. She's now 70 years old. But she still cares about her appearance. A striking woman with clean, angular features and a very straight, almost delicate nose, she disappears into her house and reemerges wearing a handsome woven skirt to her ankles that looks like it comes from Indonesia or Thailand. She has on a dark turquoise cardigan over a light blouse. The sweater hangs from her thin shoulders. She wears a patterned red headscarf drawn back and knotted above her forehead covering her gray hair. Her feet are bare.

Once a venerable community leader in addition to being a midwife, Wainoi still has a charm that draws us in. She hugs Karuana, asking her about her family. Then she invites us into her wood-framed house. We sit down on a sofa, and since there are no telephones in rural Kagumo, I explain that we're here to schedule a future visit with her when she's not so busy in her fields.

"I'd like to spend more time talking about changes over the last decade and get your opinion about the situation of coffee farmers in Mutira," I explain. "I also want to talk with your daughters, Njeri and Nancy, to learn about the differences between your life and theirs."

Wainoi nods. "Nancy married a man who lives near here so you can talk with her. Njeri is in Nairobi, but she'll be back next week."

"I'm sorry to hear about the death of your husband, Wainoi."

"Yes, things have been hard since the husband died," she acknowledges sadly. "But my sons and their wives are here."

Sons settle on their father's property, building their own houses for their families. It gives their parents a sense of security in their old age.

We make arrangements to come back two days later then go back outside. "I want to take a photo of you with one of your cows, Wainoi." I pull my camera out of my backpack. She hasn't understood. Karuana translates.

She agrees to my request then says, "When you come next, I want Karuana to take a picture of you and me together picking the tea. That way I'll remember this visit."

Thinking about Wainoi that night, I recalled her telling me about the circumstances of her own birth and how she was raised not just by her mother but her mother's co-wife, Wakaitheri, who later died.

My father Gataie had two wives. The first was my older mother, called Wakaitheri, who was co-wife to my mother. She had four children. The last-born was Wanjira, who was my agemate. My mother, Keru, which means "brown," used to take care of Wanjira after her mother died, so we were raised together. My mother was a widow when she married the man I called Baba [father]. *I never knew my real father because he was killed for stealing someone's millet shortly after my mother married him. My mother was pregnant with me when she went to live at Gataie's.*[5]

Wainoi's mother, like most Gikuyu women of her generation, shared her husband. Gikuyu men historically had more than one wife, if they could afford it, that is, if they had the land and sufficient resources. The rationale, from a woman's viewpoint, was that many hands lightened the workload. From a man's perspective, the more wives he had, the more children he added to his family, which increased his status and worth in the community. Africans measured their wealth in people. Of the 20 Mutira women I knew in their fifties in the early 1980s, half were in polygynous marriages with co-wives, despite earlier Christian missionary efforts to discourage the practice.

Missionaries who settled in Kenya in the 1920s were bent on bringing Africans' social mores into line with their own. Particularly, Protestant missionaries demanded that converts give up polygyny.[*] Some men acquiesced. Others refused. After independence, the practice persisted as it still does outside urban areas. Men in rural Kenya like to marry as many wives as they are able to build houses for and whose children they can support and educate. Legislative bills to outlaw the custom have been periodically introduced in Parliament since 1963, but each time, they have failed in the overwhelmingly male assembly. What has contributed to a decrease in polygyny is the escalation of school fees. Men cannot afford to educate many children these days.

Wainoi was lucky because her husband never married a second wife. Her family had converted to Catholicism by the time she married in the mid-20th century and she reminded her husband that the church forbid a man from taking more than one wife.

---

[*] *Polygyny* is more accurate than *polygamy* because the latter is an umbrella term that includes both polyandry (marrying multiple husbands) and polygyny (multiple wives).

CHAPTER 3

The "Awkward Practice" – Female Circumcision

Christian missionary zeal in the early 20th century led to the division of Central province into several sects. The Mt. Kenya region was split between Anglicans, Presbyterians, Methodists and Catholics. In addition to launching a campaign against polygyny, Protestants, in particular, took on another cultural tradition that was central to the Gikuyu way of life—the practice of what became known as female circumcision. It occurred at the same time boys were circumcised and was an integral part of the ritual that marked coming of age for both sexes in Gikuyu society. For adolescent girls, the genital cutting involved external genital excision, especially of the clitoris, and was performed by trained older women, such as Wainoi's mother. Circumcision was the culminating ritual event of *Irua,* the most important rite of passage in Gikuyu society, as Wainoi relates.

After piercing the ears, one knows that she has left the childish things behind. I began removing myself from childish games and began acting more grown-up, because now the days were being counted for me to go for Irua. *It was the most important ceremony among our people. To the Agikuyu, nobody could carry out a sacred sacrifice unless that person was circumcised. We say, "A goat that has not shed blood cannot offer a sacrifice."*[6] In other words, a girl who had not gone through *Irua* was not allowed to participate in adult rituals and marry. The blood and pain of *Irua* prepared a girl to accept the pain of childbirth later.

Wainoi made it clear that she *chose* Irua. She wanted to participate, but her Christian parents forbad it. Other girls her age were preparing for the ceremony and she felt left out. Girls were circumcised before they had their first menstrual period, which occurred at the age of about 15 or 16 in the 1950s.

When time reached for circumcision, I was a herdsgirl, looking after the goats. My friend came and told me that she would be circumcised. I did not want to be left behind. I decided not to tell anybody, but to just go, because I knew my parents would not allow it. I was not afraid of the pains I had heard people experienced during Irua. I was excited and eager...Before I was circumcised, I was taken to the river by many women of my clan where they washed me and threw me up in the air. Then I was carried to the big field of grass. I quickly put down the mathakwa leaves and sat down on them with my legs spread. I didn't even have a supporter! After being cut, women took me home.[7]

Adolescent boys and girls were socialized to accept the genital cutting along with other aspects of *Irua* because it was a prerequisite for a new social status that was accompanied by increased respect, attention and new privileges.

The ritual might have continued without question except that a missionary doctor, confronted with a botched example of female circumcision in the late 1920s, undertook a campaign to end the practice. It became a contentious issue that amplified the cultural divide between European settlers and Africans in central Kenya. From the 1930s through the 1960s, many Gikuyu, both women and men, stubbornly clung to *Irua* as an integral part of what it meant to be Gikuyu. Partly it was a matter of ethnic pride and partly it was a means of defying British imperialist dictates. Other Gikuyu, mainly Christian converts, began giving up the practice.

A presidential mandate outlawing female circumcision in Kenya was not adopted until 1982. Wainoi describes the quandary that adolescent girls, eager for *Irua*, faced in the early 1950s. It was an issue full of tension, as Kenyan author Ngugi wa Thiongo's novel, *The River Between*, written in the 1960s, illustrated. The practice also captured the attention of Western feminists beginning in the late '70s, a time when I first began exploring the meaning behind female circumcision with Kenyan women I knew well.

In the 1980s, I found that Wainoi was not the only woman who had been through the genital cutting. One of her agemates, Wangeci, had her own memories of *Irua*, different from Wainoi's.

Wangeci and the Knife of Fire

Both of those women [her supporters] *held me while I was being circumcised, one from behind, sitting down with her legs over mine, and the other holding my hands. But when the circumciser*

came jumping toward me, I was not watching. I had been told by my
supporters to look away so I wouldn't see the circumciser and
become frightened. So I was looking up at the sky. The first thing I
felt was a sharp pain like fire– just like you feel when you cut yourself
with a panga, a short-handled machete. *Then I felt my body numb*
and did not feel pain again until three days after the cutting when the
wound got pus.[8]   She related that her supporters took care of her,
changing the bandage on her wound until she healed enough to walk
home.

Sometimes there were only two adolescent girls being
initiated and at other times there were many. Wangeci related that in
one village 18 girls were circumcised and in another six. She said,
When you realize that men, boys, girls and women are watching you,
you make yourself brave.

Another woman who shared her story in 1984, Wamutira,
came from very circumstances to Wangeci and Wainoi's. Whereas
Wainoi's dad had been a thief, Wamutira's father was a chief, the
headman of a large village. And that made a difference in her
experience. Wamutira's mother was one of 20 wives.

Wamutira: No Gain Without Pain

I heard about Irua from my mother. She told me, "You see
so-and-so? She is circumcised now. You are also going to get
circumcised." She told me that first we would make beer for her
brothers who are my uncles and ask them for permission. The reason
that it was my mother's brothers is that my father's brothers were not
as important as my mother's brothers in this matter and they had to
be paid back the [same] *number of goats and amount of beer that*
were given for my mother's circumcision. That is the way it was
done.

I saw many people coming to my father's compound and they
drank the beer we had brewed and then a day was set for me to be
circumcised. On the day before Irua, I was told to go to my oldest
uncle's place and dance for my uncles so that they would give me
money and a goat. I went and danced, holding a wooden club and
showing my uncles my body. They gave me three shillings and a goat
and I went home ready for Irua.

I was never told exactly why I was going for Irua, but I heard
from people that a certain man, who was the first to refuse having his
girls circumcised, had daughters who would never marry. So we used

to get circumcised so we would be able to marry because no man wanted an uncircumcised woman.

I was circumcised at Giagato. In the morning, very early, we went to the river where women would smear themselves with mud, and then in the river we were washed by the newly-married women, those with one child. We were washed to make us clean and pure for the ceremony. The same women then carried us on their backs up to the field where the ceremony was to be held. They did not want us to touch the ground [become unpure].

There were so many people at the field, young and old, who made a circle surrounding the girls to be circumcised. The women would be on the inner part of the circle singing, "Ii, ii, ii, ni kiama. Yes, yes, yes, it is the truth." My circumcision mother [supporter] was Nini, our oldest mother. She helped me spread the mathakwa leaves on the ground where I would sit so that no blood would touch the soil. It was she who held me from behind with her legs over mine so my legs would stay spread while I was circumcised. Another mother held my hands away.

Kamira and another woman called Watene from Gichugu were the circumcisers. Kamira was slender and black. She had a blanket wrapped around her and tied at the shoulder. Before circumcising us, she got a small gourd and emptied muthaiga into her palm and touched herself with it on the face to cleanse herself for the ceremony.

The circumcisers used a kienji, a metal knife that was very sharp with a wide blade like an axe. But nowadays [1984], they use razor blades because there is not so much cutting done. Each time a girl was circumcised, the knife was washed in water and wiped with a special leaf.

Our father, Kuruga, had given those of his girls being circumcised some shillings. He told us that those who never cried during Irua and were brave could keep theirs but those who cried would have theirs taken away. Me? I lost my shillings. I was crying because I was afraid, and I knew it would hurt even before they started cutting.

Three deep cuts were made [to remove the clitoris] and it was very painful. They used to cut deep until a mathakwa leaf fit in. But nowadays, those who want to be circumcised, only the tip of the clitoris is removed. After the cutting was done the wounds were spread with castor oil because there was no [Western] medicine at the time. Then a soft mathakwa leaf, about the size of a woman's

*hand, was stripped of its stem and tied over the wound, using thread,
in between the legs to keep the leaf still and in place.*

*How did I walk home with all that pain between my legs? I
was being held by the supporters who were my circumcision mothers.
They were on each side and another woman was ahead with a small
gourd of water so that if I fainted she would pour water on me.*

*When I reached my mother's house, I went right inside. As I
was not able to climb onto the bed, banana leaves were spread on the
floor for me. I had to sleep on my back because if I slept in any other
way, the leaf covering the wound might come off and then I would
have to have another put in which was a painful operation. So you
see, it was no joke. I was told never to sleep on my sides as the
wound might close up the hole and then I would never give birth.
That was at night. During the day one could sit down on a banana
leaf comfortably. Each evening I would remove the leaf and smear
castor oil on the wound and then put another clean leaf on it.*

*After I had gone through Irua, I felt different. I felt like I was
a grown-up girl, ready for dances. And everybody saw us as adults.
People treated us differently and we were expected to act differently.
Nowadays, you wouldn't know who is mature and who isn't because
few girls go for circumcision, and even when a girl gets menstruation,
you don't notice because girls do not have to stay in the house as we
did.[9]*

Women in central Kenya, especially Christian converts and
those who'd been to school, began giving up the practice of having
their daughters circumcised in the 1980s. Likewise, their daughters,
most of whom had some education, were losing interest.

I didn't attend a female initiation rite until I lived in Malawi.
In that southern African country, circumcision in any form is not
included for girls, though some ethnic groups practice male
circumcision.

The initiation I observed in Malawi, called *Chinamwale*,
educated girls for their roles as adults through songs, talks and
demonstrations. It included lessons about sexuality and how to
handle menstrual periods along with other adult responsibilities.
What I experienced was a four-day celebration of 13 girls' coming of
age, a celebration exclusively for women and girls that emphasized
female solidarity and women's importance in Malawian society. Men
and boys were not allowed anywhere near the homestead where the
ceremonies were held. Property in rural Malawi is still passed down
from mothers to their daughters and granddaughters, rather than from

father to son. Children are given their mother's clan name, like our surnames. Perhaps it is the centrality of women in most Malawian groups that accounts for the difference in their initiation experience. Female genital cutting is not included in most matrilineal groups in Africa.

I did have an opportunity to attend a male circumcision ceremony in Western Kenya in 1984. It gave me a framework for understanding the cultural aspects of *Irua*. The Bukusu are a Bantu-speaking group similar to the Gikuyu. They had given up the practice of female circumcision. I was included in the community ritual at the invitation of Bukusu friends. The initiation was held during a full moon and lasted two days.

A Bukusu Circumcision Rite in Western Kenya

The ceremony began with adults drinking and the unmarried youth of both sexes dancing all night in a special field under the full moon. I could hear them from the house of my Bukusu friends. It was joyously noisy and went on all night.

The next morning, very early, the initiates (several boys aged 12-15) were led down in secrecy to an icy stream to be bathed. Circumcised men and elders smeared the boys' naked bodies with gray mud from head to toe. At the top of their heads a stalk of millet stuck straight up, symbolizing fertility. A beak-like protrusion of mud was built up over the bridge of each boy's nose so "the right eye will not see the left eye," in case one eye should begin to quiver with fear during the cutting event. Only the penis was left clean and exposed. Symbolically the boys were undergoing a transformation, and the mud signalled their re-emergence from the womb of the earth as adults.

By the time I saw the boys coming up in a single line from the river, escorted by their sponsors blowing whistles to alert the crowd gathered in the compound, they looked like beings from another planet. Their mud cocoons totally disguised them. They stared straight ahead, showing no emotion. People of all ages, men, women, boys and girls, were gathered in a ring between huts in the compound. Older women danced in a sexually suggestive way, bringing laughter from the crowd and ululations. It was to teach the boys about sexuality, my host explained. The male circumciser and his assistants were posturing too, weaving their short-bladed circumcision knives about in the air. Suddenly, the circle parted and the boys and their sponsors entered, the dancers retreating to the edge.

The initiates walked solemnly to one side of the circle and stood in a line with their sponsors standing behind them. The crowd quieted, waiting expectantly.

The circumciser, a teacher in a local primary school dressed for the occasion in a green peaked hat and a shredded shirt with cloth tassels, came leaping toward the boys. His assistants followed. All three carried the short-bladed knives I had observed them ritually sharpening and purifying in the flame of a lantern an hour earlier in a nearby hut.

The boys looked straight ahead without flinching as each one was cut. The circumcision was quick, with little blood. Wooden stools appeared and the initiates were allowed to sit down as each boy's mother stepped forward to put a special blanket around her son's shoulders to cover him. I noticed that one boy was shivering, but all had maintained their serious demeanor. None had shown fear. People came forward from the crowd and began dropping shillings at each boy's feet to show praise for his bravery. There was more dancing, and then the initiates were led away.

Having had the opportunity to observe the Bukusu circumcision ritual, I was interested to learn later that an American woman who taught English at a high school in the same area had attended a similar ceremony for Sabaot youth in 1988. Her description resonates with my experience of the Bukusu ritual, except that youth of both sexes participated in the circumcision rite she observed. She wrote:

> At dawn the initiates were led by circuitous routes to a stream, and before being bathed in its water [a restricted part of the ceremony], they were harangued by their mothers and warned not to disgrace their relatives, living or dead, by showing cowardice. After being led back to the compound, they were immediately circumcised. The cutting was public and demonstrated to the community the bravery of the initiated. The boys were cut by a male circumciser while standing; the girls were excised by a woman as they sat with legs spread on the ground, their backs supported by their sponsors. The crucial test was for the initiate to show no pain, to neither change expression nor even blink, during the cutting. Remarkably...the initiates remained utterly stoic and expressionless throughout. We were told it is this

ability to withstand the ordeal that confers adulthood,
that allows one to marry and have children and binds
one to one's agemates.[10]

That such initiations were part of the experience of five out of
the seven original women who shared their life stories in the 1980s
was no surprise. These women viewed *Irua* as a critical event that
elevated girls to adult status. In talking with younger women at that
time, I found their perceptions very different. The two women who
were mothers in their twenties that shared their life stories in 1984
had not undergone genital cutting as teenagers. They considered the
practice to be archaic, a thing of the past. Even the older women
were giving it up for their younger daughters. Neither of Wainoi's
daughters had gone through it.

Women in their 20s at the time told me they knew they'd
made the transition to adulthood when they had their first child.
Becoming a mother had become the defining event for adulthood. I
want to learn, now, how the current crop of girls in their teens and
twenties know when they have become adults. Is pregnancy still the
great event separating girls from women? Or has it changed again?
And is female circumcision truly a thing of the past?

I begin by asking Wainoi, "Do you know if anyone is
circumcising their girls here anymore?"

"*Wi!* You!" she says emphatically. "It's against the law."
End of conversation.

Despite Wainoi's emphatic denial, isolated incidents continue
to occur in the 21st-century. A letter to the editor in the *Daily Nation,*
Kenya's largest newspaper, urges that the Children's Act passed by
the Kenya Parliament in 2002 be enforced immediately to stop the
"awkward practice" of female circumcision. It is still performed in
Marakwet District in Western Kenya. "Even some chiefs allowed
their daughters to go for the ritual [in December]."[11] The writer urges
the government to take stern action to end the practice in Marakwet.
An article several days later in the *East African Standard* blames high
illiteracy rates among the nomadic Pokot as a primary reason for why
female circumcision continues in this area and cites the director of a
non-governmental organization in West Pokot who points out that
girls circumcised risk getting HIV/AIDS due to the use of unsterilized
knives by some circumcisers.[12]

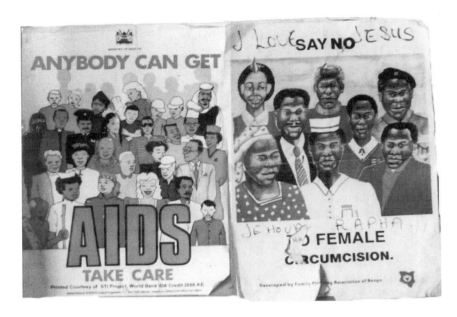

Signs of change: AIDS and female circumcision prevention posters in a Kagumo clinic.

In Kagumo, I'd seen a poster on the wall of a clinic that read, "SAY **NO** TO FEMALE CIRCUMCISION" with an illustration of a group of adults, including a mother, a pastor, a policeman and a nurse, who presumably have rejected the practice. It seems the Ministry of Health is sufficiently troubled about female genital cutting to persevere in its campaign to end the practice.

Female circumcision, or female genital cutting, as it is now referred to by international organizations sensitive to African women's critiques of the way Western women adopted the eradication of the custom as a cause celebre with almost missionary fervor, continues to be a contentious issue. Since the 1970s, Western feminist groups and human rights advocates, fueled by media attention, have shed much light on the various forms of the practice— from infibulation, the most radical form of female genital cutting that involves removal of the clitoris, as well as the labia minora and majora and stitching the vaginal opening to the size of a pea, allowing only for menstruation, to the mildest form that involves slicing or pricking the tip of the clitoris. Not all cultural groups practice the same form. Nomadic herders in Kenya, especially those located close to the border of Somalia, are more likely to practice infibulation than groups farther south, which may practice only the mildest form. Moreover, some ethnic groups such as the Luo in Western Kenya have never included female circumcision in their initiation rituals.

I remember how outraged some Kenyan women were when they returned from the United Nations Conference on Women held in Copenhagen in 1980. Western women had lumped all forms of genital cutting under one rubric, referring to it as "female genital mutilation" to politicize the issue. That inflamed African sensitivities. Ending female genital cutting will take time. I saw at the U.N. Conference on Women in 1985 in Nairobi that its eradication is most effective when those who know it best, African or Arab women who have grown up with it in their communities and understand its cultural history and significance, initiate programs to educate other women about the problems involved in the practice and why it should be abolished. I recall more recently seeing a beautiful, internationally recognized African fashion model, Iman, using the Western media as a platform for speaking out against infibulation and other genital cutting that causes so many young girls and women to suffer. She is a beacon for women and girls throughout Northern Africa. I share these ideas with Karuana as we travel back down to Kerugoya after our visit with Wainoi.

"I agree with you," she says. "African women need to take the lead. When Western women start telling us what to do, it reminds us of the British. We need to find our own solutions to problems. Anyway, *Irua* is a thing of the past here."

By the time Karuana and I get back to Kerugoya, it's after 5 P.M. We pick up Doctari at the clinic and head for the large outdoor market. Karuana wants to get some meat for dinner.

"Don't trouble yourself. I'm not a big meat eater," I remind her.

"I'll try and find a chicken." It takes a while. It's 7 P.M. when we reach home.

Dinner preparations last two hours in rural Kenya, whether a propane stove is available or not. Rice has to be cleaned (a labor-intensive process), vegetables and meat chopped and fried, potatoes peeled and diced before cooking them. Everything is cooked in pots over burners or a charcoal fire in a container. Ovens are rarely used.

While helping to clean rice, which involves removing tiny pebbles and shaft from the grain, I watch television with the family. First on is the nightly news in Swahili, the national language. It's full of the inauguration and tree plantings. I glance down at a newspaper lying on the coffee table. "KIBAKI TAKES OVER," the large headline shouts. A picture of the new president, balding with a fringe of gray circling his still-smooth dome, reveals fatigue. He sits in a wheelchair with his leg up in a plaster cast.

"What happened to Kibaki?" I ask Wang'oo, my godson.

"He was in an auto accident during the campaign. His car was hit and spun out of control on the Mombasa road. Some people blame Moi for the accident."

I ponder this news. Such "accidents" are not unheard of right before a critical election in Kenya.

Local TV news is followed by an American soap opera. Kenyans love American soaps. We watch two of them. I'm surprised I've never heard of them, but then again, I never watch soap operas. The attitudes portrayed in both dramas seem sexist to me. Is this really American life? I finally decide they must be soaps that were unmarketable in the United States so now they've been exported to unsuspecting Third World countries in the same way that drugs or pesticides that have proved harmful for Americans are often exported to such nations.

We eat a delicious dinner of chicken stew, rice, *skumawiki* (chopped kale with onions) and *irio* (a dish made of peas and potatoes mashed together) while the teenagers watch the second soap from the dining table. After dinner I bring out the gifts I've brought from America. I realize that the red sweater I've bought for Karuana based on my 1994 image of her may be a bit snug now, but her children love their T-shirts and sweaters. A third soap opera is unfolding on the TV, so I excuse myself and head for bed, poking in earplugs to block the noise of the television. I sleep like an exhausted horse that has pulled a cart all day.

CHAPTER 4

A Midwife And Her Daughters Reveal Family Thorns

Karuana and I return to Wainoi's home on Monday. Ready for us this time, she's dressed in a two-piece, short-sleeve, pink cotton suit. She takes us into her sitting room and serves tea, then asks about my sons who visited me while I was living in Kirinyaga. Having sons the same age is a bond between us. Her son Mwangi and my sons got on well.

When I visited Wainoi in 1994, she told me she'd given up midwifery, one of the world's oldest professions, because she'd grown old. This time, I want to find out if any younger women in Kagumo have taken up her skills. I ask her the question. Her answer has steam.

None, she says, *but any woman who is having problems in giving birth, I can still assist! That grandson of mine, the one born to Nancy Karuana last year, he was born here and also the one born to Lucy, Mwangi's wife. After each was born, I made out a notification, a birth certificate, and gave it to the chief.*

"Did they choose to have you as their birth attendant?"

No. It was that they called me to go look for transport to take them to the hospital to give birth. By the time I was called it was already too late. But I always leave a sufuria [an aluminum cooking pot] *filled with water near the jiko* [charcoal brazer] *to boil, and I keep a disinfectant ready in case I'm called.*

"ANYBODY CAN GET AIDS," the poster in the Kagumo clinic shouted. AIDS was in large red letters and under it was, "TAKE CARE." I didn't see such posters a decade ago. At that time, most people were in denial: AIDS didn't exist in rural areas. I am beginning to wonder whether a new openness exists about discussing the disease. Or is the concern limited to hospital staff and health officials? I decide to ask Wainoi.

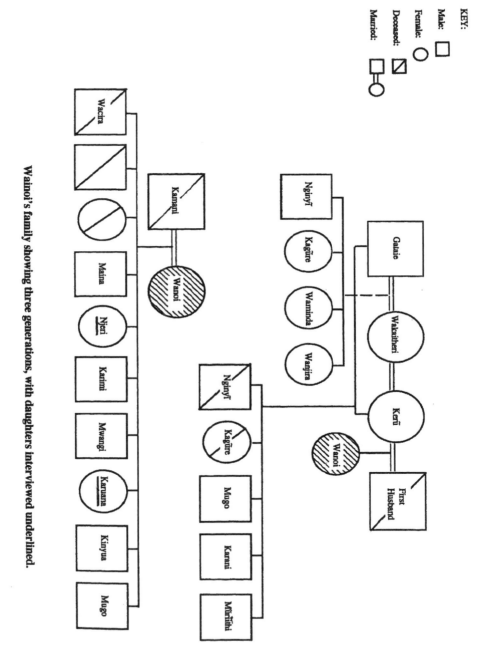

KEY:

Male: ▢

Female: ◯

Deceased: ◩

Married: ▢⃝

Wainoi's family showing three generations, with daughters interviewed underlined.

Telling her about the AIDS poster, I ask, "Are people more aware of the disease than they were when I last visited?"

I don't know of anyone with AIDS. It is not something that old people like me talk about. The most important change since you were last here is that we no longer get any money from coffee. It's been that way for the last four years, which is very bad. As you can see, we have neglected our coffee for tea.

Wainoi has dodged the AIDS issue. Darn. She would rather talk about Kenya's depressed coffee prices. In 1994, Wainoi was cultivating coffee and had little tea planted. But things have changed.

A headline in the *Daily Nation*, Kenya's largest newspaper, announced on Sunday, "Farmers earn less after drop in coffee grade." According to the article, coffee farmers in Kisii (Rift Valley) earned 40 percent less in 2001 than they did in 1999.[13] The Ministry of Agriculture attributed the drop in price to mismanagement on the part of local coffee cooperatives. However, the national Kenya Planters Co-operative Union, which controls farmers' prices, blamed the world market for the drop. All Wainoi knows is that coffee isn't worth growing anymore. It's a lost crop.

Now, she's beginning to complain about what she earns for her tea.

This month we were given a smaller bonus for our tea than the usual amount. We got 14 shilling [$0.14] rather than 20 shilling or more as we did last year. It could be that Moi used the bonus money in his campaign. That's what some people were saying.

These days we get 7.50 shilling per kilo [2.2 pounds] and that is very little. They ought to pay us more.

In 1993, Wainoi was earning 3.50 shilling per kilo for tea, so her earnings have doubled in the last nine years, though small-scale growers are still paid very little by U.S. standards. In addition, fertilizer provided by the Kenya Tea Development Authority (KTDA), which is needed to produce high-quality tea, has become costly.

We get fertilizer for the tea from the KTDA, but it is not free. We pay 1,200 shilling [$16] for a large sack. Like now I needed five sacks for my tea, so 6,000 shilling will have to be deducted from what I earn.

We only have five acres of land here and since there are five sons, each one has a plot. Before my husband passed away, he planned to have the land subdivided. Where the buildings are here, this portion belongs to me, and part for my daughter, Njeri. The sons each have a portion running from one edge [of the land] *to the other. But somebody like Njeri, she already has her portion because the husband arranged for it. But where Nancy Karuana married, the parcel of land is small, so she comes here to cultivate. Land is a big problem now in Kenya.*

I'm still a member of Winyerikia Women Group, but we want to sell the plot we own at Kiamaina since we're old now and are not able to develop it. It was bought at a good price and when we sell it, we can each get about 20,000 shilling.

Wainoi, of the seven women who shared their life stories in 1984, was the most politically motivated. When I returned in 1994, she told me she'd voted in '92 for the Democratic Party's Mwai Kibaki in the national elections. He had lost, but she maintained that the '92 elections were better run than previous ones, "with no incidents," meaning no harassment or intimidation by competing candidates' supporters. Voting had gone smoothly, but she believed Moi had won because he "rigged the votes." She said that many people she knew had not voted because they had already "sold their votes" to KANU in exchange for food or money.

I asked her in 1994 whether she thought the Democratic Party (DP) had a future.

If the opposition united and if there is no rigging in the next election, the DP might have a chance of winning, she said. These were prophetic words. It wasn't until opposition parties united under the National Rainbow Coalition (NARC) that KANU was defeated.

Now I ask her if she helped in Kibaki's recent campaign.

No. I am saved [a born-again Christian] *now, so I can't go singing for a particular candidate as I once did.* [By this she implies that mixing politics with religion would be unseemly.] *But I campaigned by word of mouth, telling my friends who I thought was the best candidate. Yes, I voted for Mwai Kibaki.*

If I could advise him now, I'd tell him to end the corruption and see that we are paid better for our tea and change the coffee board so it isn't so corrupt.

Knowing that Wainoi had had problems with her deceased husband over his drinking, I ask her if alcohol bothers her family anymore. Her response is like a dike bursting.

Let me tell you, in this home of mine I have Maina and Karimi. They are drinking terribly. They are like mad people. Even as we speak, in the neighborhood there is one who is dead from drinking, and he's not even buried yet. I keep on praying for them.

Wainoi with her daughter, Nancy Karuana, left, and Nancy's son.

Alcohol is such a problem these days. It's because of lack of jobs. Like Mwangi and Francis [her other two sons] *are educated up to Form Four and have no jobs. And alcohol hurts the family. Njeri is living here because her husband was drinking and he was beating her every time he got drunk. So she came here and refuses to go back to him in Nairobi. That's how it is now.*

Njeri's sons are staying with me here so that they can go to school in Kagumo. One goes to the primary school and the other one is in a private school called Jufred. My greatest wish is that my grandchildren get a good education.

My health is okay except for some pains here in my stomach. I've visited the doctor, but there isn't anything he can do for it except some pills. That's what happens when one grows old.

I commiserate with Wainoi. Then, getting up, ask her whether she's talked with Nancy about my meeting her. She has. Nancy will meet with us tomorrow. Wainoi will show us how to get to Nancy's home; she lives in her in-laws' compound. Njeri will be back from tying up things in Nairobi in a week. We can meet with her then.

Now it's time for you to take that photo of me with my tea. She stands up.

I laugh. "You haven't forgotten."

Karuana and I follow her down a slippery path through a maize field to her tea plot. She takes up a huge woven basket on the edge of the plot and hoists it onto her back, positioning the leather tumpline at her forehead. Then she wades out among crowded tea bushes and begins picking tea with both hands, throwing the leaves over her shoulders into the basket as she looks up at me with a half smile. I've never seen somebody pick tea in her best clothes.

After I've taken a photo, she insists that I join her so that Karuana can take a picture of us together harvesting her tea. I pick up another large tea basket and placing the tumpline on my forehead, position the basket on my back, feeling slightly ridiculous. I push my way in among the tea bushes and stand next to her. What a photo op!

Karuana takes a couple of shots of us laughing while we pick tea. The leather tumpline slips off my head because I'm not wearing a headscarf to anchor it. Usually I wear one to cover my head from the sun, but today we've come in the car and I've forgotten it. Oily sweat is accumulating on my forehead. Emerging together from the tea field, I tell Wainoi I'll send her copies of the pictures when I get home.

Nancy Karuana and her first child in her husband's compound.

Nancy Karuana, Wainoi's younger daughter

In 1984, Nancy was a beguiling young girl helping her mother out in the compound, gathering up maize stalks to feed the cows, weaving a small basket, sweeping, collecting water from the river for cooking, washing and bathing. She had a quiet energy that was appealing. I'm curious to see her again after two decades.

We meet Wainoi at her home and follow her on foot through several maize fields and along a path out to a dirt road. Then we turn off the road onto another path, passing through several compounds, greeting people as we go, until we reach Nancy's in-laws' homestead. We've walked about a mile to get there. Nancy has lived here a little over a year, since her marriage.

When a rural Gikuyu woman marries she is escorted from her parents' home to her new husband's family's place by the groom's relatives with much fanfare and celebration. Formerly, a bride was captured by the husband's male relatives and carried, willing or not, to her new husband's home. Now, especially if she is educated, she has some say about the person she marries and often chooses her own husband.

Historically, marriage was not a key life event like *Irua*, the coming-of-age rite. It was a lengthy process that began with negotiations between the fathers over bridewealth, the slow transfer of symbolic goods, beginning with tobacco, then local beer and wealth (goats/sheep/a cow) from the groom to the bride's family to compensate her parents for the loss of their daughter and ensure that any children born will belong to the patri-clan of the husband. The transfer of wealth (now cash) from the groom's family is called *ruracio* in Kikuyu and is still an important aspect of marriage, even for girls living in the United States as I discovered with my Gikuyu "daughter." Njoki's fiancée, an American, had written to her father in Mutira requesting permission to marry his daughter. Her father replied, granting Sam permission to marry Njoki but requesting that he send *ruracio* in exchange; the suggested amount was six men's suits and seven dresses for the elders in the extended family, and a sum of $50,000 U.S. dollars!

I was stunned at the audacity of the request and found it difficult explaining to an African-American who'd never been to Africa that although the sum asked for was extravagant (a male Gikuyu friend told me $3,000 would have been reasonable), the symbolism attached to *ruracio* has a cultural logic. To the Gikuyu, I explained to Sam, *ruracio* signifies a man's respect for his future wife and her family. It cements the bond between the two extended families. The amount and items included in the bridewealth are usually negotiated between the fathers of the future bride and groom, who in the process come to know each other's ways. The sum suggested by Njoki's father was a beginning, and it was not expected that it would be paid all at once.

Sam didn't seem to be hearing me and said hotly, "Well, to me it seems like I'm *buying* Njoki." Then he added, "It makes it seem like she's a prostitute!"

I cringed and looked at Njoki next to him. She'd lowered her head in embarrassment, clearly upset.

"That's not the way it is, Sam. It's a sign of respect. It's a different culture."

At that point, Njoki looked up and quietly said to Sam, "Don't you understand that it shows respect for me and my family? It's important to us."

"Well, here we don't do that sort of thing," Sam responded. "I'm not about to pay anything."

Njoki didn't respond and remained silent. We'd come to an impasse, and I changed the subject. A month later I learned that she'd broken off the engagement.

In rural Mutira the transfer of *ruracio* is still an important aspect of marriage. Though we didn't talk about it, I'm sure that Nancy's husband sent several goats to her mother and brothers as well as a negotiated sum of money paid over time. In return, Nancy will spend the rest of her life with her husband in his family's homestead. As a new bride, she was under the tutelage of her mother-in-law. Now that she's given birth to her first child, her status has improved. She has a little more independence, but she's still expected to serve and obey her in-laws. Her subservience will lessen as she grows older and has her own children to rear. Nonetheless, it is a woman's parents-in-law who usually have the final say in this age-stratified society.

As soon as we enter the paternal compound, I recognize Nancy. She's carrying a six-month-old baby boy in her arms as she comes to greet us. Though she's older, her clear, bright face and the way she plaits her hair close to her head are very much the same as when she was eight years old.

Nancy's in-laws come out of a wood-frame house to greet us and insist that we talk with Nancy in their house rather than in their son's smaller home. I'm not too happy about the arrangement, suspecting that lack of privacy and confidentiality may be a problem. I ask Karuana to explain to both Wainoi and the in-laws that we need to interview Nancy alone. Wainoi nods her head in assent and sits down on a log bench in the yard to wait for us. The in-laws agree in principle, but first the father-in-law and then the mother-in-law find excuses to pass through the sitting room where we are seated. The father-in-law remains in the bedroom next door for quite a while so that we have to lower our voices and monitor our questions. The rooms share the same corrugated tin roof and the walls don't go all the way up, which means that everything can be heard. And the door to the bedroom remains open. Neither Karuana nor I like the situation, but there's not much we can do since it's the in-laws' house.

Nancy tells me she is 27 years old. I ask whether she remembers me when I used to visit her mother on a weekly basis 20 years ago.

Yes. I thought you were studying and that you had come to my mother to learn about Gikuyu ways. Sometimes my mother used to teach students who came from the University of Nairobi about our culture.

As a child, I learned many things from my mother—how to cook, weave baskets, knit sweaters and as I grew older, cultivating and weeding. I began learning basic things when I was about three-and-a-half because my mother would involve me in whatever task was at hand. She would show me, demonstrating how to do something, and then I would try and do it. But it was my father who taught me how to pick coffee. My parents grew mainly coffee in those days.

I began going to school when I was about seven years old. I learned how to read and write, first in Kikuyu, then later in Kiswahili and English. Now I can read my own letters that people send me and write back without involving anybody. I also learned about cleanliness and cookery in home science. I learned how to make a balanced meal. I completed Standard Eight and then enrolled in a tailoring course in Embu.

The things I learned at home and at school I've applied to my home here as now I keep things clean and cook good, balanced meals, taking care of my child and husband. I married a year ago when I was 26, and I've been living here since then. My husband works in Kagumo as a clerk.

My mother never had a chance to go to school, but she has attended adult education classes. I am lucky to have gone to school.

I remind Nancy that in her mother's day, girls went through Irua to become adults, and ask, "What is the major event now that shows one is a woman?"

She thinks for a moment and then says softly, *It's when one receives the menstrual flow. These days some girls start menstruating at a very early age, even at ten. When I was young, we didn't see the menstrual flow until we were much older.*

The onset of menstruation is critically important because it signals the ability to conceive and have a child. For girls growing up during a time when *Irua* no longer has much meaning, bearing a child completes the transition to adulthood. Being a mother is still highly valued in most African groups. In Kenya, women who are mothers are looked upon with favor and given special respect, especially in rural areas. It is inconceivable to most people here that a woman would not want to have a child. However, when I observe Nancy's discomfort in talking about such an intimate topic as menstruation in possible hearing distance of her father-in-law, I change the subject to the recent elections. To ask her about AIDS at this point would be difficult, given the situation.

Everybody here is happy that Kibaki won. She smiles, looking relieved. *If I could advise President Kibaki, I would tell him that free primary education is the most important thing needed by Kenyans. But not immediately. It will take several months or maybe even a year for it to be offered. I'd advise him there should be a reduction of fees for both primary and secondary education so that we are able to take our children to school. I would like to see my children educated through the secondary level and beyond that if they are able. It would enable them to get a good job and take care of the home.*

The major changes I see in Kagumo are new buildings with many stories and more rental houses. And now there are supermarkets. The cost of things has gone up. Another change is that drinking beer has increased. You can even see young ones taking it. It's a problem. The crime rate has also gone up here. Those are the major changes.

Two things strike me about the difference between Nancy's life and her mother's. First, Nancy married at a later age than

Wainoi, and she will probably have fewer children. Whereas Wainoi had seven children, Nancy is more likely to have two or three. Family planning methods are well known to younger generations of women in Kagumo.

Second, Nancy was able to complete primary school and then enroll in a tailoring course, learning a marketable skill. In contrast, Wainoi learned her midwifery skills from her mother and added to them later through a training course. She didn't learn literacy and math skills until she was an adult.

Like her mother, Nancy married a man from Kagumo. Her husband is educated. He works as a clerk in town. Because his family has only a small plot of land, he can't depend on producing crops like coffee or tea to earn an income as Wainoi and her husband did. Education has been crucial in giving Nancy and her husband an advantage that her parents didn't have. No wonder she sees education as crucial to Kenya's future.

Njeri, Wainoi's Older Daughter

Njeri is nine years older than Nancy. She's her mother's eldest child. I remember her as a teenager who used to come home periodically from boarding school to visit her family in the 1980s. Njeri went to Mutira Girls Secondary School. Most youth who've reached this stage of their education prefer to board so they can concentrate on their studies without the interruption of household and farm chores.

When we meet Njeri at her mother's home the following week, she's dressed in town clothes, including a tailored skirt and blouse with flat leather shoes, in contrast to her younger sister who wore a simple dress when we met. Njeri also turns out to be more forthcoming with information than Nancy. Talking with Njeri in her mother's home where she's grown up gives her a level of comfort that Nancy didn't have in her in-laws' house. Moreover, because Njeri completed high school, has traveled more widely and is older, she's more confident in expressing her opinions than Nancy. We begin by talking about the survival skills Njeri learned from her mother when she was a girl.

I learned the same kind of skills my mother learned. I remember that I began to collect firewood with her when I was about ten years old and didn't begin to fetch water from the river until I was 12 years. I started working with a panga [machete] when I was about 15. Other skills were fetching fodder for the animals, especially

Napier grass, milking the cows, picking coffee and washing clothes for the young ones, my siblings.

I began going to primary school when I was about seven years. The school was in Kagumo, which was some distance from here. I learned skills like writing, reading and mathematics, how to wash the classroom floors with rags and water, and how to weed the compound. I fetched water for cleaning the classrooms like I did at home. Also sweeping the compound and weeding were things that carried over from home to school. Yes, there was a class on health. We learned about diseases like tuberculosis, measles, malaria and alcohol abuse. But we didn't learn about AIDS because it was not here then. That came later. I don't know anyone who has AIDS.

After I finished Kagumo Primary, I went to Mutira Girls Secondary School. I felt a lot of homesickness when I first went there because I was boarding and couldn't see my family all the time. But I got used to it. I took courses like history, mathematics, Kiswahili, biology and English. I also joined the Drama Club, which I liked very much. The most important subjects I learned were English, Kiswahili and mathematics because when I had my own business in Nairobi, the skills I'd learned at Mutira Girls School helped me manage the business.

Our business, my husband and mine's, was selling utensils and other things [a hardware store]. *But then we started having problems. Though the business was doing well, I had to leave it. You see I was managing it with the husband. Then I came to find out that he was taking the profit we made and buying alcohol. This went on until we did not have enough money to restock our store. I tried to get my husband to stop drinking, but he refused. Finally, I had to leave him a few months ago because he was beating me when he was drunk. And he didn't like my criticism about the shop's lack of profits. We argued a lot. I miss managing the shop, but coming here with my sons was good because now they can get an education here.*

I would like to see both my sons educated up to university because the courses they take will help them obtain marketable skills to get jobs. If I had the opportunity to go to university now, I would take law. I think it's one of the most important subjects one can take. And people who become lawyers know a lot and do well. I only took a secretarial course after secondary school—that's as far as I got before moving to Nairobi.

One of the major changes in my life was becoming a parent of two boys. I only had two children because it is costly educating them today. I learned about family planning from books and at clinics. Then I took care of it myself. Bringing my children up, taking them to school and taking good care of my home, managing it well, are very important to me.

I knew I was no longer a girl when I started having the menstrual flow. I was 15 years old and in Form One, the first year of secondary school. During the time my mother was young they used to go through Irua, but those days are over. So that's why I say I knew I was an adult when I started menstruating.

Now that I'm back living with my mother, I'm cultivating tea and coffee. I get loans from the KTDA for fertilizers. They deduct the amount from what we earn at the end of the month. We get 7.50 shillings per kilo [2.2 pounds] *and I earn about 300 shillings* [$4.05] *per day. I have three or four women that I hire to pick tea leaves, depending on how it's sprouted* [new growth that is picked], *and I pay them four shillings per kilogram.*

The biggest changes I see in Kagumo since you were here is that now we have a new tea factory at Mununga and many tea-buying centers. There are also many more schools, both public and private. Traveling is easier now because there are more matatus.

The best thing I've done is to bring my children up and send them to school.

Like her mother, Njeri married a man who turned out to have problems with alcohol. What helped her mother manage was her religious faith. Wainoi is Catholic, and belonging to the Mothers' Union gave her coping skills and support. I wonder about Njeri as we leave Wainoi's place. What gave her the courage to leave her husband? Is she finding support at home now? Njeri and Nancy were raised Catholic, but whether they attend a church and belong to the Mother's Union, as Wainoi once did, I'm not sure.

In a survey of Mutira women in 1983, I found that most were either Anglican (47%) or Catholic (42%). A few women attended the Full Gospel Church and two were members of the African Holy Ghost Church. Only two were non-Christian. I suspect it may be the same now.

I will be meeting a group of Anglican girls in the afternoon and hope to raise with them some of the issues I've talked about with Njeri and Nancy. How do these girls perceive the differences between their mothers' youth and their own? Has the opportunity to go to school affected their life ambitions? Are they more willing to talk about HIV/AIDS than Wainoi's daughters?

Later in the week, I'll go to a local clinic to take up some of these same issues with a group of girls who don't attend a church.

CHAPTER 5

School Girls: Our Mothers, Ourselves

The difference between how we learned things as small girls and our mothers' time is that in their time, there were no wells or water taps. Girls had to go to a river or stream and haul water back twice a day. Now people in Kagumo either have a well or a tap in their compounds, which makes fetching water easier.

We're sitting on benches at the front of the sanctuary in the new Anglican Church in Kagumo, talking with a dozen girls between the ages of 15 and 22. In Kikuyu, girls were referred to as *arigu*, the term used for uncircumcised girls who had not been through the coming-of-age rite, *Irua*. Customarily, they participated in the ritual in their mid-teens. They were then known as *airitu,* girls who had been circumcised and earned the honor of becoming adults. A girl retained this designation until she became a *muhiki*, a bride. Lately, the terms have become muddled as most girls, at least in Kirinyaga, don't go through *Irua* these days. And none of the 12 girls we're meeting with is married. They are *airitu* of sorts. Most are in their last year of secondary school. The three in their early 20s completed Form Four but did not have an opportunity to go on to a training college or one of Kenya's seven universities.

When Karuana and I arrived at the church, Junet Mithamo was standing at the entrance with a young woman in her 20s, who'd been charged with organizing the group. We waited for more than an hour as the girls straggled in. I got them talking by asking them what kinds of survival skills they'd learned from their mothers growing up. They named farming skills such as handling a hand plow, cultivating food crops with a machete, weeding, carrying crops from the fields to the homestead, and transporting loads of produce in a wheelbarrow—for example, harvested maize from the granary to the kitchen for processing or dried beans from the granary to the yard for husking. They also mentioned milking and taking their family's cows to graze.

Like Wainoi's daughters, they cared for younger siblings, fetched firewood from the bush and water from a stream or well. They also did plenty of cooking, washing up and laundry by hand in a plastic bucket.   Some learned how to weave baskets and make pottery.   Still, as one of the girls noted, things have changed since their mothers' time, when women hauled water up from a stream twice daily—a backbreaking task as I can testify having done it in the early '80s. Women and their daughters don't have to go nearly as far to get water nowadays, but they have to go much further for firewood, as trees closer to home have been cut down for tea cultivation. The alternative is buying charcoal for cooking at the open market in Kagumo. Few of their mothers use clay pots for cooking anymore. They use large aluminum pots, *sufuria,* set over a three-stone cooking fire or a charcoal brazer.

Education sparked shifts in the girls' lives and outlook. *We begin to notice the difference between those not schooled and ourselves*, a teenager with her hair in tightly plaited cornrows says. *Those who went to school were neat and clean. We wore uniforms.* She looks around for affirmation.

School brought more discipline, a girl with elfin features offers as the others nod their heads.

We could read letters and signs, a tall, confident teenager observes.

And also read directions, another adds.

I learned to write stories, the youngest girl says, looking sideways at her friend.

"What kind of stories?" I ask.

About growing up...things that happened to me. She looks down shyly.

A stocky girl with cinnamon-brown eyes, her hair pulled straight back, observes, *Because we know how to write, we can help our mothers by writing letters for them.*

Others nod.   Education has given these young women a distinct advantage their mothers didn't have.

They learned the usual academic subjects in primary school that armed them with practical literacy, numeracy, and science skills. When I ask them how what they've learned in school has helped them in their lives, one girl volunteers that math has helped her in daily transactions, *in getting the correct change so one isn't cheated.*

Learning about the human body and how diseases affect it in science prepared us for recognizing them and treating our families when we are older, another adds.

Some skills, they testify, have contributed to improvements in their homes, including better nutrition and cooking methods.

The gap between unschooled girls and those in this group widened as they advanced to the secondary level. Going to secondary school marked a major transition. For the four girls enrolled in boarding schools it was their first time away from home. Most felt homesick, missed their families. They had to learn how to care for themselves, keeping their things neat and washing their own clothes. They mixed with girls who came from different areas and diverse ethnic groups and who spoke a variety of languages. Swahili, the national language, trumped a mother tongue in the dorms, and English became the primary language of the classroom.

A girl who dropped out of school in Form Two (the second year of high school) admitted, *I was happier in school than I am at home. My real mother died and the situation at home with my father's new wife has not been good. I wish I were still in school.*

Of the subjects the girls take in secondary school, they agree that biology, maths, and languages are most important to them. Biology, because it teaches them about their bodies and the physical changes they will encounter and how to deal with them. It also teaches them more about various diseases encountered in Kenya, such as malaria, tuberculosis, dysentery, and a little about HIV/AIDS. Math subjects facilitate daily transactions. Languages, especially English, *are important for communicating in today's world, for instance, when interviewing for a job*, said a serious girl, pushing up her glasses. *If one speaks English well, it gives a good impression.*

Only three of the girls' mothers completed Form Four. They help their daughters with subjects such as geography, history, and civics. Other girls relate that, although they don't get coaching with their studies, their mothers are helpful in "matters related to life."

As only half the girls have been volunteering ideas, I divide them into three smaller groups. I ask them to talk about when they felt they'd made the transition from being a girl to becoming a woman, and to share their ideas about sexuality. Each group selects a spokesperson. They collect into pods of three to four girls with their heads bent toward one another. Some of the discussions look serious, but laughter erupts periodically. After a while, the first group is ready to report. Their speaker, her dark eyes looking around, daring anyone to laugh, says, *The change happens when one gets her first menstrual flow.* The other girls in her group look away, but nobody laughs.

We knew what to expect ahead of time because we were taught about menstruation from the teachers and even salesladies who sell Always *in the shops.* Some of the girls smother grins, looking embarrassed.

"What is Always?" I ask. The leader giggles behind her hand, looking at her friends. *It's a kind of sanitary napkin.* She doubles up after saying it and we move on to the next small group.

The second group agrees with the first, but adds that they learned about menstruation from books such as *Becoming A Woman.* They also learned through television and radio programs. The final group concurs, with their leader reporting, *As our teachers and some of our mothers were preparing us for adulthood they told us about the changes to expect in our bodies, like enlarging breasts and broadening hips. Some of our friends who had already menstruated were helpful, too.*

It seems, then, that these 21st-century girls agree with Wainoi's daughter, Nancy, that menstruation has become the defining event for entering adulthood, rather than *Irua* as in their grandmother's day, or with the birth of a first child, as women in their mother's generation, had argued two decades earlier.

In discussing sexuality amongst themselves, the girls relate that they learned about "the urge to be with boys" in home science and CRE (Christian religious education), a course taught in most government schools. They were taught that when the time comes for meeting boys, they should only meet in the company of others and in open places. *We should not encourage boys to touch us and should avoid having sex as it can lead to diseases like AIDS and also unwanted pregnancies,* one of the older girls says, with others agreeing. That their courses treat issues of sexuality with caution is not unusual in Kenya. Still, learning about sexuality and abstinence doesn't mean that all girls will practice what they've learned at school. Teenage pregnancy is a problem here, just as it is in the United States. But insisting on abstinence-only education, as is being advocated in several federally funded programs in the U.S., is not the solution.* It can lead to taking chances in unsafe situations, for example where a girl's boyfriend has AIDS, but she doesn't know it. It can happen in Kenya as well as the U.S.

"What are you learning about AIDS?" I ask.

Different things. In science, guest speakers from the district health office come in to talk to us about the disease, the girl with the cornrows responds.

Sometimes the speaker is a person with AIDS, which makes the disease seem more real, her friend adds.

What about prevention?

We are told that refraining from sexual relations and not encouraging boys is the best thing." Nobody mentions condoms.

The girls also have learned something about other diseases such as dysentery, tuberculosis, malaria, and alcoholism. I am impressed. This goes beyond what Njeri and Nancy learned in school. What is new since I was last here is that these girls also learn something about HIV/AIDS and its prevention, though the schools appear to stress abstinence as the primary form of protection. This flies in the face of a male-dominated society where men routinely manipulate their female partners in sexual relationships, for example, refusing to use condoms. Schools have taken up a socializing role in matters of sexuality. They teach youth about adulthood through family life courses and biology, an education that formerly took place in the community through *Irua.* To their credit, they now teach sex education with numeracy and literacy as necessary for future survival.

At the time Wainoi was growing up, education was limited to the home front, community and, for a few children, attendance in a mission school. Wainoi had to go to an adult literacy program to learn basic skills that younger Kenyans take for granted. Like Wainoi and her husband, other Kenyans wanted their kids to learn skills they never had but felt were critical to get ahead in the 20th century. The state responded by setting up government schools (like our public schools), and where these were not meeting the demand, rural communities took matters into their own hands and built *harambee* (self-help) schools, hiring secondary school graduates to teach. In the

---

* A 2004 Congressional report found that 80% of the abstinence-only curricula used by two-thirds of the recipients in a large federally-funded program (SPANS) contained false or misleading information about reproductive health, e.g, the HIV virus can be spread through contact with another person's sweat. (*National NOW Times,* Winter, 2005, p. 6).

first two decades primary education was free. That began to change in the late '80s.

By the early '90s, the Ministry of Education was cutting back on national educational expenses by initiating surcharges for primary students. The charges escalated each year. Many district education officers and headmasters took advantage of the situation, charging additional fees—"lining their pockets," as one parent put it.

Soaring school fees hit parents at a time when they were most vulnerable and feeling the pinch. They were earning less for export crops such as coffee and tea. As world market prices for these crops fluctuated, then tumbled for coffee, farmers were left with less in their pockets and bank accounts. Loans became the new savior, but with a caveat. Nyambura, a young woman who had shared her life story with me in the '80s, said it best in 2003: *For a person like me who has to borrow money to pay school fees, once the KTDA deducted what I owed them, I was left with nothing.*

That Kenyans view education as the escalator to a better life is no surprise. That they've had to get loans to provide it for their children in the wake of an economic squeeze accounts for part of the groundswell that led to the defeat of the KANU party.

Now I ask the girls at the Anglican Church how advances in communications technology have affected their education and lives. "Do your schools or families have computers with access to the Internet?" None of their secondary schools have computers. They know about computers, e-mail and the Internet because two computer centers have sprung up in Kagumo in the last decade.

I ask about television. Two girls say their schools have a TV. It is kept in the dining room. The girls watch entertainment programs: cartoons, soap operas, movies and sports such as wrestling, a Kenyan favorite. Only two schools have video equipment.

At home, only one girl's family has a television set and VCR. None has a computer. The girl with a TV says, *My family watches nightly news first, then entertaining programs like soaps and wrestling. Watching the news and soap operas improves our family's togetherness and social life, which is good.*

Another girl notes that watching news programs at school enlightens her and her friends on various world events, *like the issue about that beauty contest that was supposed to be held in Nigeria, but the Nigerians didn't want it there so it had to be moved to Britain.* Laughter erupts among the girls. Someone else says she learns gospel songs and gets Christian guidance from certain TV programs. Like

American teenagers, Kenyan youth watch a variety of programs. And some, like their Christian counterparts in the U.S., watch Christian networks, often beamed by satellite from the West, for inspiration and guidance.

Telephones also provide links to the outside world and make communication easier. Only one girl's family has a landline, but half relate that their parents have a mobile phone, much to my surprise. No mobile phones existed in Mutira a decade ago. The arrival of affordable cell phones has prompted a communications revolution.

Phone lines are confined to Kagumo town, and they are expensive to install. Only a few families can afford them, the girls admit. The advent of cell phone technology means that people living in remote areas without access to landlines now can contact one another without walking great distances. The mobile phone has become an option linking relatives, neighbors and friends. Children have benefited because their role as message runners between homesteads has shrunk.

Having witnessed how the mobile-phone revolution transformed rural South Africa's communication networks in the mid-1990s, it's exciting to see it spread in Kenya. At this stage it is far more affordable and desired than a computer because the latter is dependent on connectivity that doesn't exist in most rural areas.

At the end of an hour's discussion with the girls, I set up a simulation. I ask them to imagine they are a delegation from Mutira location that has been invited to the State House to talk with the new president Mwai Kibaki and the Minister of Education Professor Saitoti about changes needed to improve young women's lives. "What suggestions would you offer if you could talk with the new president? After you've met together, come back and present your ideas to the president, who will be played by Mrs. Mithamo, and the Minister of Education, played by Mrs. Mutiti [Karuana]."

The girls chuckle and meander down the aisle between the pews to the back of the church to debate what they want changed. The discussion is heated but good-natured, with bursts of laughter from time to time. After 25 minutes I have to call them back. In the meantime, we've set up a table with Junet Mithamo and Karuana sitting sternly behind it, waiting for the "women's delegation."

The group comes down the aisle, giggling a little. The girls stand in a rough semi-circle in front of the "president" and "minister of education." Two of them act as spokeswomen. They present the following suggestions for change.

- Women's issues should be taken seriously, with women being given more of a chance to be heard and more girls taken to school.
- The government should introduce AIDS as a separate subject in the school curricula rather than trying to cover it in a science course.
- Schools should have computers and computer courses.
- The selling of illicit brews such as Kumi Kumi should be outlawed.
- Rape cases should be prosecuted seriously and action taken.
- The Mungiki gang, which is threatening people on *matatus* and insisting that girls be circumcised, should be harshly punished by the government.

I'm startled by this last suggestion because I've read nothing about the Mungiki gang in newspapers. The idea that a gang is threatening to circumcise schoolgirls is frightening. The list gives me clues as to what is most on girls' minds: respect for women, physical security, and their education. The idea of a new AIDS course taps into both their need for increased physical security and for improved education. For their future wellbeing, they want to learn more about HIV/AIDS and its prevention.

Citing social problems such as fear of rape, threatened female circumcision and men's overconsumption of liquor (which often leads to family violence) reveals increased anxiety over physical safety. In fact, the growing erosion of public security during the Moi years is a major issue for most Kenyans. I need to find out more about the Mungiki gang. I also want to pursue the girls' desire for better AIDS education. But it's 6 P.M. and they want to leave so they can reach their homes before dark.

Later, I ask Karuana about the Mungiki gang. It's a nefarious group, she tells me, made up of disgruntled, unemployed men in their 20s who have on-going grudges over lack of employment and the poor economy. It's been rumored that before the recent elections, members of the gang went to secondary schools and threatened to kidnap girls so they could circumcise them. There was no reaction from KANU, so people suspected that Moi's party wanted to scare young female voters into staying away from the polls. KANU feared these educated girls would vote for the opposition NARC candidates. Regardless of the rumor's accuracy, it served to frighten and anger many schoolgirls.

The threat of violence is not an idle one. A week after our meeting at the church, it's front-page news that 15 people in Nakuru were murdered over the weekend and many others wounded with *pangas* and knives after members of the Mungiki gang went on a rampage in this Rift Valley town. Another attack occurred in Murang'a district, where two were left dead. *Mungiki* means "the multitude" in Kikuyu. The gang, rising out of poverty, practices fee extortion by promising protection from attacks to people along *matatu* routes and in low-income neighborhoods. It's a desperate, reactionary group that advocates returning to traditional religion, taking snuff, growing dreadlocks, and practicing female circumcision.

In Nakuru, because of the tepid response of local police to the attack, citizens began hunting down Mungiki members involved in the raid and dispensing justice. Three members were publically lynched. Finally, the police reacted and aided by the Kenyan secret service and the paramilitary General Service Unit, began rounding up sect members. The police killed four of them. By midweek, the *Daily Nation* reported that the death toll from the two attacks, which the paper referred to as "terror raids," had left 23 citizens and seven gang members dead.[14] A national search for Mungiki terrorists was on as security forces hunted down members.

The Mungiki gang is not the only group frightening Kenya's citizens. Partly due to its geographical location on the east coast of Africa, international terrorists also threaten the country's security. Kenya's second major industry after agriculture is tourism. But income from tourism dipped dramatically after recent terrorist attacks linked to al-Qaeda. First came the bombing of the American embassy on a busy street in Nairobi in 1998. Over 300 Kenyans lost their lives. And a month before I arrived in Kenya in 2002, a suicide bomber crashed a rigged car into an Israeli-owned tourist hotel on the coast, killing 11 Kenyans, a couple of Europeans and an Israeli. Kenyans, like Americans in the 9/11 attacks, bear the major costs of such incendiary acts. These costs include loss of Kenyan lives, horrific damage to their cities and the expense to Kenya's government of tracking down al-Qaeda-linked terrorists taking refuge in neighboring Somalia or the Sudan. Bomb threats are not unusual. One closed the airport in Nairobi while I was in Kenya. We

Americans are not alone in our desire for a safer, more secure homeland.

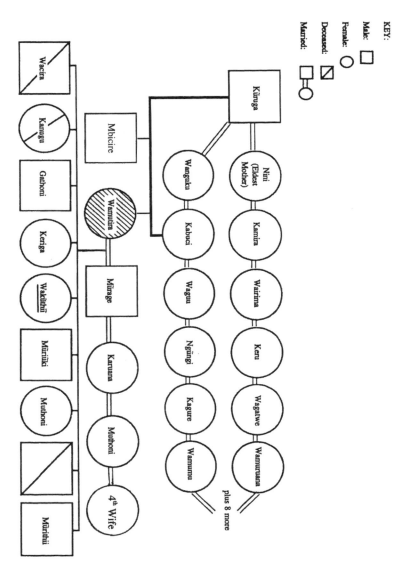

Wamutira's family showing three generations, with daughter interviewed underlined.

CHAPTER 6

Co-wives Confront a New Wife

Wamutira, the woman who shared her experience of *Irua*, the circumcision ceremony, in the third chapter of this book, is the daughter of an important chief. His name was Kuruga. He had 20 wives. Wamutira was the only daughter of his eighth wife (see family diagram). She also is one of Karuana's many aunts because Karuana's mother was the daughter of another of Kuruga's wives, which makes Wamutira and Karuana's mother half-sisters. They are about the same age. Their illustrious father had to have houses constructed for each of his 20 wives and their children. It's easy to see why both women say that growing up in their father's compound was like being raised in a village. They never lacked playmates, ate together and knew that Nini, the first wife, was their eldest mother.

I'm having trouble trying to find Wamutira. She is not at her husband Murage's homestead or in her tea fields. From Karuana's mother, I learn some startling news! Wamutira has sold her land at Murage's homestead in exchange for a larger piece in Kiomande where she has relocated. She has left behind a husband and the two co-wives with whom she'd shared most of her life. I am surprised because Wamutira is Murage's first wife, which gives her special status. She is also very close to Murage's second wife, Karuana—not to be confused with my long-time assistant of the same name. Wamutira was the one who'd selected Murage's second wife, to keep her company at home while he was active in the underground liberation struggle in Nairobi during the 1950s.

Wamutira told me in early 1984, *Murage heard about Karuana from another woman who was her neighbor. We were told that she was a very good girl—hard working and not naughty. She knew how to control her mouth. I knew she would help with the work and was one I could communicate with. So I told my husband to marry Karuana. It is me who married her.*[15]

In recording Wamutira's life story in the 1980s, I also talked with Murage's second wife about her perceptions of meeting and marrying Murage.

My people had talked with Wamutira and she told them she had asked Murage to marry a girl who would keep her company. So he had that pressure from Wamutira because she wanted a co-wife. After ruracio [bridewealth] had been brought, I stayed at home until the day Murage said he would come for me. It was Wamutira who came about three in the afternoon, carrying the child who was her firstborn on her back. We stayed at my home until dark because I would not agree to go in daylight.* We met Murage at Karia coming to get us now that it was dark. The following morning, Wamutira escorted Murage and me to the bus stop in Kerugoya. At that time there were difficulties in traveling because of the state of emergency during the Mau Mau times—the British put up roadblocks everywhere. Murage feared to stay at home as he was a Mau Mau supporter.

Karuana, the second wife, went to Nairobi with Murage in May and returned to Kagumo a year later, three months pregnant.

When I came here I met Wamutira and we stayed together in the same house. You could see me carrying her child when I needed to go somewhere.

The two women became close friends "even sharing the same cooking pot," both women testified. Then Murage came home, and he felt left out.

He would ask me, Wamutira said, *'Is it me who married Karuana or you?'* This was when he found Karuana always staying at my house.

Murage was now working as a tailor in Kagumo where he met a young woman, Muthoni. They got together and when Muthoni found she was pregnant by him in 1962, Murage went to his co-wives and informed them that he was bringing home a third wife.

At first the two wives were upset. *When Muthoni came we just kept quiet,* Wamutira told me. *But later, we reasoned that even if we three lived together feeling bad, there were none of us who had the power to take another back to her father's home. Finally, we agreed between ourselves to get united together as wives, the three of us.*

Later, Wamutira told me that she once felt resentment toward Murage when he'd ask her to do things like feeding and watering the cow. She talked back and told him to do it himself. But then she came to realize, *he is the wheel and pedals of the bicycle and if he can't take the wheel and push the pedals, then we wives can't move.*

I talked with each wife separately about her experiences as a co-wife. All three wives agreed that Murage treated them fairly. He spent the same number of nights with each wife, gave them the same amount of meat or clothing and paid the school fees for each wife's children. I once asked Wamutira if they ever felt any jealousy over the time Murage spent with another wife.

Jealousy? That would be a waste of time. Murage would spend the night with Karuana and then come in the morning and ask me to warm his bathwater, and I would gladly do it. And the same with Karuana if he spent the night with me. The thought of where he slept and what he did was never in us. When two or three wives are good friends, that home is always warm and lively.

The situation between the three wives was still amicable ten years later when I visited them in 1994, partly because Murage had given each wife an equal share of his land for her and her children. Wamutira and Karuana's oldest sons were beginning to marry and they needed land.

Now, in 2003, a new crisis has erupted in Murage's homestead. Murage, in his late 70s, has decided to take a fourth wife in her early 30s. He's recently brought her to his home. The remaining wives, Karuana and Muthoni, are furious, as are their grown daughters and Wamutira's five daughters. Wamutira's co-wives have sent a message to her, asking her to come to a meeting in Kagumo. Without her they cannot decide on a course of action. The co-wives and their grown daughters have gathered at a small shop where one of the daughters works and has her living quarters out back.

We arrive at the *nduka* on one of Kagumo's side roads late on a Monday morning. Karuana (my assistant) asks a young girl behind the counter where we might find Wamutira. "The women are inside the yard," she says, coming round to open a gate in a tall wooden fence adjacent to the small shop.

Inside, a dozen women of varying ages are gathered on pieces of *kanga* cloth spread over the dried mud yard. Right away I recognize Karuana, Murage's aging second wife. She gets up and throws her arms around me in greeting, amazed that I'm here again. She tells me they've been waiting for Wamutira since yesterday. I notice Muthoni, the third wife, hunkered down on a small stool, leaning against the side of the shop. I greet her. She is less cordial and seems very upset. Karuana, her co-wife, explains in animated detail the problem of the new wife while the family's grown daughters and nieces listen quietly, one or two nodding their heads solemnly.

"This is not good news," I tell the co-wives in Kikuyu.

Ii. They concur, looking stymied.

It is very serious, the second wife emphasizes, *but we can't make a decision about what we should do until Wamutira arrives and we have talked about it.*

Wamutira and the women gather in Kagumo.

I nod in empathy. "We will have to wait, too, until this is cleared up. But in the meantime, in addition to visiting Wamutira, I want to talk with some of her daughters and sons if I can find them. Do any of them live in Kagumo?"

"*Ii*, yes," old Karuana replies and nods her head toward a middle-age woman sitting with the others on the ground. *Wakuthii there is our first wife's daughter.* I turn to Wakuthii, who gets up to greet me. She has a sturdy build like her mother but is taller and lacks Wamutira's shyness.

"While you are waiting for your mother, would you be willing to talk with me about some of the changes you see in Kagumo since I last came?"

She agrees.

Two of the younger women pick up three wooden stools from the yard and lead us out behind the *nduka*, past the living quarters to a tea field. I notice kale growing amongst the tea plants. The soil smells moist and slightly fetid. A man in tattered shorts, bare from the waist up, is bent over, harvesting kale leaves, presumably for lunch. As we sit down on the three stools, he moves some distance away from us so we can be alone with Wakuthii.

Wakuthii, Wamutira's daughter

Wakuthii is 37 years old, the same age as Njeri, Wainoi's oldest daughter.

I am the secondborn of my mother's daughters.[*] I'm married, with three boys. The oldest boy is in Form Two, the secondborn left school after Standard Eight, and the youngest is in Standard Eight this year. I live outside Kagumo town in the homestead of my husband's parents who are still with us.

Karuana asks Wakuthii whether she remembers me when I used to live and work here in the 1980s.

Yes, I remember when you used to talk with my mother, taking photographs and such, but I didn't get the details of your talks.

After I explain that I'm trying to see how things have changed from her mother's time, I ask her what kind of skills she learned from her mother growing up.

I learned how to cook, to clean the compound, wash clothes, wash utensils and fetch food for the cattle and goats. I also learned how to weave baskets, though I cannot weave and complete a basket like my mothers used to.

Wakuthii refers to her "mothers" in the plural for a reason. Most children view their mother's co-wives as their mothers because they are raised collectively by these women rather than solely, as in a

---

[*] Actually, she's the thirdborn daughter. Wamutira's first daughter died as a child.

nuclear family. It is particularly appropriate in Wakuthii's case, because her mother shared a house with Karuana, the second wife, during Wakuthii's early years. And even when the girl was in her teens, I observed the three co-wives often grouped together with their children under the same roof.

Beginning when I was about eight years old, I followed what my mothers were doing with my eyes, and later on I would try out what I'd seen them doing. When I was older, I learned how to bake things like cakes through the women's group. My children enjoy eating these cakes, and it means that I don't have to buy such things from the market.

I went to primary school and reached Standard Seven, the last grade in those days. We used to study subjects like science, dress making, how to make sisal skirts and reading and writing. Going to school taught me to be self-disciplined, how to keep my home in order and also how to organize my day-to-day activities. That is a difference from my mother's childhood, as she never had an opportunity for going to school.

I would like to see my sons getting educated up to university level and if possible go overseas for further studies. It would make me happy to see them getting a good education so they can help themselves in getting a job and also help their parents.

In my mother's time all the arigu went for Irua.[*] It was the custom then. But these days, girls know that they have become grown up when they get the first menstrual flow. That's a big difference because girls used to go through Irua before they ever got their first menstrual flow.

Did Wakuthii endure the milder form of circumcision, the cutting off of the tip of the clitoris? She was turning 15, roughly the age of initiation, about the time that the former president signed the decree outlawing female circumcision in 1982. It's hard to know. It's a topic that I did not begin to introduce in the 1980s until I had established at least a six-month relationship with each of the older women who'd been through it.

Wakuthii's mother and her co-wives, in a discussion between the three of them, agreed in 1984 that it was a custom that not only was risky, but had outlived its usefulness. At the time, Wamutira told me about a girl who had been through *Irua* a year earlier and bled so

---

[*] *Arigu* refers to mature uncircumcised girls.

badly that she and the other participating women had to take the girl to the hospital. *When the nurse came,* Wamutira related*, she wanted to beat us when she saw Wandia, and she told us we were very foolish to be doing that kind of thing nowadays. I said we were sorry and would never repeat it again. And I pleaded with her to just give Wandia an injection. But the following morning the girl was still bleeding. What I saw that time, that was the end of it for me.*

Muthoni, the youngest wife, followed with, *I feel good because the banning of circumcision means that none of mine* [her daughters] *will be destroyed that way.* Muthoni may have been alluding to the fact that her co-wives had their older daughters circumcised, or it may just have been a general comment.

Karuana, the second wife, said, *It was a stupidity that was liked very much by Agikuyu a long time ago. The things nowadays are not the way they were long ago.*

Now you can't tell the difference between one who is circumcised and one who is not, concluded Muthoni.

Kenya's public campaign to end the practice of female circumcision over the past 20 years has made inroads in Kirinyaga district. Few younger women in the 21st century have been through any form of genital cutting. Nor will their daughters entertain such an idea: the old traditions have faded with new knowledge and education. As Wakuthii has no daughters, it's not an issue for her.

Looking around Kagumo, Wakuthii sees a host of changes since I last visited in the early '90s. Many more buildings have been constructed, including a few hotels. "Mini-dairies," small shops that sell fresh cow's milk in cartons, have mushroomed. It's because the town has grown and fewer families have the space to keep cows. People are feeling the effects of land shortage. They complain about not having enough.

She has noticed a number of new gas stations, both in Kagumo and Kerugoya.

It's because there are more matatus on the road and more people have cars nowadays.

She does not say that the single road through Kagumo has become clogged with cars, trucks, carts and people walking along both edges of the tarmac, making it difficult for a vehicle to get through the town. Walking along the road isn't as safe as it once was. People crowd the muddy paths that flank both sides of the single asphalt road, spilling onto it and crossing without looking for oncoming trucks or *matatus* that make their persistent runs between

Karatina and Kerugoya. Slow-paced carts drawn by oxen or, increasingly, donkeys take the center of the road to avoid people along the edges. It creates havoc for the faster moving traffic. And for the first time in Kagumo there is traffic! It's slowed down by speed bumps at each end of the town, adding to the clogging at the center where the open market is located and high-rise buildings are sprouting up.

Wakuthii says she's happy with the outcome of the recent elections, noting that NARC won most of the parliamentary seats as well as the presidency. In fact, NARC won nearly 60 percent of the seats in comparison to KANU's 30 percent with minor parties winning the remaining parliamentary seats.

"What advice would you give the new president?" I ask.

To have free education like Kibaki promised. But it could take time, maybe about three months, before he organizes it. I would like to see him do away with the activity fees at the primary level since we don't see the work that these fees do. In secondary school they should make the fees more affordable.

The fees that Wakuthii refers to are for activities "outside the classroom," including maintenance, that the central government and local districts began charging in the '90s to trim their budgets. As Kenyans already paid for educational materials and uniforms, the new fees were like adding an extra load to an already overburdened mule.

By the time I finish meeting with Wakuthii, it's lunchtime. We pick up our stools and walk back to the yard where the rest of the family's women have gathered. I see Wamutira, aging but still spry, sitting next to Karuana, her longtime *muiru*, or co-wife.

Nyina-wa-Stepheni! Wamutira jumps up. She throws her arms around me, hugging me tight. The first wife has arrived. Her headscarf, somewhat askew, is covered with dust and her furrowed, nut-brown face and sunken cheeks reflect the challenges of her journey. Despite her fatigue, Wamutira's blazing smile still lights up the space around her. It's the kind of smile that envelops you in its broad embrace. I have missed this woman.

"*Ii. Ni nda coka.* Yes. I have returned. And I want to talk with you, but I know that you're meeting on an important family matter this afternoon."

Her smile crashes and her eyes take on the glint of hot coals. *Yes, this is very important. That's why I came. Something must be done*, she says resolutely.

I arrange a time to visit her the next afternoon. As we leave, I wonder what the women will decide about this upstart new wife.

Arriving in Kagumo the next day, Karuana parks the car across from the small shop where we met the women in Murage's family. Wamutira comes across the road to meet us. She looks wan but shakes our hands warmly, giving us a dimpled grin. She's dressed in a maroon polyester dress with a white collar. The dress is covered from the waist by a bright blue *kanga* hastily wrapped around her middle, with the ends hanging out. On her gray head is a striped silk headscarf. She leads us through a field of spindly coffee bushes to the compound of a relative. Chairs are brought, and we settle into them. I'm eager to know what the women decided about the new wife. Rather than begin with this charged issue, though, I start by asking her about the changes she's experienced since the last time I talked with her in 1994.

Mainly the changes are in coffee. The Kenya Coffee Cooperative Authority has not paid us any money for years. As you know, the land was subdivided at home. When you last came, you saw that my oldest son, Gathiomi, the one who used to give me concern, had built a house for his family on my plot. But the plot was small, and with the poor prices for coffee, I decided to leave it and buy a larger parcel at Kiomande. I gave half of the land at Kiomande to each son to grow coffee. But Muriithi, the second son, sold his plot and went to Kirima. Gathiomi, the older one, is still there at Kiomande where I want to build my house.

Knowing that Wamutira was proud of the tea she grew on part of her acre plot at her husband's place in Kagumo, I ask her if she's growing tea now at Kiomande.

No. In Kiomande and at Kirima there is only coffee. But with the Kenya Coffee Cooperative the way it is, I don't know when we'll earn enough to build my house. I thought it would be better at Kiomande, but it was not such a good thing.

I can tell Wamutira has regrets over her decision to sell the original plot Murage had given her. She thought she was doing something to improve opportunities for her sons, but it's turned out that she has even less land available in Kiomande than in Kagumo now that her second son has sold his plot and moved away.

Generally, my children are all well. They stay with Gathiomi at Kiomande except for the girls who are married. The oldest girl, Kiriga, is married and living at Githioro with her husband. Wakuthii, the one you talked with, married at Kibuchi's [refers to Wakuthii's in-laws]. *Juliana married a man at Sagana and lives there now. Muthoni married a man in Kerugoya, where she stays.*

The problem that we have right now, she confides, *is that mzee wants to get a fourth wife who is a young woman. All those women you found there at the shop yesterday were waiting for me so that we can see what to do about it. We are either going to call the sub-chief, or we will chase her away ourselves.*

I know that these women have the strength and communal power to act on what Wamutira says, to "chase her away." Will they do it?

"How will we know what you decide?"

Ask Karuana's mother. She nods toward my assistant. *She'll tell you.*

We'll just have to wait until the decision is made and the plan executed. For us, it means waiting another day. I feel strangely disappointed, as if I've been watching a new TV drama whose emotional plot has been unfolding weekly, but suddenly I realize I might not be around to see the ending. It's frustrating and reminds me that my tendency to become impatient at crunch moments may not serve me here.

Toward the end of our time together, I ask Wamutira how she feels about the recent elections; she refused to vote in the 1992 election because she was so disgusted with Moi's corruption and past elections.

They were good. Now that we have President Mwai Kibaki we are hopeful that he is going to improve the economy so that we can get enough money to make ends meet. He shouldn't do what Moi did to our country and take away from the small farmers the money they earn for their coffee. And we should be earning more money for the milk we produce. We also want to see whether he will make primary education free, as he promised.

I tell her about the article I've read in the paper, pledging that, as of this week, primary education will be free and warning headmasters not to turn children away.

If that is true, it will be so good since we will only be buying books and uniforms. But these are all promises, and we have to wait and see if they are really acted upon. I'd like to see those things that used to be supported by the government, such as hospital services and schooling, become free again. Also I'd like to see the high taxes charged on things we buy in the shops reduced. Those are the changes we need.

"I know your mind is occupied with the problem of the new wife right now, so let me release you so you can meet with the other women," I conclude.

I'm glad you came back, Nyina wa Stepheni. Each time I think you will never come again, but you do, just like the rains we've had this year.

"Yes. I do. And now I want to give you something that will be like a seed to start your house-building project." I hand her a fat envelope with 100-shilling notes.

She opens it and looks inside. Her face opens like a sunflower. *Thank you, thank you, Nyina-wa-Stepheni.* She's pumping my hand up and down. *You don't forget us. By the time you next return, perhaps I will have completed the new house and you can visit me there—though it is some distance from here.*

"The next time I visit, I'll be sure to come to Kiomande and see what you've done." I smile, realizing she doesn't think I'll make it that far.

Wamutira grins and leads us back out along the path bordering several compounds to the dirt road where our car is parked. Now in her mid-70s, she is still illiterate. There will be no written communication between us. She does not trust her children to write a letter. It makes me sad knowing that I won't see her again for a while. Shaking her hand, I give her the Kenya farewell, "I'll see you when you see me."

As we get in the car, I watch Wamutira, who once was so shy I could hardly talk with her, confidently open the gate in the fence next to the *nduka* to meet with the women of her family. She has grown into her status as first wife with a grace and determination that I find touching. I really love this woman, though we live continents apart.

On Sunday, before going to Gatwe, we go to see Karuana's mother outside Kagumo. It has rained the night before, filling the dirt roads with slippery clay mud. Leaving the car at the entrance to the compound, Karuana and I walk up the path to the yard. Her father is bent over, cutting the grass in front of the house with a *panga*. He stands up to greet us and indicates that Karuana's mother is inside the house. She must have heard us talking with *mzee* as she comes into the front room and shakes our hands, offering us a seat on the maroon leather couch. Then she disappears to fix tea. Karuana follows her mother down the hall and into the kitchen to help.

I entertain myself looking at an album of family pictures. I recognize Karuana's older brother who'd gotten a Master's degree in Agriculture at Cornell then returned to build a new cement water tank for his family in the 1980s. Since then he's married and has a son. But six months before I arrived this latest time, he was killed in a road accident. A *matatu* in which he was a passenger lost traction on the Thika Road and overturned, killing everyone inside. Karuana and her family are still suffering his loss. Her only other brother, who was about 12 years old in 1984, is studying at a theological seminary in Kerugoya. He hopes to be a Presbyterian minister. A younger sister has married a man up in Gatwe; there's a wedding picture of them in the album.

When the two women return and we've settled down to tea, Karuana asks her mother what Wamutira and the family's women have done about the new wife.

I'm on tenterhooks, waiting for the answer.

The women took justice in their own hands, she tells us in Kikuyu. *They went as a big group to Murage's place, carrying their Sunday shoes. He was not there. They pulled the new wife out of the house and beat her with their shoes and fists. There was nothing she could do. Then they carried her back to her father's homestead.*

They actually did it! They settled the issue in their own way, as Gikuyu women have been doing for centuries within their communities and, in the last century, with their colonial overlords. In the early 20th century, they pulled up grass they'd been forced to grow by the colonial government and marched with it all the way to Nairobi, where they gathered in a formidable mass in front of the Ministry of Agriculture, shouting and taunting the colonial agents. Then, turning their backsides to them, they mooned them. Gikuyu women are, indeed, *atumia wa hinya*, women of strength, as they (and their men) have so often testified.

When I got back to the United States and told a friend about the incident, she asked why the women didn't just beat up the husband. A good question, but in gender-separated rural Kenya, women settle women's business and men settle men's business.

That's the way it is.

CHAPTER 7

Who's Traditional? Negotiating a New Century

Wamutira converted to Christianity in the early '60s *because everybody was joining, and I didn't want to be left behind like a fool.* She became a Christian so she could be assured of a proper burial when she died. But she rarely went to church in the 1980s. From my observations, cultural mores mean more to Wamutira than her church. Others in the community consider her family "traditional," that is, less oriented to Christian values associated with the West. To get a sense of what young women raised in more traditional families think about the changes they've witnessed, Karuana and I are meeting with a group of girls who don't attend a church. As we stroll along the road to town, I wonder about the differences between the girls we met at the Anglican Church and those we are about to meet at a local clinic in Kagumo.

      Turning onto the main road, our progress is slow because many people stop to greet me. I can never shake my visible *muzungu* identity, and older folks who remember me from past years want to say hello. Entering through the clinic compound's heavy wire gates, I notice a long line of women with infants and small children snaking its way from the front lawn, along an outside corridor and into one of the clinic's doorways. Other women sit alone or in groups on the lawn with their young children in tow, waiting to see a doctor. Some mothers breastfeed babies swaddled in *kangas* on their laps. Others comfort lethargic, whimpering children. A pungent mix of sweat, urine and antiseptics hangs in the stifling air.

      Junet Mithamo arrives. With her is an attractive, young woman neatly dressed in a tailored, lime-green cotton suit. Her wiry hair is slicked back and held with a broad comb.

"This is Bernice Matutia," Junet introduces her. "She's a nurse at the clinic. I asked her to find the girls and a place where you can meet."

Karuana and I shake hands with Bernice, thanking her for arranging the meeting.

As the young women arrive, eight of them, Bernice leads us away from the crowded front entrance of the clinic, down a side corridor to an office at the end. It is stark, with nothing but a solitary desk, a chair and a few cabinets. It has a slightly musty, metallic odor. Bernice and an agemate go to find benches for the others to sit on.

Karuana and I stand behind the desk in front of the only windows and put our notebooks on it. Karuana opens one of the windows to let in fresh air. Junet Mithamo is talking with one of the girls. Junet is dressed up for the meeting in a tailored dress, her pageboy wig, and newly shined, black oxford shoes. I can almost smell their polish.

Bernice and her helper return with two wooden benches and put them on either side of the rectangular office in front of glass cabinets on one side and wood shelves loaded with stacks of folders on the other side. The walls of the office are cement and painted a pale yellow. The cement floor is rust red. The young women spread out along the two benches facing each other, four on each side, with Junet sitting on the end of one bench, Bernice at the end of the other.

Bernice apologizes for being able to get so few girls; these are the only ones who were able to break away from their family's farms or town jobs to make the meeting. I tell her it's okay.

The young women look hesitant, as if they're unsure what is expected of them. After greeting them in Kikuyu, I launch into an explanation of the meeting's purpose in English, with Karuana translating so it will be easier for them to understand rather than dealing with my rough, American-tinged Kikuyu. I end by telling them to feel free to say whatever they like; I'm interested in their opinions. A couple shift on the benches, one smiles into her hand.

All of them are in their 20s and still single. As a group they are less educated than those we met with at the Anglican Church. Only three have gone to secondary school, in contrast to eight in the other group. All three have completed Form Four, the last year of high school. Muthoni, a petite young woman with clean features and an elfin grin, is a teacher. She's the most outgoing and readily answers questions. Faith, a district health worker, is model pretty and immaculately dressed. She seems well respected by her peers and contributes thoughtful comments. Keru, a heavy-set girl with a competent air, looks like she could handle a whole rugby team. She turns out to be a clerk in one of Kagumo's variety stores. This trio does most of the talking at the beginning with the other girls parroting, "Yes, that's so," or nodding their heads.

By and large, the kinds of basic survival skills these girls learned growing up are the same as the girls at the Anglican church: cultivating, weeding, fetching firewood and water, cooking, washing clothes, sweeping the compound and childcare—the same kinds of skills their mothers learned. They identify two specific differences from their parents' youth. Muthoni observes, *In our parents' time soap was not available for washing utensils and clothes, so they had to use roots or nothing at all.*

Keru adds, *Women had to spend a lot of time grinding the maize with two stones* [pestle and mortar]. *Nowadays, they can take their maize to a maize mill to be ground into flour. It saves a lot of time. For us, we can even buy unga* [maizemeal] *in a shop, already ground.* By the sounds of the other girls' *Aii...aii,* I can tell they agree with her.

The conversation turns to childcare. Muthoni relates that she learned at the age of five or six how to carry an infant on her back. Others begin to speak up now, agreeing that they were about the same age.

The reason we learned to carry babies on the back so early, Faith explains, *was to assist our mothers, and it kept the child safe and away from the ground.*

Learning how to carry a baby tied to one's back with a cloth is important because it allows a girl to do other tasks along with caring for the child, one of her less educated peers adds. Older siblings are expected to care for younger ones, all agree.

Of the social skills they learned from their parents, Muthoni says, *how to speak to wazee, the old ones, greeting them with deference and respect and following their wishes, was most important.* Other girls nod their heads with two adding, *Ii. Yes. It is true.*

Respect for elders is still an important aspect of rural Gikuyu society. Still, deference for elders is something these girls, regardless of educational level, emphasize, whereas the girls at the Anglican Church didn't mention it at all.

It may be that Christian girls, who come from less traditional, more-educated families, are more likely to question Gikuyu customs connected with age and respect for elders.

There was a time in American society when respect for older people was valued, too. But that was replaced in the post-World War II era by a new commercialism that emphasized youth and its spontaneity. Now that baby-boomers are aging, will there be a return to social norms that place a value on wisdom and old age? If the new trend toward an "older market" in advertising is any indication, it may already be happening.

One difference between American and Kenyan society is that in Kenya, three generations live together in a compound. Part of a child's upbringing is to learn who is related to whom and how to treat people of each *riika*, or age group, according to the norms of age stratification. A *riika*, in conventional Gikuyu society, referred to all one's agemates who went through *Irua* and were circumcised at the same time. This group formed a bond that provided mutual support and a safety net for the duration of each member's life. Every *riika* was given a name related to some natural or political event that happened at the time the group was circumcised. As the practice withered, the importance of *riika* ties has also waned. School ties and immediate family bonds began taking their place, as well as membership in self-help groups. For women, self-help groups enable them to raise money, on a rotating basis, for basic needs such as *mabati* (iron sheets for roofing) to replace grass thatch or for materials to construct water tanks in their homesteads. At times, the money is used for their children's school fees.

Like the church group, the girls gathered at the clinic agree unanimously that education has a profound effect on their attitudes.

When we started school, we began looking down on farming and cultivation because they are skills we identify with those who have not been schooled, observes Keru. The rest agree. It's not so different from rural areas in the United States where children who've gotten ahead in their education begin to turn their backs on farming or fishing and want to head for the city.

On the positive side, the girls agree that attending school helped their communication skills with other people and it also improved their health habits.

The teachers used to check us for cleanliness in primary school, sending those who were dirty, had lice in their hair or soiled clothing home to wash, Muthoni says. Several of the other young women giggle but don't disagree. Being sent home was an embarrassment and taught students and their parents the benefits of keeping clean.

The girls agree that some of the skills they learned at home carried over to school, such as cultivating and planting flowers around the compound, cooking and sweeping. As for cooking, in school they learned how to bake things such as cakes and *mandazi* (unsweetened raised dough, deep fried) that their mothers didn't know how to cook. Otherwise, they learned the usual academic skills of reading, writing and math.

They also had classes in which they learned something about diseases such as dysentery, tuberculosis, malaria, AIDS and alcoholism. Home science, science and Christian religious education (CRE) covered these topics.

Muthoni says, *Learning about these diseases has helped me prevent them, like maintaining cleanliness prevents dysentery and draining away stagnant water destroys the breeding sites for mosquitoes to prevent malaria.* What impresses me is how much sharper Muthoni is in citing specific measures to prevent these diseases than the girls at the Anglican Church. That she is a few years older may make a difference, but her added life experience surely contributes to her ability to apply what she learns in school to her home and the larger community. Notably, she says nothing about AIDS prevention. Is it because she hasn't faced the AIDS ogre directly? Or does village reticence about the disease prevent her from bringing it up? I feel at work again the ostrich response, head in the sand about AIDS.

What I learned in science enabled me to better take care of sick ones at home, Keru contributes, interrupting my thoughts.

Faith relates that biology and home science did have guest speakers some of whom had certain diseases themselves, including HIV/AIDS. *Someone who had the disease was especially helpful*, she says, *because that one had firsthand knowledge.*

Muthoni adds that in her school they also watched videos about AIDS.

"Were the videos helpful?" I probe.

Somewhat, but it was the guest speakers who visited the school that made it seem real, that it could affect anybody we knew. She lowers her head, giving me a clue to drop the topic for the moment.

I shift gears and ask about family life education and how the girls learned about coming of age and menarche. Muthoni tells me they learned about these things either from their parents or from their Standard Six (sixth-grade) teachers.

Another girl in the group relates, *In primary school, the teachers would take aside all the girls who were beginning to get breasts and teach them about menstruation and its social problems. We were taught how to control our desires and urged to protect ourselves against diseases that are sexually transmitted.* Could that mean the use of condoms? Possibly, but abstinence rather than contraceptive "safe sex" seems to be emphasized in schools.

When I ask about family life education, Keru says, *If it weren't for the lessons we learned in science, by now we'd all be having children.* The other girls smile in a knowing sort of way and a couple of them hide nervous giggles behind their hands. Lessons on how to control their fertility were, indeed, included in their science courses. Keru let the cat out of the bag; her comments imply that despite the campaign for abstinence as a preventive against sexually transmitted diseases, girls are sexually active in their teens. And Kenya is doing something about it by including family-planning information in courses that both girls and boys are required to take. It addresses two issues that this country has been battling for two decades, overpopulation and high HIV/AIDS rates (between 15-20% of Kenya's adult population had HIV/AIDS in 2001).[16]

Adding family-planning skills is a big step from when these teenagers' older sisters in their 30s were learning about sexual matters, either through a clinic if they were lucky (as Njeri was) or through the personal experience of becoming pregnant by mistake before learning that contraception was an option. Few women in their 30s learned about contraceptive methods when they were teenagers. Safe sex wasn't on the radar screen.

Muthoni says they learned about contraception from friends who were already sexually active. The girls agree that parents do not teach daughters about sexuality or family planning because, as one girl put it, *They think it will give their girls confidence to involve themselves in sexual intercourse before marriage.*

A contradiction exists here between the ideal of maintaining virginity and the reality that many girls do end up getting pregnant before they marry. Kenyan men want assurance that their future wives are fertile. Marriage has never been a single peak event, the way it is in Europe and the West. It is the birth of a first child that provides the glue to solidify marriage in the sense of a couple sharing a home.

Family planning is not a topic that came up with the girls in the Anglican Church, and only two of them mentioned having learned about menstruation and sexuality from parents. Kenyan girls, like American youth, learn about the biological and social aspects of sexuality in school and they turn to friends with sexual experience for further advice. Parents are little involved.

Do young women from traditional families benefit from any of the technological advances now appearing in Kagumo? All the girls have radios in their homes, and most listen regularly to the news, music and entertainment programs, particularly situation comedies. One of the less-educated girls adds that she likes a radio program that specializes in youth issues and suggests solutions to common problems. The majority of the girls also have a television set at home, in comparison to only one girl in the Anglican group. When I ask each of the girls what she watches, most say they like watching news, music, situation comedies and profiles that help them learn about their country.

Does television in these homes where the level of girls' education is lower than for the Christian girls fill a learning gap for both parents and children? I wish I could follow these girls back to their homes and observe what they watch on TV, as I'm doing with the teenagers in Karuana and Doctari's home. It would be a start.

None of the girls' families has a landline for telephones. Only two have access to mobile phones, in comparison to half the girls in the Anglican group. Lack of income may be one reason. However, that the majority of their families have a television set, an expensive item in rural Kenya and one that demands electricity, suggests that these non-church-going families may have different priorities than their Anglican counterparts. For families with few adult members able to read, an investment in television satisfies a need for learning and staying informed, along with being entertained.

The girls at the clinic view television as a "new technology." *News travels fast and we're able to get entertainment at home and don't have to travel some distance to get it*, observes Muthoni. For Faith, however, there is a downside to television: *Not all the things we watch from the West are good, but those watching just copy them anyway*, she observes. When I ask for some examples of what she means, she says, *The way Western women dress showing their bare thighs* [in shorts] *and bare shoulders with no self-respect. Another thing is men and women kissing and holding each other close in public.*

In a society where women and men value being well dressed, near nudity is frowned upon. And this doesn't just hold for Kenya's Muslim population on the coast. It applies to Christians and non-Christians in the interior. As for female/male relations in public, a sign I once saw at the entrance of a hotel on the Kenya coast says it all:

Notice to European Tourists: Please Respect Our Culture
No hand holding between men and women on public streets
No hugging and kissing in public places
No nude bathing on our beaches.

Asked what changes they would recommend to the new Kenyan president, these girls' suggestions, unlike those suggested by the girls at the Anglican Church, relate mainly to education. They think practical skills like agriculture and computer literacy should be introduced at the primary level. Topics such as family life education must be included. Keru suggests that computer studies should be compulsory at the secondary level with the costs incurred included in the tuition rather than as an extra fee.

All agree that primary education should be free as it "used to be" (in the 1970s and 1980s) and secondary education must be affordable. In addition, Muthoni complains, *They should not keep on changing the curriculum every year.* If constant curriculum change is a problem, it's plaguing teachers and students alike. No child left behind.

Computer training is a high priority for these young women. But Faith offers a caveat. She points out, with others agreeing, that in rural areas, it is only when a village acquires electricity, sufficient security and good roads that computer technology can be offered. To acquire such development, Muthoni argues, *a good political environment that is supportive and not corrupt is needed.*

A girl in matching skirt and sweater observes, *The health system in Kenya has improved but is costly.* Others note that not enough hospitals and clinics exist to serve the needs of Kagumo's growing population. More hospitals are needed, as well as more trained staff. The girls cite Kerugoya District Hospital as one without enough resources.

There is consensus that Kagumo now has adequate electricity. It is no longer localized just to the market area and shops around it. Many new buildings are going up as a result, and the market has expanded. There are more maize mills and tea-buying centers. Transportation from Kagumo to Kerugoya, Embu, and Karatina is better. These are the major changes that this group has witnessed over the past few years.

Before we leave, I have to ask these girls if they know about the Mungiki gang. They nod their heads solemnly.

That gang is no joke, Keru says. *They've scared a lot of wanachi and even killed people. But they got away with it. After the attacks in Nakuru, the government is finally beginning to do something.* She shudders.

This week the police broke into some of the places where the Mungiki meet. They arrested many members—that's what we heard on the news, Muthoni, the teacher, adds.

Ii. Yes. I saw that 92 members were arrested, Keru says. *I'm happy about the news. They were frightening too many girls.* Others in the group are nodding.

Hopefully, things will get better now that President Kibaki is there, Beatrice Matutia says. She and the girls get up to carry the benches back where they belong.

It's the end of a long day. The car is in a shop for servicing, so Karuana and I leave the clinic, accompanied by several of the girls, to search for a *matatu* heading for Kerugoya. A tall girl, who hadn't spoken much during the meeting, approaches me and takes my backpack so I don't have to carry it. Leaning in close, she says confidentially, "You know, everyone here knows somebody who has died of AIDS. But people don't like to talk about it."

"Really?" I'm astounded by her frank confession and eager to pursue the issue. Here's my chance. Just then, another girl joins us. My potential confidante abruptly changes the topic.

"What are the opportunities for education in America?" she asks.

I wilt, disappointed that my opportunity to learn more about AIDS has been thwarted.

"Every state in the U.S. has a free education system that is paid for by taxes on property. But at the university level, tuition is charged and it can be *very* expensive." I answer her question carefully so that she and her friend get the message that education in the U.S. is not totally free as Kenyans often assume.

"But at least secondary school is free."

"If one goes to a government school. But remember, people pay for it through their taxes. Parents have to pay fees if their child goes to a private school."

"I would love to go to school in America," the girl says wistfully.

"So would I," her friend says.

We are reaching the center of town, where it is more crowded. Everyone in Kagumo seems to have the same idea about catching a *matatu* to Kerugoya.

"Come on, Jean," Karuana calls back to me; she's been ahead of me with Junet Mithamo. "We're going to have to go to the other end of town to catch a *matatu* that's not so crowded we end up sitting on each other's lap."

The girl with me stops, and handing over my heavy backpack, says, "I have to leave you here. I'm expected at home. Can you give me your address so I can write to you in America?" Her dark eyes look earnest.

"Okay. But I won't be home for a while. I'm going to Madagascar after I leave Kenya. By the way, what is your name?" I take a piece of notebook paper out of my pack and hastily write down my address for her.

"Jocelyn. Jocelyn Wambui."

I hand her the piece of paper. "Nice to meet you, Jocelyn."

"Can I have your address, too?" her friend asks.

"Why don't you get it from Jocelyn," I suggest. "I need to hurry." I shake hands with each girl and run to catch up with Karuana and Junet Mithamo.

We have to walk to the far end of town to catch a *matatu* that isn't jam packed already or so empty it won't leave for another half hour. Saying good-bye to Junet, we climb into the middle seat of a dusty white minivan whose back seat is already filled. Bags and bundles begin to pile up around our feet as others crowd in. The *tout* is shouting for the last passengers. We are five adults in the middle seat. The woman squeezed next to me smells faintly of a cooking fire, wood smoke mingled with boiled milk, earthy. A mother and her two little girls, all smartly dressed, climb into the seat ahead of us along with an older man and woman. Once seated, one of the two little girls, her face full of curiosity, turns around to stare at me. I strike up a conversation with her in Kikuyu to bridge the gap.

"Have you come from school?" I ask.

"Yes," she nods, smiling. I learn from her older sister that she goes to a pre-school in Kagumo.

"Where do you come from?" the preschooler asks.

"America," I respond.

She looks at me quizzically, and at this point her mother tells her, "Turn around. Don't bother the lady anymore."

"It's all right," I reply. "Can I give your girls a sweet?"

She hesitates as I feel around in my backpack for the two wrapped candies I have stashed at the bottom. Then, "Yes, it's okay."

I give the girls each a lemon drop and ask the older one what class she's in—she's wearing a school uniform.

"Three," she replies shyly while unwrapping her small piece of candy.

"Oh, that's the year you get more math, isn't it?"

"Yes." She nods, then thanks me for the candy and turns around to face the front.

The *matatu* is speeding down the highway, anxious to beat all competitors to the next pick-up spot. The driver screeches the brakes just before he gets to a large speed bump marking a collection of shops along the road. He eases over the bump then pulls to the side of the road to let two people out. One has a bag of what feels like dried maize wedged against my feet. The *tout* asks me to pass it forward. I pull it up with Karuana's help, and we pass it over the laps of three other passengers to a woman who has just climbed down from the vehicle. She pays her 25 shillings to the *tout* and then hoists the heavy bag of maize onto her back and walks, half stooped by the load, up a eucalyptus-lined path toward a homestead in the distance. A man goes by with a small herd of goats in front of him. While we wait for him to pass, another *matatu* flies by us, its horn honking wildly to let our driver know he's going to beat him to the next drop-off.

After two more stops, we disembark at St. Michael's School opposite Doctari's clinic. Waiting several minutes for the traffic to let up, we cross the busy road and jump a sanitation ditch to another road that runs in front of the clinic. Doctari is standing outside talking with two other men. Karuana and I greet them and head downhill to the "supermarket," more like an American Mom-and-Pop store, three doors away. I buy bottled water, orange squash, matches, and toilet paper. Then I spy packages of roasted peanuts and add them to my basket to tide me over for the late dinners. We head back up to the clinic and meet the receptionist and a cleaner in the waiting room. I look over at a bench against the wall and see Wainoi with a woman in her 40s that I don't recognize.

"*Wimwega, Nyina-wa-Stepheni.*"   Wainoi greets me and introduces the woman with her. She turns out to be a sister-in-law. "My in-law asked me to introduce her to you. She wants some information."

"I see." I turn to the woman. She's well dressed, definitely a town woman. "What information do you need?"

"I understand that you are from America, and I want to know if you can find a school for my son there?" She asks the question full of enthusiasm.

It's all I can do to keep from groaning. I look at Karuana, who is talking with the receptionist, wishing we could flee. Fending off people's requests for help in educating their children drains me. It never seems to end. I have limited resources. Enough is enough!

"I'm afraid I can't help you," I tell Wainoi's in-law. "It has become nearly impossible to get a student visa since the 9/11 attack on the World Trade Center. Our government has become very strict. Some people who have outstayed their student visas are being sent home. The situation is not good. I'm sorry."

The woman accepts my explanation, and I bid good-bye to her and Wainoi as Doctari comes up.

"We'll have to walk to the shop where I dropped off the car," he explains. "Here, let me help you with your packages." He takes one of my bags. I put my heavy backpack on and take up the other bag.

"What did Wainoi want?" Karuana asks as we walk downhill through the crowds.

"That was her sister-in-law with her. She wanted to know if I could find a school for her son in America."

She laughs. "Just what you need…another Kenyan student." She knows the problems I had over the last decade with one Kenyan I helped find a college and housed for a year. He ended up dropping out.

Karuana and I follow Doctari down one of Kerugoya's side roads for two blocks and are about to cross the main road to the other side when we see Karuana's sister Mary and her three-year-old daughter June. Both are dressed to the nines in pale yellow look-alike satin dresses with full skirts and white lace trim. Mary greets me with a handshake and introduces her daughter, telling me, "I named her for the month of her birth." They have both come from town. Mary teaches in a pre-kindergarten in Kerugoya; June attends a nursery school.   Mary is a wonderful, independent woman with flipped, shoulder length hair.   Shorter than Karuana, she's five years older than her sister.   She seems thinner than when I saw her in 1994.   Very attractive, she remained single by choice.   At the age of 42, she decided she wanted a child, but didn't want to marry.   She chose the man she wanted as the father and with him produced a lovely, hesitant daughter.   It's a scenario not so different from some of my single friends at home but is atypical of most rural Kenyan women of Mary's age.

We leave Mary and June at the dusty crossroads and dash across the main street to a pharmacy on a corner, where I wait with our packages while Karuana goes to greet a friend and Doctari gets the car out of hock.   The sidewalks are crowded with people getting off work at this hour.   It's six o'clock.   The sun will set at seven, as it usually does this close to the equator.   The gas station across the street from the chemist is crowded with cars and *matatus*.   At the corner a queue of dust-laden taxis waits to take people home.   There's no municipal bus system in Kerugoya, and cars are outrageously expensive.   Most people streaming along the sidewalks and roads are walking home.   Doctari's yellow Peugeot finally pulls alongside the high curb.   Karuana appears, and we load our packages into the trunk of the car and head for home.

After taking off my tennis shoes at the doorway, I don flip-flops and go into the kitchen to see about tea.   Karuana has the kettle going, so I offer to help dice vegetables for dinner.   She gives me the job of chopping six large onions—ouch.   Halfway through tears are streaming down my cheeks.   Wang'oo comes out to check on the progress of dinner and seeing my tears asks, "What's wrong Jean? You look terribly sad."

"Onions," is all I can say, in between sniffles and blinks.

"Oh," he laughs.   "Here, let me help you."   My godson grabs two of the onions, a knife and a small wooden board and retreats to another stainless steel counter.   The kitchen is very small with room only for two people.   A yellow plastic bucket beside the stove next to me holds all the compost material—carrot peelings, banana and orange peels, paper thin onion skins, squeezed passionfruit pods, papaya skins, used tea bags, left over dried *ugali* (cooked maizemeal). A brown speckled hen wanders in from outside and begins pecking at the *ugali* in the bucket.   "Hey, out of there," I shout at her, making a menacing gesture with my knife.   Wang'oo, alerted by my shout, turns and shoos the hen, too. Squawking as she goes, she flees through the open back door.

Karuana has finished shredding the kale. "Tea's ready," she announces, then calls, "Wamuyu, come and get the tea tray." Her daughter is engrossed in MTV.

We all settle down in the sitting room. Doctari comes in and switches the channel to KCB news. The president has named his new Cabinet positions, his "Cabinet dream team," the commentator calls it. Instead of reducing the number of positions to 11, as was his goal, there are 24 ministers.

I pick up the *Daily Nation* from the coffee table to learn more. The new ministers' pictures in color parade across the front page. President Kibaki has tried to balance ethnic and regional divisions in his appointments. He's named six women to office, three ministers and three assistant ministers. One of those named is my old acquaintance Wangari Maathai, a leader of the internationally recognized Green Belt Movement in Kenya.[*] Wangari, an environmental activist, is the new Assistant Minister of Environment, Natural Resources and Wildlife. I wonder why Kibaki didn't make her the Minister instead of Newton Kulundu. She certainly has the credentials and experience. Maybe it's because she's too controversial; she actively opposed Moi on a number of key issues, including his dream of building a highrise with his name on it in Uhuru Park, the people's green belt in downtown Nairobi. Moi attacked her because she led the conservation campaign that successfully thwarted his dream. Wangari is no shrinking violet. She's a *mutumia wa hinya,* woman of strength.

Regardless of my displeasure over Wangari's appointment, I'm happy to see in the paper that Kibaki has chosen a woman as Minister of State in the Office of the Vice President and that women head both the ministries of Health and Water Resources. Long in the shadows under Moi's regime, Kenyan women are finally resurfacing with Kibaki's promise to include them at all levels. I read on.

At the bottom of the first page is a small article with a provocative headline, "Free school starts next week." Kibaki is making good his pledge of free education. "Pupils in public primary

---

[*] In 2004, Wangari was named winner of the Nobel Peace Prize for her nonviolent work to reverse deforestation in Kenya and protect Nairobi's Uhuru Park from development.

schools will not be required to pay any fees when the new term begins next week," the *Daily Nation* heralds.[17]

The next morning, on our way to Kagumo, I pick up *The Sunday Standard*. An article on page one warns all head teachers (principals) that anyone who defies the order not to charge fees for primary school children will be doing so "at his or her own risk."[18] Further, school heads and education administrators have been asked to ensure that teaching and learning continue uninterrupted. It's almost as if the president anticipates trouble once schools open their doors to all children on Monday. Another article notes the significant drop in primary school enrollments over the past decade, from 98 percent of school-age children in the late 1980s to 78 percent in 1999 as school fees rocketed.[19]

Monday will be a day to watch.

CHAPTER 8

Ascending the Ridges to Gatwe

When I get to the crossroads at the top of the muddy ridge leading to Gatwe, the one where a tea-buying center hugs one corner like a tick on a dog's ear, that indefinable scent of fermented jasmine and damp earth clinging to freshly picked tea leaves wrestles up memories of my first trip here. The scene at the tea-buying center hasn't changed in 25 years. I always know when we get to this junction that I'm nearly home. The major difference is that the number of growers and pickers across the verdant ridges has tripled as more acres of land snuggled up against the Mt. Kenya forest have come under tea cultivation.

When I first visited these highland ridges in 1977, I was on a mission: to visit our Kenyan exchange student Mararu's mother and learn all I could from her about the Gikuyu coming-of-age rite. I wanted to compare it with another group's rite for a multimedia unit on "Coming of Age in Kenya." The trip turned out to be more of a challenge than I'd anticipated.

My 11-year old daughter and 16-year old son were along that time. We settled at a church hostel in Nairobi. It took me five weeks to line up a *combi*, a VW bus with a pop-top, for the trip north. We planned to camp in the *combi* once we got up to the area where Mararu's mother lived. I'd stocked the bus with food for a week.

Mararu's 20-something brother, Karimi, who'd once been some politician's driver, came down to the capital and helped us negotiate the police roadblocks set up on the Thika road at that time. Karimi ("Creamy" to my daughter) was one of the few members of Mararu's family who spoke English and could lead us to his mother's place nestled on a ridge high above Kagumo.

At that time Kagumo was a small market center with an ancient *mugumo*, a huge wild fig tree with a knarled trunk, standing in the middle of the market. The tree could be seen from all directions.

At one time Gikuyu elders ritually slaughtered their best rams at the base of the tree and smeared the blood on its bark as a sacrifice to *Ngai*, the creator, and *Kirinyaga,* the ostrich mountain spirit. They prayed for fertile crops and the wellbeing of the clans. The *mugumo* became the hub of people's exchanges as Kagumo, the oldest continually inhabited village in the area, continued to spread. Several small shops were perched along the main road in 1977. Not much more.

People lived in homesteads, collections of thatched huts nestled together. They were broadly dispersed, like clumps of brown mushrooms protruding from the valley and along the hills. Few vehicles existed in Kagumo. We saw solitary men herding either a string of goats or a few cattle down the tarmac road, usually on their way to the market. Occasionally, a canvas-covered pickup truck functioning as a *matatu* passed us. Otherwise, everyone walked everywhere. There was no electricity. People used kerosene lanterns or candles for light and cooked over a wood fire or a small charcoal brazier on legs.

When we got to Kagumo that August of '77, we picked up a couple of loaves of bread and a one-kilo package of sugar to take up to Mararu's mother: one never arrives empty handed in Kenya. It had rained, and as we turned off the paved highway onto a dirt road that snaked up and around the green hills, the dirt turned to thick, brick-red mud. We slowed down to cross a rickety wooden bridge over a fast-moving river that tumbled over jagged rocks and climbed up and up between steep, tea-carpeted ridges the color of fresh new peas. An exotic blend of green tea and pungent earthiness came from the damp terraced fields.

As we climbed higher, the clay mud became slick as ice, and the *combi* began sliding sideways at intervals. Karimi fought to control it from pitching into a ditch. Silence, heavy as fog, filled the microbus. My daughter Ann paled to the color of old sheets. Even the live duck we'd picked up on the way, a present from Mararu's father for our first meal in the highlands, stopped squawking and wiggled to a corner of the *combi* settling down on its bound legs. It smelled foul, and Ann, a self-declared vegetarian who'd become aware of the bird's fate, sat as far away from it as possible, concentrating all her attention on the slippery road ahead and trying not to retch. She never was one for twisty winding roads. And the duck sure didn't help.

Clenching our teeth, we crested a knoll and finally found ourselves at a junction. A small cement and stucco building clung to one corner. Women and children sat on a slope of grass in front with huge baskets full of chartreuse tea leaves.

"What's that?" My son Stephen asked Karimi, as he watched a boy get up and disappear into the building.

"It's the tea-buying center. Those people are waiting for places to open up inside so they can spread out their tea leaves for sorting and grading. Do you want to see what they're doing?"

"Yes," we said at once, anxious to get out of the cramped VW bus.

Inside, raised smooth cement counters at waist level lined three walls. Women, a few men, and some older children were standing in front of the counters sorting tea leaves into different piles. They looked around at us curiously, startled to see a trio of *wazungu* (whites) in their neck of the woods then, embarrassed, returned to their work.

"There are three grades of tea," Karimi explained, holding up a tea stem. "A stem with a new growth bud at the end and two small leaves on either side, like this one, is the highest grade of tea. We earn the most for two leaves and a bud. More mature leaves without a bud are the next grade, and lowest are slightly older leaves." For a few minutes, we watched the pickers, young and old, sorting the tea. They were very fast, with no wasted motions.

"How long does it take to sort a whole basket of leaves?" I asked.

"It takes about an hour or more, then another 15 minutes to have it weighed by the KTDA supervisor, with the picker watching to make sure he has weighed it properly and not cheated the picker. At the end of the day, each picker gets a chit with her name and KTDA identification number at the top, showing how many kilograms have been picked, the grades and the amount earned for the day."

"How much does someone pick each day?"

"It depends. An experienced adult can pick between 60 and 80 kilograms [132-176 pounds], but children and beginners pick less."

We saw that the harvested and sorted leaves were being put into huge burlap bags that were lined up near the entrance.

"Where do they take the tea from here?" Stephen asked.

"It's taken by lorry to the Kangaita Tea Factory. It's one of the oldest and largest tea factories in the country. I'll take you there to see it one of these days. It's a bit of a walk from here. We're almost home now."

After leaving the tea-buying center that day, we drove slowly along the top of an emerald-green ridge. The sun was beginning to sink over the Sagana Plains far below, brushing the valley with strokes of mauve and plum. We turned off the mud-clogged road. Karimi maneuvered carefully downhill along the top of a cleared and grassy ridge edged by clusters of eucalyptus trees. We came to an abrupt halt next to a fenced-in compound. We could see the thatched roofs of three small mud-and-wattle houses inside. After scrambling out of the *combi*, Karimi led us through a makeshift gate and called, "*Hodi?*"—the Swahili equivalent of "Hello, anybody home?"

A small, wizened woman, her wiry gray hair wrapped in a large blue headscarf, came from the doorway of the nearest hut. She had penny-brown eyes, a flat face with a button nose and a slightly quizzical grin. As her smile broadened in recognition, her lips spread back on a row of large protruding teeth, like kernels of white corn, cushioned by dull pink gums and a prominent jaw.   She was obviously a woman who led with her chin. Her expression took on a look of amusement as Karimi introduced us.

"*Karibuni,*" she welcomed us enthusiastically.   Having *wazugu* in her highland compound was not an everyday event. She shook my hand with vigor, looking us up and down all the while. She and my daughter were the same height.

"You can call me by my Christian name, Jessica," she offered through Karimi.

I nodded and asked, "What is your Kikuyu name?" Karimi translated.

"*Wanjira.*"

"*Wan-jir-a,*" I repeated it slowly, trying to roll the *r* the way she had.

She giggled then said something to Karimi in Kikuyu. It made him laugh.

"She wants to know why you and Ann are wearing trousers."

"Oh," I grinned.   "Anyone can wear trousers in America, whether you're male or female."

"*Ni gwo* [Is that so]?" Her skepticism was palpable. "What's the news of Mararu in America?" She changed course. Mararu was her son.

"He is well and studies hard. He sends you his greetings and love."

"Come in. Come in and have a cup of tea, Nyina-wa-Stepheni."

Stephen ducked his head to go through the low doorway. The room was small with a pounded earthen floor. At one end was an open cooking fire dug in the floor. Three large stones were placed around the edge. A well-worn aluminum pot without a handle or lid sat balanced on the stones, steaming. Inside the pot, fresh cow's milk was coming to a boil, filling the room with warm fragrance. It blended nicely with the smell of the fire's cedar wood. With a deft movement, Jessica took a large pinch of tea from a tin and dropped it into the boiling milk, stirring it a little, then with her bare hands took the edges of the blackened pot off the cooking fire and put it on a burlap bag to cool a bit before pouring it through a strainer. This is how Kenyans make tea. No water, just straight milk. And when it's served, a generous helping of sugar.

While we were having our tea with pieces of cooked arrowroot, Karimi moved the *combi* through the gate and into the compound next to Jessica's small house "for safety," he told me. I was astonished to see later that the VW bus with its top popped up for camping was nearly the same size as Jessica's house.

A small group collected in the yard to meet us, including Jessica's brother and another son, Mwangi, and his wife Mariam, who held a chubby, toddler girl. Karimi made the introductions, explaining that Jessie's brother lived in one of the compound's houses, and Mwangi and his young family in the other. Earlier, we had learned that when Jessica's husband took a second wife in Mwea, on the Sagana Plain, Jessica did not like the arrangement and opted to move back to her father's homestead in the highlands to be near her older brother who was a widower. Mwangi and his wife decided to relocate with his mother to the highlands rather than stay in the mosquito-infested lowlands.

Karimi handed the bound duck we'd brought to Mwangi and asked Stephen if he'd like to see how they killed it.

"I guess so," my son said dubiously.

"Do they cut off its head?" Ann asked, looking worried.

"No," Karimi said. "We twist its neck. It's very fast."

Ann groaned and turned away in disgust, but Stephen perked up and followed Mwangi with the duck to the back of the house.

In the meantime, Jessica emerged with a large pot of boiling water and put it down on a bench under the eave of her house.

"It's for the plucking," Karimi explained.

Mwangi and Stephen, who now looked a little green, returned. Mwangi carried the dead duck by the neck. Its head lolled to the side over his brown fist, but there was no blood to be seen. Mwangi dipped the bird into the pot of hot water. Jessica and her daughter-in-law sat down to pluck the bird once its feathers had loosened in the hot water. This was more than my daughter could bear. She retreated to the *combi* to read, muttering under her breath, "I'm not going to eat any of that duck, Mom. Please tell them I'm a vegetarian."

The plucking went quickly. Then Karimi and Mwangi took the naked bird out back to butcher it. It later wound up in a stew pot for our dinner, adding flavor to the vegetables and potatoes but little meat. I fixed spaghetti for Ann in the *combi* and took some to share with everyone. But Jessica would have none of it. She thought the pasta looked like intestinal worms!

Even though Jessica and I did not speak the same language in 1977, over the next several days we found we could communicate, for the most part, through a combination of miming and gestures. We got on famously, and as Mararu had promised, she was a "traditional" Gikuyu woman who knew her culture inside and out. She explained the purpose of *Irua*, with Karimi acting as translator, and even acted out various scenes from the ritual. It was difficult for me to understand and accept that excising or cutting off the tip of the clitoris of girls, as well as circumcising boys, was part of this climactic and most important coming-of-age ceremony for Gikuyu. It seemed like such a cruel practice. But something happened up there that week that gave me pause.

One morning as Stephen, Ann and I were finishing up an early breakfast outside the *combi*, Jessica appeared and observed for a moment what we were eating—omlets, made by Steve, and sliced pineapple—and how we were eating. She went up to Ann, looking closely at my daughter's mouth. The sun was shining at an angle that reflected light off Ann's braces. Jessica pointed with her finger towards Ann's mouth and asked something in rapid Kikuyu. I was perplexed. Then it suddenly dawned on me that it must be Ann's braces, that she'd never seen someone with braces on their teeth.

Ann obliged her curiosity by grinning broadly to show her hardware.

"Where's Karimi? We need him. Ka-ri-mi," I called.

He appeared from the doorway of his uncle's house.

"We need you to translate."

Karimi ambled over, and Jessica repeated her question.

"*Cucu* (pronounced Shosho, meaning grandmother) wants to know what those metal things on Ann's teeth are," he explained.

"Those things are braces. They put metal caps over children's first permanent teeth and attach bands across them to straighten them so they'll have a better bite." I tried to explain the process of orthodontics in as simple language as I could muster.

Ann chimed in. "Each time you go to the orthodontist, they tighten these wires," she pointed to the wires connecting the metal caps in her mouth.

Karimi translated the explanations into Kikuyu for his mother with some misgiving, a perplexed look on his face.

Jessica examined Ann's barbed teeth closely. "Does it hurt?" she asked, a scowl of concern on her face.

"Yes, sometimes. When they're tightened," Ann said.

The old woman, her dark, flat face twisted in pain, looked incredulous. She turned on me with an angry sputter of words.

I backed up, flinching at the force of her tirade, not comprehending the meaning.

Karimi hastily translated. "She says, 'How can you be that cruel to your children? It must be too painful to have all that metal in the mouth. How can they eat?'" He shuffled uncomfortably, quickly looking from me to his mother.

"They have no trouble eating. It's to help them chew food better," I said, trying to explain.

"Humph! We would never do such a horrible thing to our children." She's standing with her arms akimbo in front of me, scowling like an angry cat, as Karimi translates this. "Such a cruel practice! And you white people call yourselves civilized!"

I was startled into silence. For a small woman Jessica could pack a wallop. I'd never thought of braces in this way, from the perspective of a people whose teeth are naturally strong and white from a fibrous diet with few sweets, and to whom orthodontics is unknown. Here I'd been thinking female circumcision, which the Gikuyu historically practiced, was the worst pain I could imagine, and Jessica was thinking the same about orthodontics.

Do we ask our children if they want their teeth straightened? Not always. We do it for their own good. Partly it is a question of aesthetics—we believe that our children will look better with straight teeth despite the pain involved. But Jessica was aghast, shocked by the practice. It was a good reminder of how we tend to see things through our own cultural lens without realizing the lens is there. Personal relationships within the same culture have their own liabilities, as we all know, but in intercultural encounters they are magnified.

My confrontation with Jessica over Ann's braces taught me to withhold judgment of another person's cultural values and practices until I understood their meaning for the community involved. The lesson was a gift, the first of many I was to collect, like unusual stones, in the Kenya highlands.

Over the next few days our walking tour of the ridges between Gagathoma and Gatwe, which are small market centers roughly three miles apart, took us to the 15-foot-deep, 12-foot-wide trench that had been dug by the British using Gikuyu forced labor. The trench was constructed in the early 1950s to prevent Mau Mau guerrillas in the Mt. Kenya forest from coming down to homesteads to get food, arms and recruits for the liberation struggle. The trench encircled Mt. Kenya for 200 miles. An engineering feat, it was originally filled with bamboo stakes sharpened into knives at the top. A similar arrangement was used later by U.S. forces in Vietnam as a deterrent to Viet Cong guerrillas. The trench was still there in 1977, although the bamboo stakes had been removed and the walls of the trench were beginning to erode. Grass grew at the bottom. We visited several homesteads near the trench and in one I learned that a couple of years earlier a child, hoeing in his mother's garden, had his lower leg blown off when his hoe hit a buried land mine.

Among the survival tricks we learned that week were how to pick tea, to haul water, and each evening before we went to bed to bathe out of a bucket to protect ourselves against chiggers, I was told. I'd heard about chiggers plaguing people in the U.S., especially in the south, but I'd never run into them myself. For those of you who've never had the pleasure, the pale mite larvae begin as eggs carried by fleas attached to goats and sheep in Kenya. They drop off into the soil. People pick up the microscopic eggs and larvae with dirt and dust on their feet. The larvae, minute white worms, burrow into the toes and begin sucking blood. The larva's lunch produces an intense itching, burning irritation that hangs on until the worm is extracted. Tiny larvae, no longer than a staple, once left my toes an itchy, stinging mess in 1983. Karuana had to dig the flesh-eating chiggers out of my toes with a pin. I learned to take precautions after that incident.

Carefully washing our feet of all dirt and dust at night, we learned, would reduce the chances of getting these nasty little parasites. Ann got one anyway. I found later on that wearing closed shoes was the best prevention.

One day that August we took a long hike to the Kangaita Tea Factory. A truck passed us carrying huge burlap bags of tea on each side hanging from hooks that ran the length of the truck bed. When we got to the factory, we followed the burlap bags inside where they were removed from the hooks and the leaves were shaken and spread out on large metal trays for wilting. The tea leaves had to be wilted under carefully monitored tropical conditions, then roasted on slowly revolving trays over ovens using huge amounts of wood from the nearby forest.

Going outside to the ovens at the back of the factory, we found a whole team of men, sweat dripping off their faces, chopping up long logs and feeding them to three giant ovens in the factory's exterior wall. The men kept the ovens going all day. By 1983, the factory had made the transition to electricity, new modern ovens were installed, and the men had found other jobs.

To meet the increased demand for tea, more neighborhood tea-buying centers began springing up. In addition, after the tea growers' three-month strike for higher prices and more production facilities in 1992, several new tea factories were built, and farmers began earning more for their tea.

Our time in the highlands in 1977 had given me a tantalizing glimpse into the Gikuyu's world and how it was changing. I thirsted for more. By 1983, having returned twice (once in 1978 and another in 1980) to visit Jessica and her extended family, I decided to make my base in Mutira. The location's cooler elevation meant I was less likely to encounter malaria-bearing mosquitoes. Still, one got me on a trip to the coast, and back in the highlands, I battled chills and a ferocious fever that left me drained of energy for ten days.

I lived in Kagumo during the last quarter of 1983 while doing a modest survey of the location's women farmers, then moved up to the Gatwe region at 5,000 feet in January for the remaining year and a half of my field work because Jessica's sister and her husband invited me to stay with them in their compound. I became their third "daughter" and inherited a whole extended family in the bargain.

Of the seven original women who shared their life stories with me in 1984, three lived within walking distance of Kagumo. Four, including the two youngest women, lived up in the highlands between Gagathoma and Gatwe. The oldest woman Wanjiku died at the age of 89, six months before I returned at the end of 2002. I planned to visit three of her grown granddaughters living in the family compound. The two youngest women, who were in their 20s at the time I collected their stories, were now in their 40s. My most recent visits with both had been in 1992 and 1994.

The older of the two, Wanja, has daughters whom I hoped to meet with this time, but the younger woman, Nyambura, has five sons and no daughters. As a result I decide to enlist her 17-year-old son, Kiragu, to help me bring together a group of his agemates for a session similar to the ones I had with the girls in Kagumo. I want to compare the boys' perceptions of change with the girls' views. I've recruited my godson Wang'oo to facilitate the discussion so the boys will feel freer to talk. He's agreed to help and I've given him a few pointers for his role. Still, like other people in Kagumo and Kerugoya, he perceives Gatwe, due to its location and lack of modern amenities, to be a remote area.

People picking tea in the highlands when we first visited in 1977.

Welcome to the New Year, 2003

The morning Karuana and I set out for Gatwe, it's a holiday—New Year's Day. I plan to spend it with Jessica and other members of the extended family that I lived with in the 1980s. They've heard I am back again. Karuana wants to see them, too. We have to take a *matatu* from Kagumo to get to the junction and then hike up to the ridge where Jessica lives, because Doctari needs the car. He has promised to pick us up at the tea-buying center at the end of the day.

Maitu, my "mother" in Kikuyu, who was Jessica's younger sister, had died two years earlier but *Baba,* my "father," is still alive. One of their daughters, my "sister," lives on a nearby ridge. She's a close friend, and it was her daughter, Njoki, who came to live with me in hopes of getting her diabetes treated. I also want to set times to meet with Wanjiku's granddaughters, as well as Wanja and Nyambura, the youngest life narrators.

"Happy New Year," Selena, one of Jessica's daughters-in-law, comes to greet us as I stop on the ridge, glancing around for Jessica. "James is here. I'll go call him."

While we wait for her husband, who is one of Mararu's soft-spoken brothers, I look down the ridge in search of Jessica's house. It's gone. In its place, a little higher on the ridge, is a lovely stone and wood plank house with vertical three-inch wood ribs painted alternately blue and white against the dark brown planks. It gives the siding the look of a striped house trimmed in blue.

The house has a firm cement foundation with two rows of rectangular stone masonry bricks above it that support the wood siding and keep the termites at bay. Windows with glass panes are encased in wooden frames of the same sky blue as the rest of the exterior trim. Under each window the rectangular stone masonry has been brought up to the sill. The house has a stylish *mabati* roof set on a blue frame. It has a peak with a slightly lower roof set under it covering the other half of the house. From the back, the angular roof appears to have two halves that fit together, one tucked under the other, covering what looks like a three-bedroom house. The design is lovely, reminiscent of Frank Lloyd Wright's early adaptations to nature—though on a simpler scale.

I figured in the late 1980s that with two sons now in the United States, it wouldn't be long before Jessica would have a modern house. But when I returned in 1994, she still lived in a mud-and-wattle house, though the thatching had been replaced with a corrugated iron sheet roof. Her sons, ever loyal, had finally convinced their mother to upgrade her housing.

"*Karibu, Nyina-wa-Stephen*," James arrives to greet me then switches to English. "We didn't know you were coming. My mother will be very pleased to see you."

"Is she here?"

"Yes, she's in her garden down by the stream. I'll send a girl to fetch her."

"Thanks. How are you and your family?"

"We are well. The oldest girl is now married and living away, but the other two are here. Things are better than when you last came. We're not depending on tea alone now."

"Really? What else are you growing?"

"We have a project here to grow passionfruit. The fruit will be exported to Europe. We can get a good price for it. It's better than depending on just one crop."

"That's great. I love passionfruit," I tell James excitedly. "We get passionfruit juice from South Africa in the U.S. Show me your project."

"This is our first year," James explains, leading Karuana and me downhill to a place where two rows of cedar posts, one at either end of a rectangular garden, have been driven into the ground. The two lines of posts are about 20 feet apart. Long wires have been strung between the end posts like the horizontal lines of a music staff. Staked passionfruit vines grow in rows between the end posts and spread out along the suspended wires strung between them. I can see unripe green and some ripe purple egg-shaped fruits hanging in places along the vines. The crop looks healthy.

"I can remember when passionfruit just grew along a fence in the compound and we ate them one at a time as they became ripe," I reminisce as we go down an aisle between the vines.

"Yes, but now we're growing them to make a profit," James smiles serenely. He's still a handsome man, even with graying hair and a creased brow. His quiet, disarming gentleness combined with a remarkable command of English have always put me at ease. I like being around James.

"Did you know my mother visited Mararu in America?" he asks, as he picks a ripe passionfruit and hands it to me.

"I do. But I live very far from Mararu and Kamau now, so I didn't see her. I had a long conversation with her on the telephone instead."

Jessica at her homestead on one of the many ridges near Gagathoma in 2003.

At that point, Jessica crests the hill, leaning on a long wooden walking stick. She's dressed in a cornflower blue dress with an oversized green cardigan sweater over it. On her head is a white headscarf with another in brown stripes twisted into a rope around it to hold the headscarf in place. Her elongated ears, made longer by the hollow holes in each lobe (*matu* in Kikuyu), hang limp. At one time, they held large bone plugs. Whereas some older women have had *matu* stitched up now that women no longer wear plugs, Jessica has left the holes in her lobes, vestiges of another era. On her feet, characteristically bare in the past, are dusty brown loafers. Jessica has come up in the world, but her smooth face is the same, and she is laughing now to see me here.

"So you have returned," she says in Kikuyu. Then she embraces me. "We were wondering when you'd be coming next."

"Happy New Year," I greet her. "I always come back. And this time I came to see your new house. I knew one of these days that old one of yours would no longer be here even though you liked it so much."

She chuckles. "Well, these sons of mine insisted that I have a new house. What could I do? I sleep there and there's room for the grandchildren. But I still cook in the other place." Her eyes twinkle. Despite her 92 years, she exudes amazing vitality.

"I like your new house, Nyina-wa-Ndegwa. It's beautiful and so well-designed."

"Come and see it then," she leads me around to the front with Karuana and James following. The front veranda faces a tea-carpeted green ridge and hills beyond.

"*Karibu*," she welcomes me, beckoning us through the open doorway. Instead of a flimsy beaded entrance, this house has a solid wooden door with a lock. The sitting room is small but cozy with a couple of sofas covered with a printed cotton material. I sink into one of the sofas opposite a handsome raised fireplace in the corner. It's painted a dull brick color. It reminds me of the pueblo-style fireplaces I used to see in homes on the Hopi mesas in the Southwest. On the side mantles are family photographs. But there is no firewood in the fireplace. It looks like it's never been used, clean as a new day. A central hallway leads away from the sitting room.

"This house has three bedrooms," James says. "It's well made."

I nod, noticing that Jessica has disappeared, probably to the cookhouse, while we survey her new digs.

She returns a few minutes later with a thermos of tea and three pottery mugs instead of the old tin ones. Things have indeed changed since I first visited her 26 years ago. The only vestige of her previous life is the privy. It's still perched on the steep hillside below her house.

"We're going to visit Wambura [her niece]," I explain to let her know we're not staying.

After tea, we make our way down the steep grassy flank in front of her house. Its mud-clogged path is tortuous. Coming to the bottom, we weave our way through a stand of maize growing adjacent to a stream. We cross the brook on rocks that are none too stable and jump to the other side. I follow James up a trail through Wambura's terraced tea field. The clay path is nearly vertical and worn slick as a slide. James gives me a hand to prevent me from slipping backwards. Karuana, I notice, is literally digging in her heels to get some traction. We arrive at the top, out of breath, and traverse a vegetable garden planted in sweet potatoes and beans.

Stepping through a breach at the rear of the compound, we pass the cement water tank built as part of a women's group self-help project in the early 1990s. When we arrive in the flower-lined, pounded-earth yard, I notice the front door of Wambura's house is open. But no one is around. I smell milk tea brewing. Hearing voices and laughter, we follow the sound along a hedge toward the entrance of the compound near the cookhouse. That's where the action is.

Several teenage girls and young women are gathered on chairs with their friends under the eave of the dark wood cookhouse. To celebrate the holiday, they're braiding one another's hair, using extenders. It's a time-consuming process. I barely recognize Wambura's teenage daughters among the girls. It's been nearly a decade since I last saw them. Then I see Njoki, my Gikuyu "daughter" in California, in one of them. It's Nge'ndo. She was an infant in 1984. Now she's 18. Her oldest sister, Wangui, is also around. She's in her 30s. Wanjiku, the one named for her grandmother and the girl who used to follow me around like a small shadow in the '80s, isn't there. She's visiting a married sister.

The girls shout as they see Karuana and me, scrambling off their chairs to embrace us before Wangui goes in to get her mother. It sounds like a huddle of chipmunks as the girls explain to their friends who we are.

Wambura emerges from her house with a friend and stands for a moment observing the scene before she throws her arms around me laughing. She's a big woman with a broad forehead and prominent buckteeth that surface when she smiles. "Happy New Year," she exclaims. Then to Karuana, "*Wimwega. Ni atia?* How are you?"

"*Ndimwega muno.* I'm well," Karuana answers, shaking her hand.

Wambura turns to me again. "We heard you'd come, my sister, but we weren't sure when we'd see you."

"I'm sorry I didn't write and tell you. I didn't know until December that I was actually coming." I'm still smarting from my role as go-between in the *ruracio* negotiations between Wambura's husband and Njoki's former fiancée. I'm not sure that Wambura isn't holding me responsible for the marriage being called off.

"It's good that you came. You are family," she reassures me, taking my hand. "Come and have some tea." She leads me, still holding my hand, back to the front entrance of her house. "Do you remember this house you designed for me on that paper of yours? It's still here, even with the guest room. *Karibu*."

As we enter the house, I notice a piece of lined notebook paper tacked to a door to the left of the sitting room. On it is written in carefully-scripted black letters, "Office-Guest Room." The door is slightly ajar. I push it open. The last time I visited, the room was a jumble of bicycles, bicycle tires, stakes and farm equipment. I slept in one of the bedrooms the daughters shared. This time the room has a double bed, a desk and chair. It's freshly swept and clean, waiting for a visitor. There's still no electricity here, so the room is musky dark without its shuttered windows open. But it does serve its original purpose.

"Now I know where I can stay," I tease Wambura as she comes in carrying a tray. On it are a large gray thermos and porcelain mugs ringed by a pattern of pink flowers.

"Of course. You're always welcome. Where are you staying now?"

"With Karuana. We're doing some follow-up work with the women and now their daughters."

"I see. Well, we hope you'll visit us, too," she chides. " I want to have at least a whole day together. When can you come and spend time here so the rest of the family can see you?"

"On Monday I'd like to come and talk with the girls. Then on the following Saturday I'll come without Karuana and spend the whole day with you."

"Good. We have much to talk about. Now let us pray." It's a prerequisite before drinking tea in Wambura's home.

As we sip our tea, *Baba* comes in. I'm excited to see my Gikuyu father. He looks the same, a diminutive man with bristly gray hair, but fine looking in his own way. We greet each other warmly. A few minutes pass while Wambura tells her father the story of my arrival. Then I offer my condolences over the death of *Maitu*, my Gikuyu mother, who died two years earlier.

"Don't feel sad," he replies lightly in Kikuyu. "She is resting peacefully with no worries now." He smiles benignly.

Wambura and James burst out laughing. It's not until later that I learn that *Baba* has a girlfriend he keeps in Gagathoma. The grandchildren who live at his place refuse to let him bring her home out of respect for their grandmother's memory, so *Baba* commutes between his homestead and Gagathoma, often spending the night there. At 78, he's found life pretty spicy.

But I miss *Maitu*. In my mind's eye, I see the awful day when *Baba* was trapped under the horns of an angry red bull in the pasture, pinned to the ground and yelling for help. Suddenly, *Maitu* was there. Though small, she was incredibly strong. She grabbed a four-by-four post left over from a building project, entered the pasture and began pounding the bull on his withers with the post, shouting at the animal in a string of angry Kikuyu until the frustrated beast, distracted by her blows, released her husband. In that few moments *Baba* rolled away and ducked under the fence. *Maitu* dropped the post when the bull turned its head toward her and scrambled to the fence, squeezing under it just in time. *Baba* owes his life to her.

After finishing our tea, I take Wambura's daughters aside and tell them that I want to meet with them on Monday. They agree. We bid *kwa heri*, good-bye, to everyone after a round of picture taking and head up the road to Nyambura's homestead.

A small, lively boy about three years old comes out on the road to greet us. He's adorable, with eyes that dance from one to the other of us. He turns suddenly and runs, his legs pounding with irrepressible energy, up the path to his family's compound. He must be Nyambura's "mistake."

In 1992 when I visited her, Nyambura had had a difficult Caesarean birth with complications when her fourth son, a whopper of a baby, was born in 1991. She'd been forced to undergo further surgery the following year. After that, she'd decided to leave her family at four boys and forget about trying for a girl. But Munene, as this last son is called, put in a surprise appearance. I'm curious to learn what happened.

When we arrive at Nyambura and Wacera's house, it's full of visitors who've come to feast the New Year. Nyambura's sons are around for the holiday. They range in age from nearly three to 21 years. The oldest, Mwangi, who's always been the spitting image of his beautiful mother, is washing his laundry in a plastic bucket out front. The middle boys, Kiragu (17) and Mugo (15), are gossiping with friends in their *kithunu* (boys' house). At 12 years, Magondu is hanging out, not doing much of anything, while little Munene is everywhere, charming the adults and getting into mischief.

Nyambura runs out to greet us when she learns from Mwangi that we've arrived; the news had spread from one homestead to another along the ridge. Like Karuana, at 42 Nyambura has added a few pounds, but her face, dominated by beautiful amber eyes and a sparkling smile accented by dimples, is still lively and smooth as a penny. She practically knocks me down with a large warm embrace, kissing me on both cheeks.

"*Nyina-wa-Stepheni.*" She holds me back to look at me as she says it. "*Ii*, it's still you, but you're older by now."

I shrivel, then recover, knowing she's right. And besides, age is respected here.

"Come in and help us celebrate the New Year," she says in undulating Kikuyu. She leads me, holding my hand, to the doorway of her house, Karuana following. "We have visitors. Come and greet them."

As Karuana and I enter, Wacera, her husband, stands up. He has spread at the middle, like a doughboy, and is graying around the edges. Both he and Nyambura have honey-brown skin. Their sons range from honey to ebony black. Wacera introduces us to his neighbors, explaining where they live on the ridge. He invites me to sit down on a sofa next to a neighbor in a gray, worsted suit. Nyambura disappears into another room and returns with tea. Glass bowls of stew, *ireo*, rice and *skumawiki* (minced collard greens) cover a dining table pushed against one wall. Magondu brings china plates, forks and spoons and sets them near the food.

"Eat, eat," Nyambura urges us. "You must be hungry. The rest can wait."

Karuana and I get up and fill our plates and return to the sofas.

"I was getting hungry," I admit, savoring the delicious food.

"This day is a blessing," Wacera smiles. "We have a new year, a new president, and our friends have not forgotten us."

After we've finished our lunch, the conversation picks up with everyone talking about the election and how much better things will be.

"Nyina-wa-Stephen," Wacera says in English as I finish my soda, "I am no longer at the Kerugoya post office. I have shifted. I was posted to the one in Karatina. That's where I am now."

"Do you like it there?"

"It's a bit farther to go, so I stay there during the week and come this way on weekends. But today, because it's the New Year, you've found me here."

"I'm glad. I can talk with you in English." Wacera was one of my informal bilingual teachers in the 1980s. He loved to tease me by running a stream of rapid Kikuyu by me, then waiting to see whether I'd understood what he'd said. If I hadn't, he'd laugh and translate with a hint of amusement. It was a way of keeping this *muzugu* in her place.

"Your tea crop looks great. What are you doing now?" I ask Nyambura, who is standing in the doorway, pulling at the front of her headscarf, observing me.

"Several tea growers up here formed a farmers' group to improve our production. We're keeping cows for milk and also to collect their manure for the tea bushes. That's why they are growing so well. I'll tell you more about it when you come to see me next. Today is a holiday. When will you come back?"

"On Monday afternoon – around 2 P.M. Is that all right?"

"That's fine. Do you have that camera of yours?"

"I do. Do you want me to take a picture of you and your tea?"

"*Ii.* Yes." She tightens her headscarf and follows me out.

After we've taken care of the photo op, Nyambura leads me down a slight incline to a shed she's built for her cows. It has a cement floor with a shallow trough in the middle that allows the cows' waste to drain down into a sump below. "The manure stays here." Nyambura shows me the hot, smelly pit where a pool of heavy brown manure mixed with urine is stewing. Steam rises from it. The stench is overpowering.

"Wow!" I hold my nose.

It doesn't faze Nyambura. "We take the manure from here to fertilize the tea bushes and our gardens," she bubbles with enthusiasm. "It's much better than depending on [chemical] fertilizers from the KTDA."

"What you've done here is impressive. But now Karuana and I have to leave, or we won't get back to Kerugoya by nightfall. We still have one other woman to visit."

As we're saying good-bye to everyone, I remind Kiragu that I'm counting on him to get his friends together for a group session on Monday.

"You don't have to worry," he says in English. "You'll find them here when you come." Kiragu, of all the boys, looks the most like his father. His eyes are smaller and his nose longer than the others. He wears his hair cut in a flat top. He's clad in jeans with fringed patches, each with a logo at the center, sewn on the legs. A leather belt holds up his jeans. His tailored white T-shirt with a navy-blue collar sports another logo. "AUTOGLASS" is written under it. Kiragu has a sense of style that he undoubtedly got from his father.

As an infant, Kiragu had a life-threatening heart valve problem that unnerved his parents. After trying a doctor at the district hospital in Kerugoya with little success, I got a rental car and took them to Kenyatta Hospital in Nairobi. The doctor there diagnosed Kiragu's heart problem and treated it. His parents say I saved his life. They've told Kiragu the story enough times for it to become a legend. Since that time, our lives have become linked in Nyambura's mind. In 1989 when I visited the family and Kiragu was five, she teased, "Since it is you who saved him, he is your son. You ought to be taking him to America with you now that your sons have left home." I could tell at the time that Kiragu wasn't sure this was a good idea. We all had a good laugh.

Kiragu has written me from time to time as he's proceeded through the Kenyan school system, hoping I might sponsor him for higher education at some point. I've had to turn him down. The cost and complications of sponsoring a student have multiplied exponentially over the last decade.

Karuana and I finally break away from Nyambura and her family. Kiragu and Mugo accompany us as far as James' house on the next ridge. James comes out to escort us to the corner where the tea-buying center sits. Wanja, the other woman in her 40s whom I want to revisit, lives on a knoll just north of the junction. She's been a single mother for as long as I've known her. I have difficulty finding her home.

It has been nine years since I last came (without Karuana that time), and for some reason I can't remember Wanja's father's name. It would help in finding her place. After talking with a couple of people in neighboring homesteads, I find out where her parents live. No one is at home except two young grandchildren, a girl about ten years old and her younger brother. The adults have gone to visit relatives. I ask the girl to convey our greetings and deliver a written message to her aunt. Taking out a pad of paper, I write the message asking Wanja to contact us and write down Karuana's mobile phone number. Karuana hands the message to the girl, instructing her to make sure that Wanja gets it. The girl nods solemnly.

We retrace our steps to the tea-buying center and find Doctari there with the car. As we get in, a man runs up. He wants a ride to Kagumo. He and his wife climb into the back seat with a large plastic bag filled with bananas that fill the car with their fragrance. We descend to Kagumo, dropping the couple off at the junction to the main road.

It's been a packed, emotion-filled day. I look forward to getting home and vegetating in front of the TV. When we arrive at Doctari's house, we find Wamuyu, Wang'oo and Jumbe deep in discussion in *Shang'* (pronounced Shan-ga), a pidgin language that combines Swahili words, some of them turned backwards, with a few English words. It's a language that Kenyan teenagers created in boarding schools to differentiate themselves from adults. They've carried *Shang'* back to their villages.

Wang'oo explains that they've been practicing their roles as facilitators for the groups they will lead in Gatwe and Kerugoya, but they have some questions about what to do if the talk breaks down or one person dominates it. Wamuyu and Jumbe are more concerned than Wang'oo, who has some peer counseling experience and has been a leader of several clubs. He's been coaching the other two. I get a soda from the fridge and sit down to answer their questions. To involve Wamuyu, I've suggested she organize a group of her agemates and lead a discussion so she gets an idea of what we're doing.

"I'm going to line up the guys for my group tomorrow," Jumbe tells me.

"When are you meeting?"

I learn they are meeting on Sunday in the boys' *kithunu* at the house. It means that snacks and tea will have to be provided, something I hadn't anticipated. I assure Karuana that I will buy the snacks and help with any cooking necessary.

Later, after dinner, we watch a CNN interview with President Bush. I try to explain to Jumbe and Wang'oo, who raise the question, why the president got the U.S. involved in Iraq when most countries, including some of our allies, were against the invasion. It's an uphill battle. And I don't convince them. They think Bush is in Iraq for the oil.

"Don't Americans see that?" Jumbe asks.

I shrug, feeling powerless since I'm among the minority who didn't think we should have gotten involved in the first place.

Jumbe gets up in disgust and turns the TV to another channel.

CHAPTER 9

Death of a 20th Century Woman

Wanjiku was born in 1910, just as British and South African adventurers looking for cheap land began to settle in and around Nairobi, then a small railroad town. She died in May 2002. Her life spanned nearly a century. During that time the British forcefully colonized Kenya, African men assisted their colonial masters in fighting two world wars and many of the same men fought for liberation during the '50s and won Kenya's independence in 1963. For Kenyans it was a cataclysmic period that saw ethnic divisions sharpen under British "divide-and-rule" then wither under Jomo Kenyatta's initial *harambee* (self-help) movement, only to be replaced by more ethnic tensions when Moi came to power in 1978 and exploited tribalism as a political tool for silencing his opposition.

Growing up in Kirinyaga, Wanjiku was relatively untouched by the invasion of foreigners. The ridges above Kagumo were still fairly inaccessible. It was only as an adult that she felt the sting of colonial occupation.

I was born at Kiaritha, Wanjiku had related in 1984. *My father was called Gacoki. He was a big, black man. He did not have a temper for he never beat my mother. He and my mother, who was his first wife, had eight children. Wamini and Muthungu, his other two wives, each had three children that I can remember. Muthungu was not a Mugikuyu. She was a Kamba with lighter skin. There were many children growing up together in my father's compound. We would all eat together...One year, when I was about Njoki's size* [Njoki was her eight-year-old granddaughter], *we did not have much to eat because no rains fell. People called it "Ng'aragu ya Kimotho," the Hunger of Kimotho. Kimotho was an important elder in Kirinyaga at the time* [1918]. *We were very hungry. Even our cows died. But the next year the rains returned.*[20]

Wanjiku's three older sisters took care of her in the early years when their mother was working in the *shamba* or cooking. As

The Ostrich Wakes

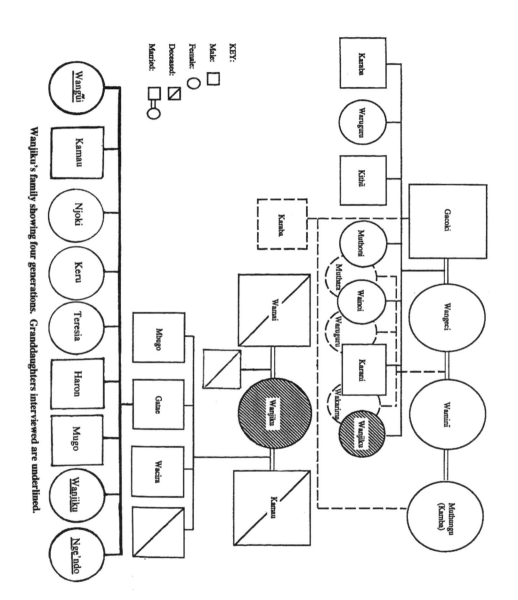

Wanjiku's family showing four generations. Granddaughters interviewed are underlined.

soon as she was walking they gave her a small gourd and took her with them to a nearby stream to fetch water. As a small child, she wore a goatskin gathered and tied at one shoulder. She realized she'd become a girl when her mother gave her a *mwengu*, a goatskin skirt decorated with beads with pointed flaps in front and back.

As she grew, Wanjiku learned how to collect firewood with a *mukwa,* a tumpline, and how to fetch green vegetables and carry them home in a *kiondo,* or basket. She and the other children also were taught some useful math.

We were told to collect sticks. Then we would count one to five and tie a bundle of five sticks together. We counted bundles of five sticks until we got to the number needed. We also used our fingers. It was important to learn [to count] *because of buying and selling goats and for trading in the market.* They also learned to measure lengths and widths with string, skills they put to use later in house construction.

When Wanjiku was older, her mother gave her a *kibanga,* the machete that serves as an all-purpose tool for most rural Kenyans, and taught her how to use it.

You see this scar on my leg? After I was married I found that the kibanga can be dangerous if used without care. My husband's mother hurt me with a kibanga when we were cultivating close together, so it taught me not to go near anybody using one.

The way children were taught to use their brains was through oral stories, puzzles and riddles that adults gave them around the cooking fire at night as they waited for their dinner. Riddles taught children problem-solving skills. I learned while living in Kirinyaga that to solve their riddles and puzzles, one needs a grasp of the culture and environment that locals gain from birth. Here are two Gikuyu riddles to ponder.

(Riddle)	(Answer)
Ciariranira [They cry at each other.]	*Thara murima uri noyu ungi* [Napier grass on both sides of a riverbank.]
Kanya gatune rware. [A red pot in the field.]	*Thathi wamuhiki.* [Red soil smeared over a bride.]

Gikuyu riddles, like our own, depend on metaphor. It would be a challenge for most Kenyans to answer the American riddle "What is black and white and read all over?"

Rites of passage were an important aspect of Gikuyu society in the last century. It was Wanjiku who taught me the name for each life stage and the transition ritual identified with it.

When I was growing up, there were terms given to girls for the stages they went through-- from the time they were small until they matured to become women and then became old. "Kaana" referred to an infant of either sex. Then came "karigu" for a small girl. The next was "kirigu" which applied to a big, uncircumcised girl. After a girl went through Irua and was circumcised she became a "muiritu." When she got married and had young children she was known as a "muhiki." A woman with three or more circumcised children was known as a "mutumia." "Muongia" referred to an old woman like me who had no teeth and could no longer give birth. These are the terms that were used when I was a child, but "karigu" and "kirigu" are not used now and even are considered abusive, like an insult. "Muiritu" is used for any girl child before she gets married and has children. [*] *"Mutumia" refers to all married women with children.*

For a girl who went through *Irua*, the period after she had healed and become a *muiritu* was the happiest, most carefree period of her life. She was treated with greater respect and was able to move about more freely, going to harvest dances and participating in other ceremonies. Historically, Gikuyu women didn't marry until they were in their 20s, some five to eight years after *Irua*.

After Irua, I was counseled to wait for my first menstruation. When I saw blood, I went to my mother and she cautioned me to stay in the house until the days were over. Then my mother gave me water and I washed and she started telling me to be careful around men when going to dances.

When we went to dance ceremonies it was usually at night. We'd hear somebody playing a flute and we knew there was a dance. We'd dance "mugoiyo," a dance held on a night when there was no moon and the beans had been planted. A circle of fires was made and the dancers encircled them. Men stood with their backs to the fires, each holding his partner who stood with her feet on his. The two bounced up and down slowly in time to the music. We also danced

---

[*] Often children precede formal marriage in Kenya.

"mweretho," which was just for unmarried youth. Each man would toss his partner in the air while she shook her body [erotically]. *Mweretho was later forbidden by the missionaries.*

Wanjiku met her future husband at one of the dances. *Wamai was a man whom we called "kiumbi." It means "one who is attractive to girls." He is also a good dancer, can talk well and laughs a lot. Girls would go and visit him together for the night at his kithunu but he could not touch their wrapped thighs* [undo the wrapped cloth around them]...*If a man raped a girl and she became pregnant, he had to marry her and no one else. The relatives of the girl made sure it happened.*

Courtship began with an elaborate series of signals and covert encounters.

When Wamai first started showing an interest in me, he came near the granary at our home and blew his nose, which was the traditional way of getting someone's secret attention. I went out to see who it might be. We talked. He said we ought to cultivate together. Yes, young men and women often cultivated together...Wamai visited several times this way, blowing his nose, then one time he told me he wanted tobacco—you know, the kind you pinch up in the nose [snuff]. *I went to my father and asked for tobacco and told him to whom I was giving it. I would not have asked if I had not liked Wamai—a girl has her own mind. My father gave me tobacco and I took it to Wamai. Love started from there.*

But that was just the beginning. Once Wamai took the tobacco to his father and informed him whom it had come from, his father began a search of clan ties and past relationships in their village that might prevent Wamai from bringing Wanjiku to his father's homestead. Marriage is an event that involves two sets of extended families and their respective clans. Just like Indians in the film "Monsoon Wedding" or the Greeks in my "My Big Fat Greek Wedding," one marries the whole tribe, for better or worse.

The next milestone on the Gikuyu marriage road is called *guthokia.*

Wamai's father told him to tell his mother to brew beer, the local one made from sugar cane that we call "njohi," and to take it to my father in exchange for tobacco. A man carries the beer in a very large gourd to the father of the woman he will marry. With guthokia, Wamai's parents and mine became "athoni," meaning that as their children are marrying they will be joined as parents.

It was only after this ritual was completed that negotiations for *ruracio,* bridewealth, began. They could drag on for several months. In the meantime, Wanjiku's mothers were counseling her on how to be a good wife, being respectful of her husband's wishes, washing his clothes and heating water over the cooking fire for his bath, and how to treat people in her husband's home, showing them that she was hospitable. There was no formal marriage ceremony. Rather, the girl was "captured" from her home.

Then one day Wamai came and took me from my father's place to his home. He came alone because there was no need for anybody else to help him take me as I loved him and had agreed to go. I felt sad about leaving my home that day because I realized that I was separating from my family.

Once I went to live at Wamai's, I became a member of his clan and from that time I have remained Unjiru. When I first came here I stayed in Wamai's mother's house, learning things about the treatment of my husband from her, until my husband built a house for me and I was officially put into it. I found marrying was a big change—learning about sex and my husband's habits once I moved to the new house. And after staying together for a while, I found I was pregnant.

Wanjiku gave birth to her first child, a boy, and was happy being a new mother. Then her life took a turn for the worse.

The baby was not even a year when my husband died. When one loses somebody like one's husband through death, she experiences a lot of changes and differences. Like me, I was married to Wamai, who died and left me with only one child. Then after a short while, the child died, too. The husband's parents refused to let me go back home to my parents' place [after her husband's death].

The reason that Wamai's parents refused was that by having a child who bore the clan affiliation, Wanjiku became part of the husband's family and clan. An underlying reason in her case may have been that her mother-in-law didn't want to be deprived of the labor and company that Wanjiku provided. As they begin to age, many women depend on the labor of daughters-in-law.

When I asked Wanjiku if she'd been with her husband when he died, she said, *Yes, I saw Wamai die.*

What happened is that one day he went to the marketplace and he was given a piece of cooked meat that might have been poisoned. When he came home, Wamai was seriously sick. His father told him to sleep at his mother's house because I had a child.

Wamai slept that day but with a lot of stomach pains. The following day it was recommended that "kubibo" should be done. Kubibo is when a person, not a traditional healer, is called and he makes cuts using a kienji on the sick person's body and then sucks out the sick one's blood and spits it out...Though kubibo was practiced on Wamai, he never recovered. He died the following day. I felt a lot of pain and cried to see him dead, thinking that now he was leaving me all alone. My friend, I was really shocked. For a time, I was feeling lonely and found myself with no energy to do anything. And then soon after, the child died too. First the husband, and then my child—life was grim for me.

I wanted to go to my father's home, but my husband's parents were not eager to see me gone. At times, I did go home then my husband's parents would come and take me back. So I finally decided to stay here as I had been given some land to cultivate. They told me that I should never marry elsewhere because they liked me so much.

A substantial investment had been made to secure a daughter-in-law through *ruracio*. Those goats and sheep weren't given away for nothing. In transferring bridewealth to Wanjiku's father, Wamai's parents got the right to her labor and her children. It was part of the deal. To protect their investment after Wamai died, they figured the only solution was for her to marry Wamai's brother. The sticky wicket lay in the brother's age-stage. Kamau was too young for marriage at the time Wamai died. He hadn't even been circumcised. He couldn't marry her until he'd tasted the knife.

That boy loved me, but he kept his love in his heart. Other boys used to tease him after Wamai died and tell him that if they were him, they would have gotten circumcised so as to marry me...Finally after Kamau got circumcised, then we were able to marry. With Wamai, we got married in the Agikuyu tradition. But with Kamau, we married traditionally when I moved into a house with him, then later we went to church and he put on this ring you can see on my finger.

It was customary for a deceased husband's brother to marry his widow so that she and her children would have continued protection and sustenance. Referred to as leverate, or wife inheritance, by anthropologists, this is a custom that is being challenged throughout Africa by more educated women, who want a say in choosing their marriage partners. Because wife inheritance can be an added financial burden for a man who is obliged to care for his deceased brother's family, men, especially in urban areas, support the move to get rid of the practice, arguing that it's a custom that has outlived its day. This is as true in Zimbabwe as it is in Kenya, Tanzania and much of Malawi.

It was common in those times for a man to marry his brother's widow. And you can read in the Bible where it says that one can take his brother's wife if the brother happens to die...With Kamau I had three sons. We would have four, but one, born after Wacira, died when he was not yet a year old. So there were two of my children who died, the firstborn and the lastborn.

Wanjiku was alone with her sons when the liberation struggle, or Mau Mau, as the Gikuyu refer to it, broke out in the 1950s. Her husband, Kamau, was away working for the colonial government in a railway station at Voi in Eastern Kenya. *He was the one who swept the station and kept it clean*, she said.

She was interned with her children in a government "village."

We had to stay in one of the villages that the [colonial] government had assigned us to. Nobody wanted to go. We were forced to stay in a village, which was surrounded by a high wire fence. When going to the toilet or to the river for water, we were taken by Home Guards, Gikuyu who were appointed by the colonial government as local police, carrying their guns. A lot of times we would hear the airplanes coming to kill the Mau Mau freedom fighters in the nearby forest. Then we became frightened.

While living in the villages, we had to dig a big trench up here to keep Mau Mau fighters out of the villages. We would wake very early in the morning, before the cock crowed and the trumpet sounded. It was still dark. The British soldiers came round telling people to open up their houses and come out. If you were met asleep, you could be killed. Then we would start walking all the way from Kiaritha up to the place where the trench was being dug and arrived after sunrise. We were each given a portion of the trench to work on. We would dig with our jembe [hoes] all day, removing the soil until the trench became deep. If we started to drag behind working, we were beaten. Later the trench was filled with bamboo sticks, sharpened at each end, to keep the Mau Mau from crossing. But some came across anyway. Nobody knew where or how they used to cross to the village for food. It's like if a human being is closed in a house, he/she will find all means possible to get out.*

---

* The Kikuyu language does not have gendered pronouns. That is why I've used *he/she*; pronouns are inclusive of both genders.

During that time, Wanjiku's sons were going to a school run by Anglican missionaries at Karaini. Attendance was poor because people feared that Mau Mau might come and burn down the school, beating or killing teachers and students. They never burnt down Karaini, although they made a raid there once. Going to school was a challenge.

The day that we got our independence we started shouting "Uhuru na Umoja" [Freedom and Unity], *and the news traveled fast from one person to the next. No one slept and we spent the whole night before dancing and singing, "Munyao, raise the flag on Kirinyaga." We were so happy because we would never be ruled by foreigners again.*

Wanjiku's husband returned to Gatwe and found that his industrious wife had cleared a portion of the forest and was beginning to plant tea and coffee. Their sons completed secondary school. The oldest had an additional two years of education and went abroad to study teacher training. He lectures in a teachers' training college in Embu. The second son works at a local tea factory, and the third is a retired assistant chief. The granddaughters I'm going to visit are the daughters of the former assistant chief, who now works informally as a community organizer for development projects. I've known his youngest daughters, Wanjiku and Nge'ndo (pronounced Nyen-doe), since they were babies.

Karuana and I and Wang'oo, my godson, head back up to Gatwe on a Monday morning. It's the day the schools reopen. Kibaki's free primary enrollment scheme is to be initated. I wonder how it will go as we leave the main road and begin to climb toward Mt. Kenya. The low clouds have cleared. Kirinyaga, the mountain, has shed its ostrich feathers. Suddenly I see it, the snow-capped double peak shining in the early morning sun, perfect in every detail. It looks so close I want to jump out of the car and run up the jade velvet folds cushioning its angular peak to touch the dazzling snow that nearly blinds me this morning.

"Look! You can see Kirinyaga. How brilliant! It's so clear."

Karuana and Wang'oo nod their heads patiently, as if to please me.

"Aren't you impressed?"

"It's something I've seen all my life," Karuana says. "I guess I take it for granted. Yes, it is beautiful."

"Never take a mountain like that for granted. I can almost see its ostrich shape."

"It *is* startlingly clear today," Wang'oo admits. It's the first time he's been to Gatwe. And now, as we ascend the steep hills with chartreuse tea-studded ridges on either side, he says, half to himself, "I had no idea it was so beautiful up here...and peaceful." Then to us, "You really walked all the way up here from Kagumo?"

"Yes," his mother says. "We were walking up and down all these ridges."

"This is the first time we've used a car to get up here," I add.

"Well, I'm glad you're using one this time. It would be a long trek."

We still haven't heard from Wanja about our meeting with her, but Karuana has her mobile phone in case Wanja tries to reach us. We park the Peugeot in Nyambura's compound, nestling it in between two banana trees, then walk up the short path to the yard with Wang'oo trailing behind. Nyambura is there, winnowing rice in a large flat basket. Little Munene runs up excitedly and grabs onto my jacket. He's looking for sweets like the one I gave him the other day. I reintroduce Wang'oo to Nyambura, who hasn't seen him since he was small, and explain that he'll be leading the discussion of the young men's group Kiragu has organized.

"You have grown big," Nyambura observes, turning to Karuana. "He's as tall as you. I didn't know you had such a big boy now, Nyina-wa-Wang'oo."

Karuana smiles. She and Nyambura have always gotten on well.

"Kiragu is not here," Nyambura says. "He's getting the boys. They should come soon." Then to Wang'oo, "Why don't you wait in the *kithunu*. I'll bring you some tea in a moment." She nods her head towards the small house where her older sons stay.

"That's okay," Wang'oo responds affably. "I don't mind waiting."

Leaving Wang'oo, Karuana and I walk down along the ridge slowly, enjoying the view, to meet with Wanjiku's granddaughters and learn about their grandmother's death.

Jemimah Wanjiku and Faith Nge'ndo

Faith Nge'ndo and Jemimah Wanjiku, Wanjiku's youngest granddaughters, are 18 and 22 years old. Wanjiku is the older of the two. Neither is married. I'm eager to find out how these girls, whom

I've known a long time, are getting along and what they have to say about the situation in Gatwe. My guess is that their lives are dramatically different from their grandmother's. Their sister, Wangui, is older and a single mother with two children. She's in her late 30s. She had her first child when she was 17. Her son was born a few months before her mother gave birth to Wangui's youngest sister, Nge'ndo. One of the ways I got to know the girls' grandmother and gained her confidence was by helping her with these two infants plus another daughter-in-law's baby. As the oldest woman in the compound, Wanjiku was often left with the responsibility of caring for the three babies while their mothers were laboring in their tea fields or gardens.

The granddaughters come to greet us as we arrive at the compound. Their mother has left for the day to work in her *shamba*. All three speak English, so I decide to meet with the younger two while Karuana talks with Wangui.

Wanjiku takes me into the house, where I settle down on one of the sofas facing each other across a coffee table. I pat the sofa next to me and Wanjiku sits down next to me. She is a lovely young woman with dark skin, sensitive features and a shy smile. She doesn't resemble either of her parents. She looks like the grandmother for whom she was named must have looked in her youth.

Gikuyu customarily believe that a child named for her paternal or maternal grandmother becomes that person, assuming her identity, her soul, and taking her place in this world after she dies. A woman who was named for her maternal grandmother once explained, "It was me who gave birth to my mother." The child and her grandmother form a special bond. The same is true for a boy named for his grandfather.

It became Wanjiku's responsibility to care for her blind, lame and incontinent grandmother at the end of her life. I ask Wanjiku to describe what she did for *Cucu* (grandmother) to complete this oldest woman's story.

Every day I would get up early and prepare porridge and carry it over to Cucu's house. I'd light a fire to warm water for bathing her, then sweep out the house and yard around it. Her house smelled bad because she couldn't control her bladder or bowels. As soon as the water was warm, I'd remove the soiled bedding and her nightclothes and put them in a karai to soak and wash later with Omo [a detergent]. *Then I would give her the porridge I'd brought. She*

Ngen'do, on right, with her married sister's children.

Wanjiku's granddaughters plaiting one another's hair on New Years's day.

was very weak and confused at times. I'd talk with her, asking her if she needed someone to pluck her tea. She'd agree. But she got confused about taking her medicine and asked me to help her with this. "You stay here to give it to me so I don't get confused," she'd say.

Sometimes I spent the night with her using a fold-up bed. I'd prepare the food and tea then wash the utensils. Afterwards I washed her body again and helped her get into bed. I can tell you she was really helpless. It was like caring for a sheep.

On May 29, 2002, I was making porridge in the early evening and I asked my mother to go and check on Cucu. She went over to see her and found her cold and dead. I was very sad, but relieved she was out of misery, as she'd become so weak and helpless.

My father went for the doctor and then to the headman to make a report of the death so the body could be taken to a mortuary. My mother and aunt wrapped the body in a blanket while my father went to his brothers and asked them to come and help him take his mother to the mortuary in Kerugoya while a coffin was being made.

About a week later the wooden coffin was ready. All the family and neighbors contributed money to get her fixed up in the coffin, so she looked alive and well dressed. We put photos of Cucu around the body. My father hired a preacher to come for the burial. It was on a Wednesday when we buried her in Mugo's [her oldest son's] farm. We still miss her. She was a very wise person and managed her three sons and their families well. She even made sure that the land was divided evenly between them, each having his own title, so that there would be no fighting after her death. That is how orderly she was. We can never forget her.

This granddaughter, who "became her grandmother," looks wistful.

"Let's bring in Nge'ndo so I can talk with you together about the things you learned from your grandmother, growing up."

"I'll go fetch her," Wanjiku rises softly.

CHAPTER 10

Hilltop Granddaughters

The view out the doorway of the hilltop house is of carpeted tea interspersed with blotches of color as pickers bend to their work, framed by large straw baskets on their backs. The smell of the damp fields is earthy, almost fetid this morning.

Nge'ndo appears in the doorway and enters her mother's house. She plops down on the couch across from her sister and me without a word, as if sizing up the situation.

"I thought we'd begin with you telling me about your early childhood," I explain to her. Nge'ndo looks like a clone of my "daughter" Njoki. She has lighter brown skin than Wanjiku and almond-shaped eyes in a classically beautiful, smooth face. She looks the way I imagine Nefertiti, the ancient Egyptian queen with the high forehead and straight nose, must have looked. She nods and looks at Wanjiku to take the lead.

Wanjiku: *I was about three years old when I first learned how to fetch water from the stream; you probably saw me collecting it with my sisters since you were staying near here then. I was also helping my sisters to collect firewood from the forest and getting charcoal for the jiko from that pit where our uncles used to make it. When I was four, I watched how my mother chopped onions and put them in a sufuria with oil, then she added meat with salt, stirring them together, and finally the potatoes and vegetables. When it was almost ready, she'd put in tomatoes and grated carrots.*

At this point, I turn to Nge'ndo who agrees with her sister that she was about three when she first went with their older sisters, Keru and Njoki, to the stream for water.

Nge'endo: *They put a small rope on my forehead for carrying the plastic container, like the ones that cooking oil comes in, and showed me how to hold the rope taut so the container wouldn't slip out of the rope on my back. I also went with them to pick up small sticks for firewood. Another thing I learned was knitting. My older sisters gave me small knitting needles and wool strings and showed me how to knit. At four, I could carry a baby on my back and at six years I was looking after small children. I began plucking tea at five years. Maybe tea wasn't here in Cucu's time.*

I was sent to preschool, and there I learned how to mold toys with clay, and more knitting patterns. At home I guess we learned the same things as Cucu learned when she was a child, but at school we learned different things.

Wanjiku: *I was seven or eight by the time I started plucking tea. We'd go out amongst the bushes and watch what others did. If we made a mistake when we tried, we were corrected. It was at this age that we first were sent to take messages, like to a shop.* [Nge'ndo nods her head in agreement.] *At 10 or 11, our mother would give us money for shopping and would tell us, "Now you plan the meal and decide what to purchase for it, because it is you who will be cooking it."*

Nge'ndo: *Did we take a written list?* She and Wanjiku laugh. *No. We just kept it in our head.*

Wanjiku: *In primary school we had math and English, so I could read labels on things, and Swahili, so I could speak with people from other areas. We also had GHC* [geography/history/civics], *CRE* [Christian religious education], *science and agriculture. Science was important because it taught us how to prevent diseases. And agriculture taught us about crop diseases and how to prevent them, how to use fertilizers, both manure and the chemical kind. We also had arts and crafts, music, PE and home science. Arts and crafts, music, and home science reinforced things I learned at home, but PE, that was mostly a school thing. I liked GHC because it taught us where different African countries are, and where each province and district is in Kenya.*

Nge'ndo: *I liked civics because it taught me the positions of ministers in the Cabinet, how they talk, and what they do. It taught me about the political offices and helped me understand what an election is.*

Wanjiku: *I went to secondary school in Kagumo, at Mutira Girls Secondary School. That's where I learned how to socialize with others. I was very homesick the first year, but then I got over it. I joined the debate club and the geography/environment club. I liked debate club best. We had no TV in our classrooms, only one in the dining room. We used it for recreation.*

Nge'ndo: *I went to a mixed government secondary school at Ngiriambu, Kabare. It's beyond Kerugoya. The first term in Form One was awful. I was unable to cope with boys because I feared them. The Form Four boys were forcing themselves on us. The boys and girls' dorms were far apart, but the boys would see us in the compound and at meals. There were no matrons in our dorms, only prefects who were older girls, so it was difficult. The first year I was scared, but by Form Two, I started feeling more comfortable. I had a cousin at the school. I was glad she was there to help me.*

We had the same subjects as in primary school: mathematics and languages, sciences like biology, chemistry and physics, agriculture and CRE. We also had clubs. I joined the law club and the Science Congress. In Form Four, I became a games prefect, and I was chairlady of the law club. That club taught me a lot, and I learned to speak well in front of others.

Wanjiku: *In Cucu's day, girls knew they were big when they went through Irua, before they ever menstruated. I was in Form One when I first menstruated. I was 15 at the time. But I knew what to expect because in Standard Six, we learned about the biology of our maturing bodies in science.*

Nge'ndo*: I learned about menstruation from Teresia* [an older sister]. *I was in Form One, too. It was in 1999, when I was 14.*

Wanjiku: *But nowadays things are different. In the 1990s, when we were in school, girls were waiting until their mid-20s or later to get a child. But by 2000, they were getting babies much earlier, even from 12 years old when they were still in primary school. Too many are having babies at an early age. No. They are not forced into sex by the* [male] *teachers. It's that they want to have babies. You'd think that fear of getting AIDS might stop them from having sexual relations. But it doesn't.*

Nge'ndo nods her head in agreement. *It's a big problem*, she adds.

I wonder how accurate Wanjiku's assessment of teenage girls' wanting to have babies is. The girls' groups in Kagumo didn't say that younger girls were becoming promiscuous and having babies. Are Wanjiku and Nge'ndo exaggerating? Or is teen pregnancy a problem unique to Gatwe? In either case, this is the first time I've heard AIDS talked about in this homestead. I want to pursue it. "Are there many people up here suffering from AIDS?" I ask.

Wanjiku, lowering her head: *Not so many, but it's hard to tell. We hear of one person dying but the family claims it's something else.*

Nge'ndo: *Some people still think AIDS is an evil disease so they don't want to admit that some of theirs have died from it. They might say, "So-and-so has died of cholera." That's sort of a code word for AIDS. Then people know.*

I first learned about sexual relations in Standard Eight, in science class. But we didn't learn about AIDS until Form One. We should have learned about it earlier. We learned about AIDS from teachers and videotapes, and sometimes from somebody from outside who was sick with the disease and came to talk about it. School is the only place we could learn about it. But it made me sad to hear someone with AIDS talk about it. It seems hopeless. If only there was some medicine that could cure it.

"People are working on that," I assure her. "How about young people your age? Are they afraid to talk about it?"

Nge'ndo: *Yes. It's sort of an embarrassment. Families who have someone with AIDS feel shame because people know it is sexually transmitted.*

I shift gears. "In your grandmother's day girls went through *Irua* to become adult women. How did you know when you'd become an adult?"

Wanjiku: *It was in secondary school, in Form Two. In Form One, I was fearing to talk with people. I was afraid of the prefects and afraid of the headmaster. I was very shy. But in Form Two, I began to feel comfortable with others and even had the courage to become head girl of my class. So that's when I grew up—when I gained confidence and learned to stand on my own feet.*

Nge'ndo*: I agree. When I went away to secondary school, that's when I made the change from being a girl to a young person. I learned how to handle myself with others and not to be afraid. By Form Two, I had changed and knew my way.*

Wanjiku: *When I left secondary school I hoped to become a nurse. But I only got a D+ on the KCSE* [Kenya Certificate of Secondary Education] *exam because I took it in eight subjects. It was too many. I was not encouraged to go for more education, so I took a tailoring course. Also, my parents didn't have money for further education because Nge'ndo was still in school, and the fees are very high at this level.*

Nge'ndo: *I completed secondary school in 2002, and I'm waiting for the results of my KCSE exams. I'm hoping for a B+. If I do well, I will go for teacher training at Kagumo Teacher Training College in Nyeri for four years. My goal is to be a secondary school teacher of either math or English.*

Wanjiku: *If I could find the means, I would like to go to Nairobi Nursing School. It's a three-year course. Then I'd like to be posted to the general hospital in Kerugoya.*

"Have there been changes you've noticed up here in the last ten years, like more telephones or computers?"

Nge'ndo: *There have been some developments, but there are still few landlines for telephones, and there's no electricity. My father is working to bring electricity to people here. They have a harambee* [community self-help] *project started to bring it to Gatwe. Everyone has radios, and some people have mobile phones. Njoki calls us from California almost every week to talk with us. We have a landline that she helped us with, and now a mobile phone. In my secondary school they had a video but no TV.*

Wanjiku: *There are a lot of changes. Down in Kagumo one can see many computers and even a computer-training center. We have better roads up to Gatwe and better transport.*

"Have you missed Njoki since she left for the U.S. in 1987?[*]"

Yes, the girls answer.

Nge'ndo: *But we have seen advantages, too. First, it has brought us new knowledge of America that we didn't know. And another thing, Njoki helps us by sending money here to better our lives. When my parents miss something, they let Njoki know and she gets the money to us.*

Wanjiku, nodding her head in agreement: *We miss her, but she has done well and even sent for Teresia* [another sister] *to join her—though my parents had to pay someone in Nairobi to get her a proper visa. Teresia wants to join a nursing school.*

"You two have been really helpful." I stand up and put my notebook and pen back in my pack. "Now I'm sure you have things you want to do."

Wanjiku: *It was interesting to talk about these things. Thanks for coming.*

---

[*] Njoki had returned twice to visit her home in Gatwe after she came to live with me. She had problems with her visa the second time and has been reluctant to visit since then.

Nge'ndo takes my backpack, and we walk toward the front of the compound. Karuana and Wangui are sitting in the shade of the cookhouse, drinking tea.

"I heard from Wanja," Karuana tells me. "She can't meet us today. She'd like us to come on Wednesday morning."

"Oh. That's fine. We'll have more time with Nyambura." I look from Karuana to Wangui, wondering how their session went.

Phoebe Wangui, Wanjiku's Eldest Granddaughter

Wangui is the eldest of nine children. As a teenager, she was the one who organized her five younger sisters and three brothers to carry out the tasks that needed doing around the homestead. She was quietly efficient. Without her help her parents would not have had the flexibility to be community leaders. Her mother is a retired nursery school teacher and chair of several self-help groups, including one to provide water tanks in every homestead. Wangui's father is a prime mover in a *harambee* project to bring electricity to the ridges.

Wangui was a single mother when I first met her in 1983. Her son is now 19 and her daughter 12. They share the same father. When I saw Wangui in 1994, she was working for a chemist in Kagumo. Middle age has caught up with her since then. She looks more matronly. Wangui has the same high forehead and straight nose as her mother but lacks her mother's buckteeth and broad chin. Wangui is blessed with a pretty mouth and full lips. She wears her hair pulled straight back and oiled to keep it from frizzing. She's more introverted than either of her gregarious parents. In a word, Wangui is responsible, someone you can count on. This is what Karuana gleaned from her.

I'm 37 years old now. I was 17 when Jean first came to stay here. I had just given birth to Munene, my firstborn, and was living at home since the boy's father refused to marry me.

I live up here at my grandfather's homestead, where my brothers stay. It's on the next ridge over, as you may remember. I stay in the stone house that was completed in 1983 just before Jean came to live with my grandparents. Each of my brothers inherited land there because my father does not have enough land here to divide between my three brothers. Michael, as the oldest, will inherit most of my father's land. That's why my son, Munene, has inherited a piece of my grandfather's land. My mother's father had only two daughters, and the other daughter is married some distance away. So my grandfather is helping my father and mother in this way.

Like my grandmother, I also learned some survival skills growing up; skills like cleaning the compound, cultivating, picking tea, cooking and washing clothes. Apart from those things I also learned to talk well and respect the old people.

As I grew older, I was allowed to fry food and learned to pick tea using a small basket. It was much later that I advanced to carrying a large basket and learned how to pick the right leaves. My grandmother didn't learn how to pick tea until she was older. Neither my mother nor grandmother fried foods like we do today. I can remember frying chapatis for Jean when she used to visit us. She liked them so much.

In primary school I learned how to read and write, to keep myself clean, and how to keep the school compound tidy. I also learned how to socialize with other people.

I went to Karaini for secondary school. I liked it there because the learning environment was good and the teachers cared about us. If I didn't understand something I could take it to a teacher and she would take time to explain it all over again. It was a good school.

The things I learned there turned out to be useful, especially in my business, because I'm able to account for my finances and know when I have increased my income from tea and when I've had losses. I cultivate tea on my grandfather's land. I gave up the job at the chemist's when I came back to Gatwe.

The major changes I've seen in Gatwe include people building two-story stone houses here and there. Many children have had a good education. Some even go outside the country for further studies after secondary school. The roads are much better up here, and transport to Kagumo is easier. We have a project here for getting electricity.

I would like to see the new president do away with school fees. I know it's possible to have free education because it was there before [in the 1970s]. The president must have known about it and thought about how he would begin it before he promised free education in the election.

What I want to see changed is the practice of primary teachers caning and mistreating students, especially those that perform poorly. In secondary school the change I'd like to see is better health care so that when a student falls sick or says he/she is not feeling well, the teacher takes it seriously and doesn't just think the student is faking it. I'm saying this because when I was in secondary school, a student died because the teacher thought she was only pretending. It affected me greatly. The girl was a friend of mine.

I want to see my daughter and son educated up to university level. This would enable them to get good jobs, and that way they can help themselves and not rely on gifts from other people. You know, Munene, my firstborn who is 19 now, was lucky. He inherited a piece of land from his great grandfather. But not everyone is so lucky. Those who don't have land need an education to get good jobs elsewhere.

Look at Njoki. When she went to America, I was very happy for her. To me, it was like a miracle. I'm also proud of her because she works hard and did not forget us. She has become a nurse and sends us money from time to time. She even helped us get a landline. Our life has changed for the better. We're thankful for that.

Having a first child at 17, by a man who refused to marry her, shaped Wangui's life. Her children's welfare came before her own. Because she was seduced in her teens, Wangui doesn't want the same thing to happen to her daughter. She wants her to have more options than she had.

After talking with old Wanjiku's granddaughters, Karuana and I prepare to leave and return to Nyambura's place to meet with her and see how the boys' group went. But Wangui asks us to wait a minute and disappears into the garden with a plastic bag. She comes back with the bag full of passionfruit.

"How did you know I love passionfruit? It's one of my favorites! Can you believe that *one* fruit costs $2 in America? And here, you can just eat them off the vines. You're lucky." I give her a hug.

"That much? *Haiya.* One could become rich at those prices," Wangui grins. Nge'ndo and Wanjiku accompany us partway up the road before turning back. Kenyans call it "giving a push."

Talking to Wangiku's granddaughters makes me realize how much things are the same and yet how they've changed since their grandmother's time. They've learned many of the same survival skills, such as hauling water, cooking and childcare, but their lives are dramatically different because of schooling. Education has reinforced some of the old skills, and it has given them a bundle of new ones that will contribute to their survival, development and self-reliance in this new century.

Nyambura winnowing rice in her compound

CHAPTER 11

Nettles, Honey and Sons

In 1983, Nyambura was one of 16 women I surveyed whose birth anticipated Kenya's independence. In their 20s at the time, this cohort had had more opportunities for education than their older sisters born under the yoke of colonial occupation. Schooling made a profound difference in their lives. Yet within this age group, there were some startling disparities.

The average number of years of school attended was six years. Only three women had reached secondary school. None had gone to university. Nyambura and Wanja, the other woman in her 20s who shared her life story, took two different paths. Nyambura was educated through Standard Five (fifth grade) before she was forced to drop out of school. She was typical of women in her age group, most of whom had left primary school between fifth and sixth grade because their parents needed their labor at home or had run short of money to pay for school materials and uniforms.

Wanja, on the other hand, was lucky. She was one of only two women who had completed high school. Her options were broader because of it, and so were her children's. She was a single mother and a nursery school teacher. She belonged to the Anglican Church in Gatwe and sang in its choir. Nyambura had been raised a Catholic. She had two small sons when I first met her, and planned to have as many children as she could. She mistrusted contraception and the new family planning ideas sweeping Kenya at the time.

At 20, Nyambura typified her age group in 1983-84. She was "married" according to Kenyan convention, which means she was living with someone and already had a child by him. Her first son, Mwangi, was three at the time. Her second son, then an infant with a heart valve problem, was Kiragu. She had three more sons over the next two decades. Mugo was born in 1987. Magondu was born by Caesarian section in 1991, and Munene, the unexpected, came in

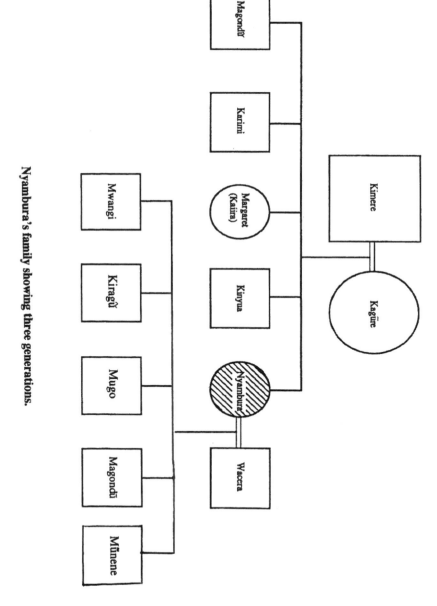

Nyambura's family showing three generations.

2000. Over a 20-year period, Nyambura's views on contraception changed dramatically.

Like her youngest son, Nyambura exudes joy. It radiates from her pores, enveloping those around her. She makes light of the work she does. And she is hardworking. The only time I saw her in the doldrums was in the early 1990s when medical problems threatened to overwhelm her. In 1992, she was in the hospital having surgery for a rupture between her uterus and colon when I arrived in Gatwe. I returned a week later and found her still very weak and in much pain. But she wanted to show me the X-rays the doctor had given her to explain where the problem had been. She winced, explaining that the pain was unbearable before the surgery. By 1994, her health had improved and she was her cheerful self again. She and her husband—he had become more solicitous of her after the medical crisis—planned to renew their vows in a church wedding. When I asked in 1994 how things were going with Wacera, she told me:

Ii, those days are gone when he used to beat me. He has not beaten me for some years now. He has to take on more work with the children and the mashamba since I had this problem.[21]

My own reading of the situation was that Nyambura's medical problems scared the living daylights out of Wacera; he was forced to ponder what his life would be without Nyambura's joyful nurturing. It was a wake-up call.

When I first knew Nyambura, she delighted in teaching me the rudimentary skills of fetching water from a stream and cutting wood for a cooking fire. During our initial session, when she began to talk about her life, she was shy. As we spent more time together and I got to know her in various settings, she started to reveal the nettles as well as the honey in her life. She was born on the eve of Kenya's independence and was the baby of her family. I have chosen to let Nyambura tell you about her early life, because, frankly, she tells it best.

I was born at Kamuiru, the lastborn of Kimere and Kagure. My father, Kimere, was a tall, slender man—slightly taller than me—and he had a quick temper like Kinyua, my brother. Kagure, my mother, is a cheerful woman and hardworking.

I was named Nyambura for my mother's mother, who was born during the Long Rains. I am of the Unjiru Clan, and my Christian name, the one I was baptized in the Catholic Church, is Meri. I have three brothers, the youngest being Kinyua who is eight years older than me. Magondu is the oldest. He's talkative and polite. I cannot remember too much about my brothers because they were already big and married when I was little. I also had an older sister, Margaret Kaiira, who followed Karimi, the middle brother. Margaret and Kinyua were the ones who took care of me, but Margaret loved me the most. I could tell she did because she would bathe me, make up my hair, wash my clothes and give me food. At times she would carry me around tied to her back.

Margaret and Kinyua were the ones who used to tell stories and give riddles around the cooking fire. I can't remember any of the stories, but here's a riddle.

	[Answer]
Wathii na njira wathekio nu?	*Mwatuka wa thi.*
[Who smiled at you as you walked along the road?]	[A crack in the earth].

I liked to hear riddles and try to figure them out. I also liked to try new things. If people went to the shamba to cultivate, I did not want to be left behind—I wanted to go, too. I learned how to cultivate with a kibanga, go for water, and wash clothes from my mother.

Like most Kenyan children, Nyambura learned about her kin from her parents.

We would go visit some relatives—like when my mother carried me on her back to visit my uncles and aunts. When we met them, I was told who they were and how they were related to me. It was important for us as children to know which people we were related to and who were clanmates. *

When we were little girls, we used to play games like mbiya, where children try and hit each other with a ball made out of strings...We'd also sing songs and jump, using a rope. Sometimes we made toys out of maize stalks and string or bottle tops.

I can remember the first day I went to school because it was my oldest brother Magondu, who took me. His children were like my agemates, so he took all of us together. We spent the first day there trying to reach our one hand over the head, like this, to the other side of the head. Anybody who was able to reach her/his hand over and touch the ear on the other side with her fingers was big enough to go to Standard One. As we were chosen, we entered the classroom. We spent the day like this, then it was time to go home.

---

* Knowing clan names and whom one is related to is still important.

The school that Nyambura attended was made of mud bricks. *We used to sit on long benches and we wrote on cut pieces of chalkboard. Later on we started writing in notebooks. If a child forgot her notebook, the teacher would punish her with a beating. By my last year of school—in Standard Five—I was going very early in the morning to sweep the classroom and then pour water on the* [cement] *floor to clean it. After cleaning the floor, I'd go for parade with the rest of the kids, where the teacher on duty inspected us. Anybody who had lice on her hair was shaved over a portion of her head and sent home. Those who were dirty were pinched hard and sent to the river to wash.*

Class would start at 8 A.M. By the time we had reached Standard Four, we got each lesson from a different teacher who would come into our classroom. The lessons lasted about 30 minutes. We'd go home for lunch after the fourth lesson and come back at 2 P.M. We'd have three more lessons before going home at 4 P.M.

The way math was taught is that the teacher wrote numbers on the chalkboard and we copied them down in our exercise books. After solving the problems, we took the book up to the teacher who would mark the problems we had done. When we were learning numbers or words, after the teacher wrote them on the chalkboard, she would call someone's name and that student would wake up [from the boredom of rote learning] *and read what was on the board with the other students repeating after her.*[*]

After school, I would run home to help my sister go for water at the river or to collect maize stalks for the cows. On Saturdays we helped in the shamba, weeding the vegetables, or during the coffee harvest we'd pick coffee berries. On Sundays nobody worked. We'd get up, bathe and get dressed in our best clothes, then go to church. We'd have Bible lessons and singing. Afterwards, on the way home, we'd visit our relatives and neighbors. We were fed well on all those visits.

I stopped going to school in Standard Five. What happened is that at that time, the local brew called "karabu" was on the increase and my father used to drink so much of it that he was unable to take all his children to school. We were sent from school often because the parents had not contributed to the harambee fund for building another classroom, or we didn't have writing materials. I

---

[*] This scenario has changed little over 40 years, and rote learning is still a drag.

could spend the whole term without going to school. I never lacked for school fees, but my father was a drunkard and never viewed education as something important. I felt badly, but there was nothing I could do.

Soon after leaving school I went to live with the Mwais, who are relatives. Ever since I was little I used to go to visit the Mwais and I liked the place. So when they wanted me to go and stay with them, I was ready to go. *

I went to the Mwais when I was about ten years. I was taught by Mrs. Mwai things about how to care for the children, to cook, and to keep the house. This was a big change because at my house I never had to do much work, being the lastborn. But aside from the work, Mrs. Mwai used to treat me like one of her own children. She had two small children, one a baby and the other about four years. The baby was put in a woven baby cot, and my work was to put the cot outside and after some time to bring it inside again.

Mrs. Mwai was a teacher so I put hot tea in a thermos for her to take to school. After she left, I would start preparing the lunch, peeling the potatoes and carrots carefully so as not to cut myself. After preparing lunch, I would wash the baby's nappies and other clothes [in a bucket]. *Then everyone would come home for lunch and afterwards I would wash the dishes and look after the baby.*

When I asked Nyambura if she had gone through Irua, she was emphatic. *Wi! You! Those days are over! I am a Christian and we do not believe it is a good thing. Why? Because it is a thing of the past. Going to school and learning some things helped us see the difference...You know the president made it against the law. There are some who still do it, but not many. No, I didn't get my ears pierced either. That was for our mothers. Some of those old women used to hurt each other's ears when fighting. I once saw a woman grab another woman's matu* [gaping hole in the earlobe] *and pull it until it ripped. That woman was screaming very hard from pain. No, I would not want matu.*

Nyambura met her future husband during the time she was staying at the Mwais.

---

* At this moment, Nyambura's mother-in-law, hearing our exchange, explained, "People used to ask for young girls to help them in bringing up their own children. Usually the girl was a relative. She became an *ayah*." Mrs. Mwai went to Nyambura's mother, who was a relative, and as Nyambura was the lastborn and didn't have younger siblings to care for, Mrs. Mwai asked for her.

I used to go to the post office down at Kutus to collect the mail for them. That is where Wacera worked—at the post office. So we used to see each other that way. Then one day he asked me where my home was and I told him.

When Wacera first came to the Mwais, I ran away from him. But then I came to like him as he continued to visit. Then I noticed he was not coming as much and maybe had found another, better girl. After he stopped coming, I found I was two months pregnant. I went home and told my parents what had happened. My mother was not happy.

My parents called Wacera to see them, but he refused to go. I have never had such mistreatment. He didn't deny that he was responsible for the pregnancy, but he didn't say anything about marrying me either. Now that I was pregnant, he ignored me completely. To me it seemed that everything was over between us. I was really angry with him.

Her firstborn son, Mwangi, was born while she was staying with her parents.

Things really changed for me after that because I suddenly became conscious that I was totally responsible for this tiny human being and what the future holds for him...I started my knitting business so I would get money to take him to school. That's when I knew I was a mutumia, a full-grown woman. When you are a girl and then give birth, you find that you have changed. Your body features change, too. The breasts drop, and the features show that you are no longer a girl...The woman with a baby on her back signifies she is a mother. When I became a mother that was the biggest change for me.

While she was at her parents' home, Nyambura's father gave her a piece of land to cultivate, and her mother helped her plant maize, beans and skumawiki. *I worked very hard to keep my mind off my problems and to get plenty of food for those at home. Sometimes my mother would look after Mwangi so I didn't have to work in the shamba with him on my back. Then I would make sure I returned to the compound in plenty of time to suckle him.*

During that time, Nyambura's sister, Margaret, married a teacher and moved to Embu. *We'd go down by matatu to visit, staying there the afternoon, eating and dancing with the women of her husband's homestead, then return home by dark.*

Her sister's husband was doing well and had planted coffee, hiring several workers to help with the harvest. He was saving some of the coffee profits to build a stone house. *Margaret is lucky to have such a good husband,* Nyambura told me wistfully in 1984.

Toward the end of 1982, I went to Kutus to start my knitting business. I set up my knitting machine in the shop of one of Mr. Mwai's friends. I was making sweaters and jackets. People liked what I made, and I began to sell the sweaters. During that time, I stayed with my sister and her husband near Embu.

While Nyambura was in Embu, Wacera started visiting her again with the result that she became pregnant. Wacera was living by himself and wanted Nyambura to come and stay with him, promising her parents that he would not mistreat her. She decided to take two-year old Mwangi and stay with him in Embu. The beatings returned and were violent, especially as she became more pregnant. She gave birth to a second son and then made a decision about Wacera.

I had two children by him and decided to come here to Wacera's parents' place and tell them I was leaving after all. When the parents found out about the problem, they called Wacera and talked to him about the other girls he was moving with and asked him if he wanted any of them for a wife. Wacera kept quiet. The father said, "I have known Nyambura for some time now. I think she should stay here with us. If you have anything to say, then say it." Wacera was going for a course in Nairobi and so I came to Gatwe.

When I got here, I found the father had recently died and Wacera's mother was very sad with nobody to fetch water for her. And the cows were a pathetic sight. Wacera's mother was so happy to have me here. She talked to Wacera, and he cooled down and vowed not to mistreat me again. When we have a problem, I go and tell his mother and she comes and straightens it out.

You have seen me picking tea here. It is only recently [in 1983] *that I learned. At home we had coffee. It was my mother-in-law who taught me. The first time I picked only five kilos* [11 pounds]. *Then I was able to pick more as the days went by. Now when I start after my morning work of the homestead, I can pick about 25 kilos* [55 pounds]. *Most of the land on the hillsides here is planted in tea. Who owns it? Not Cucu. It belongs to Wacera and his brothers. But Wacera does not have much to do with it except when it needs pruning.*

Does Wacera ever help me in the shamba? Yes. When the soil needs to be prepared for planting vegetables and maize. Also, at harvest time. But by the time he reaches here from Kutus on Saturday afternoons, all he wants to do is rest from the week's work—so I don't count on him. When he comes, he usually brings some meat and bread or some other things we might be missing here. Last month, you remember, there was a shortage of sugar. Not even the shops down in Kagumo had any. But Wacera found a shop in Kutus that had sugar, so he brought some to us. The same with maizemeal; Wacera knows where to get it when there's a shortage.

I asked Nyambura about her hopes for the future in 1984 and she told me, *I want my children to grow up healthy. Right now I am worried about the baby. The doctor at the clinic says he has a problem in his lungs. I see him struggling and breathing hard and wonder what is to be done. I want to take him to the hospital in Nairobi, but I'm told one needs a recommendation from a doctor here. Sometimes I become fearful wondering if this baby will survive. Then I pray to God for an answer.*

I would like to have as many children as God gives me. I do not like these family planning ideas. It is not good to put chemicals into the body. My husband would not allow it either. Children are a blessing to the Agikuyu.

Looking at Nyambura's declaration in 1984, it is remarkable how medical circumstances she couldn't foresee changed her viewpoint. By 1992, she had four sons. Kiragu, the baby she'd worried about, was a strapping youth. She had been in the hospital for surgery after Magondu's birth. In 1994, she told me she and Wacera had decided against having more children. *I started using the pill. Wacera was against my having a tubal ligation in case he wanted a daughter. I see no problem in using the pill; I have to take care of myself.*

In 2003, she confesses, *The last time we talked, I had gone through a difficult birth because Magondu was very large. As you know, the husband and I decided not to have any more children. But then we made a mistake and had this small boy, Munene, in 2000. I had him by Caesarian section, too. After that I decided to go and get a tubal ligation at the hospital in Nyeri. Bringing up these children has been hard because of the difficult economic times.*

Now, I can say my physical health has improved. This past year I had only one large burden—that of paying for school fees.

Wacera and I are more settled. We renewed our vows in February 1994. We'd been saving our money for a church wedding for a long time. You know it takes a lot of money to pay for a proper wedding.

The biggest change since you last came is that Cucu [her mother-in-law] *died a year ago. I miss the happiness that was there between us since we used to share a lot and she helped me with ideas. If I had a problem with money, I would borrow from her and pay her back later. I have nobody to borrow from now. Mwangi and his father were hospitalized at Jamii Nursing Home in April for two weeks. They had malaria and typhoid fever. We were charged 40,000 shillings* [$556] *and had to get a loan from the KTDA that we were unable to pay back at first. Finally, our good friends, whom you met on New Year's Day, gave us the first 30,000 shillings to clear most of the loan. That helped us get another loan for school fees for Mwangi's college and Kiragu's secondary school and pay the fees for the other boys' primary school. They attend a private primary school, so it costs more.*

I'm proud of the tea I grow here. From where you see the boundary of my in-laws' land, I inherited 300 plants from Cucu's tea. The rest went to another daughter-in-law. I have hired three pickers who come about four times in a month. The schedule is they pluck four days in one week, then rest for eight days so the tea can sprout again, then pick for another four days and rest. I pay each worker four shilling per kilo after I get paid by the KTDA at the end of the month.

When I pruned the bushes back last time, I called a KTDA field extension worker to come and show me how to spread out the new growth, pegging it so that it sprouts well in a horizontal direction. He advised me to put manure around the bushes. I made the big hole [sump] *where all the cow's dung collects, and it is enough for the fertilizer I need. Before I had seven cows, but I have reduced them to three since it became hard to buy feed for all of them. I also had chickens but sold them. With only three cows I have enough manure for the tea. You see, I mix the dung with wastes from the cattle feeds, and it makes enough. We also use some chemical fertilizer that we get from the KTDA.*

In 1994, we were paid about 3.50 shillings per kilo for our tea, but now we get 7.50 [US 10 cents]. *The KTDA should pay us more. What they pay is not enough. This year we got a bonus of only 14 shillings* [20 cents] *per kilo. I know the bonus depends on the world market. In 2001 the bonus was about 25 shillings per kilo, which was good. But this year what I got is not enough because I have children in secondary school.*

For a person like me who has to borrow money to pay school fees, once the KTDA deducted what I owed them, I was left with nothing. The KTDA also provides credit to its tea-growing members but then deducts so much a month from their earnings until the loan is paid back. I did not have enough to pay the other debt that remained for the nursing home bill. I had to borrow 60,000 shillings for school fees and 10,000 for food and to pay the pickers at the end of the year. These are my worries.

We formed a farmers' group called Mutira Maziwa, which has projects like keeping cows and chickens. We've been visiting agricultural projects in other places where we get ideas. Our members come from all over Mutira. The group has both men and women, but the women are only five out of the 38 members. To become a member, one pays 200 shillings monthly.

We started with a project for building a cow shed for every farmer using the merry-go-round [pooling their money, then giving the sum to a different farmer each month]. *Each member got a cow. The next project is to have AI* [artificial insemination] *so it will be easy to fertilize our cows. We visit each other to make sure that when a member is given the money for a month, they put it to the use that it was intended for. Like when we started giving each member resources for the cow shed, then we made sure that we visited each one to see with our own eyes that they had built a shed before we went to the next project of buying the cows.*

Our group taught me how to improve what I was doing, like the cow that I had before was only giving me five liters of milk, but after I was taught how to take care of cows properly, giving them the correct amount of animal feed, I began getting about 25 liters from the same cow.

Since 1994 the children have grown up, except for Munene. The relationship between my husband and me is good. But it will be on my shoulders to educate all these boys. You see, the father [Wacera] *is retiring next year and so I will have to work harder to accomplish my goals. As far as the in-laws are concerned, we are putting in a lot of effort to live together in harmony. This is because when the grandmother was alive she insisted that we live peacefully with one another. The land is already divided, but the new toilet* [pit latrine] *and well for water I had constructed are on my sister-in-law's land. We talked, and she agreed to have that portion of land included in our plot when the title deeds were written.*

Nyambura in her tea field up in the highlands.

The Boys' Group in Gatwe with Wang'oo and Kinyua at far right.

When I saw that Mwangi is not a very high academic achiever after Standard Eight, I sent him for a course in welding after secondary school. It was a yearlong course. He is going for another course in publishing. He has to get skills that will help him earn a living. Kiragu is in Form Three and Mugo is beginning Form One. Magondu is now in Standard Eight. My wish is that they all get a good education, and then get good jobs so they can move from this small piece of land because it will not be enough for all of us.

The changes in Kenya are many since 1994. One is the increase in poverty. Another is the increase in crime. *If I could talk with our new president, I would tell him to improve our economy so that we can get more money to send our children to good schools. Kibaki should improve the security in this country and reduce the high crime.*

In 1994, Nyambura told me that she'd heard of AIDS and that people were being urged to use condoms when they had sex. But she believed it was something that affected people in Nairobi more than in Mutira. *People in Nairobi tend to have loose morals so they are more apt to get AIDS than people here,* she'd claimed. Ten years later, although she is aware that some people in Mutira have died from AIDS, she is reluctant to discuss the problem. *It is not something people like talking about because it involves sexual relations and wearing condoms, which men don't like to do.* She lowers her head, and then looks toward the doorway, her lips set in a tight line.

"Well, I'm glad to see that your tea is prospering," I change the subject. "This is a healthy farm, and you and your children look healthy, too. Congratulations."

A dimpled smile returns to her face. *Yes, we have no complaints.*

In late 1984, Nyambura had told me at the end of our year together, *The things I'm proudest of are that I'm able to pick tea, I cultivate and cook well and look after my children. At times I keep quiet and know that if I work harder, one day I will be rich.*

Nyambura may not be rich, but she is definitely better off than she was 20 years ago. She's able to hire workers to pick her tea; in 1983-84 she was picking the tea herself. She's a member of a progressive farmers' group that has made it possible for her to keep cows and improve her tea quality. It shows when you look at her fields. The tea forms a thick, luxurious green carpet. She also has enough combined income with her husband to pay for two of her sons to attend private schools, though at times she has to take a loan to cover all the fees. She and Wacera built a timber house in 1991. Their relationship is better than it was in the 1980s. They are "more settled," as she puts it.

With Wacera retiring from the postal service next year, however, and the usual delay before a government pension is released in Kenya, next year will be difficult for Nyambura. It means that for a year, she and Wacera will be living off the proceeds of her tea until the pension money begins to come in. At a time when four of their sons are in school, she and Wacera may have to increase their debt burden if they want to continue sending the younger ones to private schools. Rural Kenyans like Nyambura have little in the way of savings. They live day to day, barely keeping up with demands on their financial resources. Yet they continue to be hospitable to visitors, sharing what they have with dignity and grace, as Nyambura does when the boys her son Kiragu has brought together meet in her compound.

Gatwe's Sons Speak Out

Seven young men between the ages of 17 and 22 have gathered in the bachelors' hut to discuss generational differences and changes in Gatwe. None is married. Their educational backgrounds are similar to Wanjiku's granddaughters and the Anglican girls in Kagumo. Three are in the third form and three are completing secondary school. One is in the second year of a training college. Only one is a non-Christian.

When Wang'oo asks them what kinds of survival skills they learned growing up, they cite milking cows and "cleaning up around the compound." Four mention cultivating tea and/or coffee and food crops such as yams and maize. Half learned to dig with a hoe, often preparatory to planting. Two cite collecting fodder for cows. The majority of them say they still do these tasks when they're at home. But they are away in boarding schools or college most of the year.

The Gatwe boys and the girls learned some survival skills in common, but there were also differences. None of the boys mentions fetching water or wood, whereas all of Wanjiku's granddaughters and the girls in Kagumo (both groups) had to collect these essentials at an early age, as did their mothers and grandmothers.

The boys learned to milk cows, and two said they collected fodder as children. Wanjiku's granddaughters did not milk cows or collect fodder because their family didn't own cows when they were growing up. But two Anglican girls in Kagumo said they milked cows, and one mentioned herding. Likewise, cultivating and picking tea or coffee berries were skills girls and boys learned in common. Cleaning the compound and house and doing dishes were domestic tasks children of both sexes were taught. They also learned how to do laundry by hand—there are still are no washing machines in rural Mutira.

None of the Gatwe boys cites learning how to cook, although I have seen boys cooking when no woman or girl is around to do it. In the Kerugoya group that Jumbe facilitated, the majority named cooking as a survival skill they learned. Because it is a task culturally identified with women, perhaps the boys in isolated Gatwe are less willing to admit that they can cook than their urban counterparts.

Things have changed for the Gatwe youth since their fathers' time. Two survival skills their fathers learned but the boys did not acquire were hunting and gathering. With Gatwe close to the Mt. Kenya forest, their fathers gathered wild yams and hunted gazelle and waterbuck. Today, they buy meat at the marketplace in Kagumo. Some Gikuyu still raise goats and sheep, but these animals are mainly used for ritual feasts or to honor visitors.

When the boys began attending primary school, they found themselves washing the classrooms and cleaning up the compound like the girls. All of them were involved in cultivating crops through 4K clubs and Young Farmers clubs. At the same time, their perspective on life skills needed for adulthood changed. Reading, writing and math became the ones they sought for survival in the future. At the secondary school level, the boys have added new skills in the sciences and commerce. They'd like to see a computer course added.

Information about diseases such as dysentery, tuberculosis, malaria and AIDS was learned through set courses at the primary level. However, the group agrees that what they learned about HIV/AIDS wasn't worth much because it was too vague. It was taught mainly through films, leaflets and health facilitators who came as guest speakers.

Going away to secondary school made these boys feel more independent. They had to cope with new people, demanding teachers and dorm life. Maintenance of school grounds and classrooms, being responsible for washing their own clothes and keeping their space in the dorm decent looking were mandatory.

New clubs provided greater opportunities for learning and socializing. One boy says he learned organizational skills by being the treasurer of his school's wildlife club. A couple of them learned new sports.

Biology classes, social ethics, and guidance and counseling sessions taught them about the biological and social aspects of sexuality. However, they have not had an opportunity to apply family planning lessons because, they argued, they aren't married yet. Do they perceive contraception only as a device for couples with families? Help! Certainly, most of these boys are already sexually active. Nyambura noted that for a decade now people have been warned to use condoms to prevent getting AIDS, and Wanjiku and Nge'ndo were worried about girls becoming pregnant at a young age. What are these young men doing to protect themselves and their partners against getting AIDS and other sexually transmitted diseases? Their responses are vague. I still don't have a sense of how Mutira youth respond to the specter of AIDS.

One boy notes that going to a mixed boarding school, where they can mingle with girls, is a problem. He thinks single-sex schools are better because mixing means that each sex *has more distractions from their studies, and the temptation of being in close proximity to one another breeds problems that don't exist in single-sex schools.* His observation has some currency. I remember well the big bruhaha in the early '90s over the violent rampage of older boys against a group of girls in a mixed boarding school that resulted in at least 17 girls being raped and two left dead. It was a large enough incident to hit the international news.

Educational reforms the Gatwe boys recommend include dropping music, art and home science. They agree that the present timetable for the lower grades ought to be changed to give younger children more rest time. One boy observes, with the rest agreeing, that the frequency of punishments (such as beatings with a cane or rapping a child's knuckles with a ruler) for minor infractions should be reduced or abolished.

When asked about telecommunications, the boys volunteer that none of their homes has a landline. They view mobile phones as an alternative. Still, only two of their families have a mobile phone. Though they are coming down in price, buying a phone credit card adds to the expense. Because the boys are away at school, being able to telephone their families would enable them to maintain a link with home. In addition, they acknowledge that having a telephone speeds up communication. When they were young, they were often the ones who carried messages between homesteads when there was a birth, a special event, or a family crisis. It meant running long distances up and over ridges at times.

The majority of their homes do not have electricity and, consequently, no labor-saving appliances. Nor are they able to have computers even if their families could afford them. Instead, they go down to Kagumo and use a computer at one of the two new computer centers. They have to pay by the minute for using a computer unless they are enrolled in a computer course. Having to pay for use discourages them from using one very often. None of them, except the one enrolled in a business college, has taken a computer course. The enrollment fees are costly. Yet all of them believe learning computer skills will enable them to get a job in the future.

The seven boys in Jumbe's Kerugoya group, whose families in this peri-urban area do have electricity, also felt that computer literacy has become increasingly important and should be made a compulsory subject at the secondary level because it has become a necessary skill for getting a job nowadays.

There's general consensus among the Gatwe boys that once young people become computer literate they will most likely have to leave Mutira to seek job opportunities in urban centers such as Nyeri or Nairobi.

The major problem in Gatwe is that computerization is impossible because most homesteads don't have electricity. *If power were made available*, one youth argued, *new businesses could be established in centers such as Gatwe and Gagathoma with cybercafes, card printing, and duplication services.*

Computers would assist big businesses that need record keeping and accounting. The secret, they conclude, is to find a means of attracting big businesses to Gatwe so young people won't have to leave the area. *The rural areas should be targeted for development by providing them with the necessary infrastructure to encourage new business*, the oldest participant, who attends a business college, says. The others agree.

Whereas the Gatwe group has linked computer literacy with "big business," the young men in Jumbe's Kerugoya group, who were in their 20s, linked it to specific record keeping and accounting functions related to improved farming, trade and small businesses. Both boys and girls see computer literacy as their ticket to securing a job.

Just as I'm completing my session with Nyambura, Wang'oo comes to tell me that the guys in his group want to talk with me and find out more about the project I'm doing. *Ah ha. I'm being held accountable*, I think to myself. *I'm sure they want to know how the information they've provided will be used.*

I get up, leaving Nyambura and Karuana to their own devices, and walk with Wang'oo across the yard to the *kithunu*. It's dark inside and takes me a minute to adjust my eyes. I sit down on a small bench near the doorway. The group makes a place for me in their circle around a coffeetable. After answering a question about the purpose of my visit, someone asks, *What advice can you give us about preparing ourselves for jobs or further education?*

"To prepare for getting jobs," I suggest, "it's important to know the job market, to be aware of which occupations have a shortage of skilled workers. For example, with more cars on the road, more skilled mechanics are needed. When electricity comes to Gatwe, people trained as electrical engineers and technicians will be needed. Kagumo has computers and even a computer center now. Technicians are needed to maintain the computers so they don't break down. It would be less costly to hire local technicians than hiring ones from Nairobi. Not everyone can be a computer programmer or clerk. I see more people using mobile phones here. Someone should know how to maintain them and fix them when they break down. The secret is not to get the same kind of training everyone else has, but to anticipate what kind of skills will be needed in the future and get training in those skills."

They take it in, some nodding their heads in agreement, then thank me, each one shaking my hand as I prepare to leave. Wang'oo and I return to Nyambura's house to collect his mother.

We walk back to the front of the homestead, where the yellow Peugeot is still parked between the banana trees. Wang'oo gets into the back seat after shaking hands with each boy. Karuana hands me the car keys—I've discovered that she has trouble putting the car in reverse and backing out of places. With an audience watching me intently, I carefully back the car out of its niche, maneuvering over the lumpy grass to a fairly even spot where I make a Y-turn. Shifting into first, I drive out through the open gate onto the road and, waving out the window, head uphill toward the tea-buying center at the corner junction. A woman in front of the center has huge avocados spread out for sale on a burlap bag. Karuana and I get out to buy some. I hand her the car keys.

On the way down to Kagumo, Karuana asks Wang'oo how his group went.

"There was no problem once it got started," he says, "but it took a long time for the guys to arrive. At first, it was hard to get them talking. I finally had to go around the circle, getting each one's opinion. What surprised me most was their discussion about change in Gatwe. I expected them to say that because the place is still so undeveloped they plan on going to Nairobi or Nyeri to find jobs after they complete school. Instead, one of them said that development should be brought to Gatwe so they won't have to leave. And the others agreed. They started talking about what is needed to improve the place, beginning with electricity. They discussed how they could help Gatwe to change rather than trying to escape from it. I liked what they said. It was quite a revelation."

"Very different from the girls' groups," Karuana says.

"Sounds like it went well, Wang'oo," I add.

"What did they want to know from you, Jean?" Karuana grills me.

"How to get a job." I grin.

She and Wang'oo laugh.

In talking with Jumbe that evening about how his group went the previous day, he tells me that six out of the eight youth were either in a training college or in a university. Only two had ended their education with secondary school. *What concerned them most about their primary education*, he relates, *was the use of physical punishment for nonperformers*. Fear of being beaten acted as an incentive to do well. Otherwise, their descriptions of their primary and secondary educations sound similar to those of the Gatwe boys. Their critique of their education was that *too many subjects were included in the secondary curriculum. Students should be allowed more electives, especially in computer science and commerce courses*. He says there was little discussion of AIDS or its prevention.

"Is the topic mainly handled by visiting public health officers?" I ask.

"Yes. That's the way the schools introduce it."

"Do you know if teachers get any training in how to present the topic so students feel comfortable discussing it?"

He shrugs his shoulders. "It's hard to know." He gets up to turn on the TV.

There's a sub-text going on here that I'm not picking up, I'm thinking. And I know better than to ask a Kenyan a question that requires a Yes or No answer. "No" is not an answer in the view of most Kenyans. It is considered impolite. "Perhaps" or "Maybe" act as proxies to save face. But again, I feel frustrated that my attempts to ferret out information about AIDS are getting nowhere. It's like a leopard in the trees—every time you think you see it, it disappears.

I want to bring it up with Jumbe again, but realize I'll have to wait for a moment when I'm less tired and there are fewer distractions.

The next day I decide to work at home, while Karuana reports to her school for the pre-term meetings. I walk up to town and get a couple of newspapers to catch up with the news of the free education initiative. I've been tracking the issue all week.

"Confusion marked the first day of free education in primary schools," the headline in the *Daily Nation* announces on Tuesday, January 7.[22] "A flood of parents demanding that their children be admitted threatened to bring the education process to a halt," the accompanying article proclaims. It seems that most school heads found they couldn't cope with the increased numbers and closed down for the day. A popular school in Kibera, Nairobi, shut its doors after enrolling 2,000 new students, according to a *Daily Nation* article.[23] In another school a deputy headmaster was kicked out of his office by angry parents. They maintained he was failing to observe the government's directive to admit all school-age children. The teachers closed the school doors against a press of parents, but over 100 of them sat down in the school compound and began registering new pupils themselves. "We are not going to walk out of this compound until the government deploys more teachers," an irate father explained.[24] That was the first day of school.

At a school just over the ridges in Nyeri, a local Member of Parliament was called to bring parental furies under control. He assured parents that arrangements would be made to construct temporary classrooms to accommodate the new influx of students. Some parents camped overnight to be first among those to secure a place for their children in school. A picture in Wednesday's *Daily Nation* showed a group of children behind the locked gates of a school that closed down under the pressure.[25]

EAST AFRICAN STANDARD, Saturday, January 11, 2003

President Kibaki makes good his pledge to provide free education
causing an enrollment jam as children of all ages rush to enter school.

Corruption and educational mismanagement are prime topics
in the media. Local authorities' "greed and personal aggrandizement"
are blamed for education's problems. A cartoon in a newspaper
shows a headmistress "looking the other way" as a parent sneaks his
child into a top-ranked school through an open window.[26] Even in
this new era of free education, the cartoon suggests, a school's leader
will have a say in who gains admittance and who does not. In the
recent past, *chai* (a bribe or payoff) was used to gain a child's
admission to a prestigious school. Part of the problem this past week
is that some parents whose children have been enrolled in mediocre
schools in urban areas have switched them to higher-ranked schools,
adding to those schools' burdens. This is a twist the new government
didn't anticipate.

In 1980, primary school enrollment nationally was 98
percent. It was similar in Kirinyaga when I was working here in the
'80s. However, since then enrollment has dropped in the district, just
as it has across the country. To get an idea of recent enrollment in
Kirinyaga, I stopped one day at the district headquarters in Kerugoya

and got the latest census figures from the Central Bureau of Statistics so I could calculate the enrollment and dropout rates for children ages 5-14 (see Table 11.1).

Table 11.1. School Attendance in Kirinyaga by Age Group and Sex, 1999-2000 (by percentage)

Age Group		Enrollment rate	Left School	Never attended
5-9	**Male**	82.3	3.0	6.3
	Female	83.6	2.7	5.7
10-14	**Male**	86.5	8.5	2.5
	Female	88.8	6.7	1.9

Compiled from Table 1, Population by Sex, Age Groups, and School Attendance, Central Bureau of Statistics, Ministry of Finance & Planning, 2002, pages 1-5.[27]

Enrollment rates for both boys and girls in the two age groups fell by 15 percent over the last 20 years. Parents who were forced to keep their children out of school for economic reasons over the past decade were lined up to enroll them at local schools on Monday. With a third of the population in Kirinyaga under the age of 15, the demand for education is intense and will not go away.

Kibaki's free schooling has been launched like a kite without reliable cross spars or a tail to keep it flying. More trained teachers and classrooms are desperately needed to accommodate the sudden spike in students. Teachers are unhappy about the situation, insisting that they are already overburdened because of a hiring freeze and government cuts in education in 2001-2002 that arrested any increases in their salaries.[28]

In addition, not all parents are jumping for joy. Some had false expectations about what the new program would provide. They thought the government would pay for everything—uniforms, textbooks, notebooks and pens—even though the education minister warned parents that the government would allocate money only for essentials, including textbooks and desks, but not uniforms or pens. The days of government handouts are gone, warns an editorial in the *Daily Nation*.[29] Parents seem unconvinced.

One large obstacle is the absence of government guidelines for admitting students under the new system. Over-age students, that is, children over the primary-school entry age of five, who were denied an education in the past because of the cost, began flooding the schools.   In one case, parents demanded that their 13-year old child be enrolled in first grade.[30]   That's a challenge for any teacher but not unheard of in rural African classrooms.   In Malawi, I recall a fifth-grade classroom with a front row of students that included one who towered above the rest.   He was 22.   The students' ages ranged from 12 to 22.   I saw similar discrepancies in South Africa in the mid-1990s as then President Nelson Mandela and his education minister struggled to overcome the educational disparities between black and white South Africans, wrought by years of apartheid.   "Leaving no child behind" takes on new meaning in African schools.

Kibaki has his work cut out for him.   But knowing how international donor agencies love a good cause, I'm sure the World Bank, USAID and the European Union will jump into the fray offering advice and further loans now that Kenya has a new democratically elected leader.

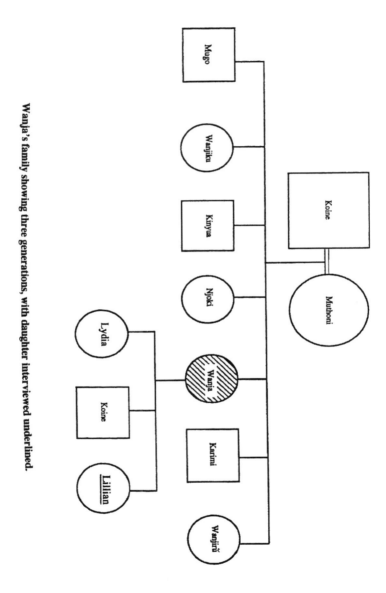

Wanja's family showing three generations, with daughter interviewed underlined.

CHAPTER 12

An Independent Woman of Means and her Daughter

We're about to leave for Gatwe to meet with Wanja when I discover that the Peugeot has vanished. I'd come out earlier and put my backpack on the back seat so as not to forget it. It's stuffed with my precious notebooks bearing questions and ideas for our meeting, as well as my tape recorder and camera.

"Where's the car?" I call to Karuana, still inside the house. Panic deep in my gut is rising swiftly, engulfing the reasoning cells further aloft in my head.

"Jumbe and Wang'oo took it." She appears in the doorway. "They're taking a friend of Jumbe's to the bus station. They won't be long." Her voice is light, calm.

"Damn." I groan. "My backpack was in the car. All my notes and the tape recorder are in it. If I lose that, there goes everything." I can hear my voice escalating toward shrill as I conjure up the bus station, not a safe place to leave a car—even for a minute.

"Calm down. Your backpack is safe. They're only dropping him off. They'll be right back," she says, barely concealing the maternal amusement puckering her face.

Her motherly voice irritates me. *Sure*, I think to myself, knowing how Kenyans spin time, and teenagers' sudden whims. Anxiety bursts into anger. I begin pacing between the fruit trees in the front yard, hoping to dispel it. We're already late.

"They know we need the car. It'll be okay." Karuana, the "not-to-worry-kid," casts a look of annoyed bemusement toward my footwork and disappears into the house.

A fretful half hour goes by as my pacing mutates into jogging. I begin circling the house, ignoring the surprised looks of the watchman as I go by him. Running always helps me control panic attacks, especially when I'm confronted with small crises over which I have no control. I make several circuits, feeling better.

I hear a motor and a door slam as I'm rounding the house to the front yard again. The Peugeot, hard to miss for its color, pulls through the gate.

Slowing down, I call to Karuana, "They're back. *Tuthii.* Let's go."

Jumbe parks the car in its customary spot and slowly gets out, followed by Wang'oo, looking relaxed and happy.

"Is my backpack in there?" I ask before they can greet me.

"Yes. It's there," Jumbe assures me. "Were you worried about it?"

"I was, because everything I own is in there. I didn't know you were going to take the car before we have to leave for Gatwe."

"We took Justin to the bus station. We didn't leave the car long," he says with a beguiling smile.

"Your backpack was safe," Wang'oo adds. "To tell you the truth, I didn't even know it was there."

"Thanks," I grin despite myself. It's hard to stay mad at these two for long.

Karuana comes out with her bag. Seeing that my mood has brightened, she says to the boys, "You two make sure that you and Wamuyu do the dishes and lock up if you go anywhere. We won't be back until dinner time."

Finally, we're off to see Wanja, only a little late by Kenyan standards.

Wanja is an exceptionally resourceful single mother. She's a teacher, a tea farmer, and a part-time shopkeeper. When I first met her in the early '80s, I was struck by the advantages that completing a secondary education had given her. It meant, for one, that she and I could converse in English as well as Kikuyu. This proved useful. I was able to clarify things I didn't get in her native tongue.

In earlier years I was able to converse with Wanja alone. But this time Karuana has come along; I suspect that Wanja's English may have become as rusty as my Kikuyu.

When we get to Wanja's house, I introduce Karuana and ask Wanja which language she would like to use. She says, "My English is not so good these days. Kikuyu is best."

Wanja was a mother of three young children in 1984 when she first shared her life story. She told me two of her children were by a man with whom she had lived in Kerugoya and hoped to marry him. I learned later that her second child actually was the result of having been raped by an uncle of the man she wanted to marry. When Wanja revealed to her boyfriend that his uncle, a widower, had forced himself on her, causing the pregnancy, her boyfriend became angry. Disgusted by the situation, he refused to take responsibility for her or either of the children. He abandoned her. Wanja was humiliated and deeply disappointed. From that time on, she vowed to go her own way. She had accepted her life as a single mother by the time I met her in August 1983.

At that time, Wanja lived at her parents' homestead, depending on her father for access to farmland. Her father gave her a small garden to grow vegetables, and Wanja helped her grown brothers pick tea. She was also teaching nursery school part-time.

Wanja is the fifth child and the third girl in a family with six children, three boys and three girls. During her childhood Wanja's parents treated their children equally. *There was no difference between the way my parents treated the boys and the girls in our family*, she told me. Children of both sexes herded the family's goats, gathered wood, and fetched water. It was a close family, with storytelling and games, as well as the usual chores expected of children whose parents farmed.

During the liberation struggle, however, her father was sent to a British concentration camp for Gikuyu suspected of being Mau Mau sympathizers. The rest of her family was sent to an internment village. Her mother was away from the village much of the time, helping to dig the trench around Mt. Kenya. *We were left with my oldest sister during much of that time because both my parents were away. She would tie me on her back and do her work of gathering wood and fetching water and cooking.*[31]

In 1984, Wanja felt that having acquired a secondary school certificate, she deserved more than the tedious job of picking tea. Like Wanjiku's granddaughters later, achieving a secondary education changed her feelings about farming as a way of life. Her dream was to become a businesswoman with her own shop. The small salary she earned as a part-time nursery school teacher, however, did not fully support her children. She depended on help from her parents, something she hadn't anticipated. It nagged her. Yet she acknowledged her role as a single mother, telling me, *Nowadays a woman has to be self-sufficient because you can't depend on a husband. Whether a woman is married or not makes no difference, you are still responsible for your children.*

She had hoped for a full-time teaching position when she came home with her high school diploma. None was available at the time, so she settled for the part-time nursery school position. Her immediate goal became to own land like her brothers. By having her own land, she could hire pickers and earn enough from tea to become self-sufficient.

Until the 1990s, Kenya's inheritance laws did not permit daughters to inherit land. The legal norms were that sons, not daughters, inherited their father's property, according to the patrilineal precepts of Kenya's ethnic groups. But in 1991, under pressure from Kenyan women's organizations and women leaders who had attended the United Nations' Women's Decade conference held in Nairobi in 1985, the Kenya Parliament passed a new law allowing daughters equal rights with sons to inherit their father's land. Based on the new law, in 1992 Wanja's aging father divided his farm equally among his three sons and his remaining daughter at home, Wanja. In 1993 they went to Kerugoya to register the parcels, each in his or her own name, and were in the process of getting the written deeds when I returned to Gatwe in January 1994.

Wanja told me then, *The thing that satisfies me the most now is having my own land. We were each given an acre. The parcel that my father gave me is down near the river. The soil is fertile there. I plant vegetables and maize that we sell in the market, and I have tea planted further up. I also rent tea plants from a neighbor so I can have them picked to earn additional income...I am doing well enough to pay for my daughters' schooling and even to pay the taxes on one of my brother's parcels.*

Nine years later Wanja holds a title deed to her land. It gives her a sense of security she didn't have before.

When I visited in 1994, Wanja was teaching pre-school full-time. She also managed a shop for her brother in Gatwe, and she had hired two women to pick her tea.

I have now become the major breadwinner in our family, she confessed with a certain pride. *My parents are too old to be of much help in the gardens. Yes, when you last saw us, my mother was trying to grow pineapples to sell. But the weather gets a bit cold up here, so she decided to give that up. She helps out with my brothers' children now. I saw that my parents needed someone to take care of them, so when I built this house* [of stone] *I made sure it has a place for them.*

Wanja not only had land of her own and a full-time job, but she'd built a permanent home for her family. She was also helping to manage her brother's shop in Gatwe. It may not have been her own shop, as she'd dreamed, but it was close. She managed it for four years and was responsible for taking inventory and ordering new goods. On weekends she worked part-time in the shop and loved it.

By 1994, Wanja's children were nearly grown. Lydia, her oldest daughter, had recently completed secondary school and was away in the mandatory one-year National Youth Service (NYS) program that all postsecondary students were required to enroll in at that time. The program combined community service with some military training. She was scheduled to attend a secretarial course in Nairobi once she completed her NYS commitment. Wanja's son, Eastus, had applied to Kenya Polytechnic in Nairobi for science training. He had completed secondary school that year. Her lastborn, Lillian, was in Form Three and doing well. The girl was home for Christmas holidays when I visited, helping her mother, so I had a chance to see her. As a teenager, Lillian impressed me as being industrious and self-contained as I watched her doing tasks that made her mother's work easier. As it turns out, Lillian is the only one of Wanja's children who settled back in Gatwe.

Now in 2003, Wanja tells me, *Things are going well, even though I am old now* [She's 47]. *I am a grandmother. My firstborn, Lydia Wangithi Gitonga, is now 29 years old. She completed the three-year sectretarial course and in 1997 got employed in the Office of the President.*

"That's quite an achievement," I commend her.

Wanja nods, smiling. *Yes, she is doing well. She married Allan Gitonga, who works with the Kenya Association of Travel Agents. They have one daughter, age five, and live in Nairobi. Lillian Wangu Wanjohi, whom you saw when you were here last, is now 27 years old. She completed Form Four and went to a catering college for two years where she learned about beverage and food processing. After that she took a one-year pharmacy course but is still not employed. She is married to Wanjohi Ngaca, who has a Master's degree in teaching. He was teaching at Nyeri Technical College, but it has been closed for two years, so he and Lillian stay at his parents' homestead. They have a small daughter who is not yet two. Eastus Mwangi, my son, went to Kenya Polytechnic and got a diploma in applied biology. He's now enrolled in a computer course in Kagumo. I have no money problems now that I have educated all my children. Even though not all of them have jobs, the last two are hopeful of getting one.*

I am still teaching in the nursery school in Gatwe. It is okay. I no longer work in my brother's shop. It became too much. I am too occupied with my tea. I have three to five tea pickers employed at a time now, depending on how fast the new tea sprouts. The KTDA is paying 7.50 shillings per kilo at this time, which is not enough because the bonus has been reduced. We got only 14 shillings per kilo for the bonus in November [2002] compared with 25 shillings in 2001. I also started growing a little maize to sell in debes [large five-gallon cans], as the tea bonus was less last year. I get 200 shillings [$2.78] per debe in the market. I've never grown a lot of maize as some do who sell large bags of it.

Even though Wanja's dream 20 years ago was to leave farming behind, in the end she has returned to it. Having her own land has made a huge difference: she can depend on what it produces to supplement her income from teaching, and her tea will provide a source of income once she retires. Like American teachers, Kenyan teachers often have to balance two jobs to make ends meet.

You can see there have been some changes here at home, she says. I no longer live in the same compound with my parents. I moved over here on a nearby hill and built this timber house we're sitting in. I also bought the furniture. Before I moved from my father's compound, I had a well dug and through the Matangi Women Group I belong to, I was able to build a water tank. We contribute money and each woman builds a tank in her compound when it is her turn to receive the money. Having a water tank in their homestead has made a big difference to my family. And I use it, too. It saves us the work of hauling water up from the stream.

Here at home I have a radio, but no telephone or mobile phone as you are seeing in Kagumo. I listen to the news and sometimes education programs, such as ones about health or how to get better crops. The mobile phone I used to call Karuana, your assistant, the other day was my oldest daughter's. She brought it when she came to visit last weekend. We also have a neighbor who has one, and he allows me to make calls with it for a fee. It's important now to have a phone as it helps me to contact my daughter in Nairobi, the one who works in the Office of the President. You can see we don't have electricity here yet, but we have a project to get it now.

I am physically healthy, but nowadays my parents are sick. My father cannot walk far because of his weakening bones. My mother has diabetes and goes for treatment at Tumu Tumu Hospital. That is where I was the day you wanted to meet with me; I was taking my mother to a hospital where I know she will be given quality care. With the Kerugoya Hospital one can never be sure. A big change up here, though, is that the Gatwe dispensary has been modernized, so people do not have to go all the way to Kagumo for treatment.

In 1994, I asked Wanja if she'd heard of AIDS or knew of anyone who had it in Mutira location. *Yes,* she responded. *I have heard of AIDS. But up here people are not thinking too much about it. Malaria is a problem for us now. We never used to have malaria-carrying mosquitoes because it was too cold up here. We thought we were safe. But these days there is malaria here, so it looks like those mosquitoes got immune to the cold. Also pneumonia and TB are problems, especially in the cold season.*

At the time, Wanja, like others in Mutira, viewed the problem of AIDS as a distant disease, located someplace else—an urban problem. Now, when I ask her about malaria and other diseases, she says:

I've had malaria several times since I saw you in 1994. You know it's a disease that one can get from time to time. I went to Gatwe to get medicine for it each time. Also, my brother had tuberculosis two years ago, but he was treated for it and is now cured. But this problem of AIDS, I know little about. We are taught through the radio and posters that it is a disease one can get if one is loose in her ways, but I do not know anyone personally who has had it or has it now.

Alcoholism is getting to be a big problem. I can tell you one of my brothers here and another brother's son are both alcoholics. Maybe if they got educated about it and got jobs they might be able to be cured. With AIDS, we don't hear directly about it until someone dies, but with alcoholism one can see how it affects the person and the problems it brings to his family.

When I ask about changes in Gatwe, she tells me, *The major changes I see in Gatwe are better transport to Kagumo, and we have the project to get electricity up here.*

Wanja has settled into her own skin. The former doubts and bitterness she experienced as a single mother 20 years ago have dissipated. She has overcome the obstacles that faced her then. Her well-educated children are grown and making a place for themselves in the new century. She has come to terms with her own education, recognizing that now that she has title to land, she doesn't mind managing its production. And she makes enough to hire laborers to do the most tedious work. She has helped her brothers and parents, making their compound more comfortable with a stone house and readily accessible water. And she has built a home of her own for her old age. Her teaching job has become mundane, humdrum. She'll retire in another eight years. What she is most proud of is her land and her children. She enjoys being a grandmother.

After the conversation, I ask Wanja if we can meet with her daughter, Lillian, who lives about two miles away, in the homestead of her husband's parents. It is just north of Gatwe, next to the Mt. Kenya Forest. We make arrangements to fetch Wanja on Friday and she'll show us where Lillian lives.

Wanja in front of her new house on the hill.

Journey to Lillian's Homestead

Friday turns out to be an overcast day with rain threatening. I'm glad we have the Peugeot. We park the car at the side of the main dirt road above the tea-buying center and walk to Wanja's place to fetch her. She is ready for us, wearing a scoop-neck pink T-shirt that has *Americano* written across the front in shades of pink, red and blue, and a long dark skirt with a pattern of stained glass chips in the same shades of blue and dark pink. She wears a sky-blue cardigan, unbuttoned at the front, over the T-shirt. On her head is a pale blue silk headscarf with a flowered pattern of the same colors in her skirt. She has artfully knotted the headscarf at the top of her head in a manner worn by many West African women. Wanja has a sense of style, but she is also practical. On her feet are the same black oxfords, without socks, she wears to church every Sunday. She is ready to go visiting.

When we get out to the road, Karuana offers to sit in the back of the Peugeot so Wanja can show me where to go once we have passed Gatwe village. Wanja seems pleased to be given a front seat.

We traverse the ridge, descend down a steep hill bordered on both sides with folds of rich-looking emerald tea, then cross a creaky wooden bridge over a swiftly moving river and climb the hill on the other side. After a curve, we come to a row of small shops strung along the road like children's blocks. They mark the beginning of the village. Gatwe has spread out; it consisted of only a few shops, a primary school, a minimal clinic, and a church a decade earlier. I can see a couple of two-story dwellings among the cluster of stucco buildings with iron-sheet roofs that cling to the hill.

We have passed several prosperous-looking compounds nestled among the tea fields on our way to the village. Dominated by large stone houses with glass windows, these compounds are surrounded by sturdy stone fences with imposing grillwork gates. They are a far cry from the thatch-roofed mud and wattle clusters I saw in the late 1970s or the collection of timber houses with iron-sheet roofs that characterized Gikuyu compounds in the 1980s and early '90s. Timber houses still predominate, but they are slowly giving way to large stone houses and defining fences. As tea has become the crop of choice, highland farmers, at least those with three or more acres planted in tea, have begun to prosper. Whether this trend will continue, given the vagaries of Kenya's export sector, remains a question.

Leaving the main dirt road, we climb what looks more like a broad, grassy cow path. I am glad to be driving. The track is slippery and maneuvering over the raised spots, deep ruts, and occasional rocks takes some doing. We traverse the side of a knoll for about a mile and a half, with nothing but verdant green hills sloping away on our left and an occasional fenced compound on our right. I can smell wood-fueled cooking fires in the distance mingling with the scent of damp eucalyptus. The trees line the track on the uphill side, acting as a windbreak for some homesteads. When we get to the top of the knoll and look down the other side, I see that the track narrows steeply, becoming a single muddy path. It disappears around a curve.

"How much farther is the homestead?" I ask Wanja, who has been silent.

"It's just around the corner after we go down that hill."

"I think we'll walk the rest of the way. Why don't you two get out, and I'll turn the car around and park it on that little spot of grass so we'll be headed downhill toward the main road in case it starts to rain."

"Okay." Karuana grabs my backpack. She and Wanja get out of the car and stand in the grass next to a fence to watch me. I pull partway up into a steep, rutted driveway and gingerly begin reversing onto the grassy spot across from it. Several children have suddenly appeared at the gate of the compound. Climbing up on the gate, they stare at the *muzungu* lady as she negotiates the slippery U-turn. Sweating over the stubborn steering wheel, turning it this way, then that way, I finally get the car onto the level spot, heading downhill. I set the parking brake and get out, wiping my brow with a Kleenex.

Karuana hands me my backpack. "I'm glad you were driving, Jean. I never could have done that. Let's hope it doesn't rain before we get finished."

"I didn't know this would be so hard for a car," Wanja adds meekly. "We don't have far to walk now."

Karuana hands a few shillings to a boy about ten and asks him to watch the car until we return. Looking down, he nods his assent respectfully. The three of us wave good-bye to the kids, telling them to greet their parents, then walk down the steep hill towards the entrance to the forest. Adjusting the weight of the pack on my back, I take a deep breath of the cool air and suddenly notice how extraordinarily beautiful the surroundings are, even in gray light. A muddy red track leads into the forest, passing through enormous old growth cedars and evergreens. Carpeted tea fields have given way to fecund green scrub brush gathered in dark clusters against closely-cropped kikuyu grass.

Remembering that Mararu, the first Kenyan I had brought to the U.S., had once told me about being treed by an elephant in this same forest, and knowing that elephants can cause infinite damage to farms not only in Kenya but in other African countries such as Malawi and in Zimbabwe, where I had lived, I ask Wanja, "Do people living up here have any trouble with elephants raiding their gardens? It's so close to the forest."

"Yes, occasionally when they get hungry and can't find enough in the forest, they will come."

"There are no fences here like I saw in northern Zimbabwe to keep them out...Not that it did much good there."

"No." Wanja laughs. "A fence isn't going to keep elephants out. They'll just step over it or knock it down with their tusks."

"How do people protect their gardens?"

"Just pray that if an elephant comes, it doesn't trample down the whole *shamba*."

Shuddering, I recall my feelings of awe and dismay when I saw the damage elephants had done to the fenced maize garden of a farmer outside Kariba Wildlife Preserve in Zimbabwe. And I remember the time my sons and I were backpacking along a trail on the eastern side of Mt. Kenya Forest in the 1980s and suddenly heard elephants swishing through the underbrush, then saw them tearing up whole trunkfuls of bamboo as if it was spaghetti for dinner. Both incidents left me with a humbled respect for the power of an elephant's appetite. Beautiful as it is up here on the ridges, I'm not sure I would want to live this close to the forest preserve.

"Some day I'd like to hike into the forest on that track to see where it goes," I tell Karuana. "But I'm not sure what I'd do if I came face to face with a bull elephant."

"There's not much one can do when they come but let them pass," Wanja says. "But they don't see them too often here. Mostly they stay in the forest."

"But what will happen if more of the forest is cleared, the way it was in the 1990s, when President Moi wanted to plant tea for his Nyao Tea Plantation scheme?"

"Let's hope that will stop now that we have a new president," Wanja responds. "We're nearly there," she adds, as we round the corner and walk up another hill toward a cluster of plank houses with *mabati* roofs. "This is where Lillian's in-laws live. The first house belongs to the husband's older brother."

As we approach the compound, a girl about 11 and two small boys dressed in tattered shorts run out to greet us from behind the first house, staring at me with curiosity. Wanja greets each of them with a handshake and asks for news of their parents. As we make our way through the maze of small houses that form the compound, we come to a fence. A man and woman are emptying tea leaves from two large baskets into a burlap bag to be carried to the tea weighing station. They stop briefly and offer us a wrist to shake, as their hands are unclean from picking tea. The two turn out to be the children's parents.

"We have come for a visit with my daughter and her husband," Wanja explains. "This *muzungu* wants to talk with Lillian. This is her friend, Mrs. Mutiti."

They nod their heads, looking from one to the other of us.

"Wanjohi is at home," the brother tells Wanja. "He is expecting you."

We nod and follow Wanja through the fence opening as she begins calling, "*Hodi...hodi?*"

A tall, dark, well-dressed man with his trousers tucked into rubbers boots comes to greet us. "*Karibu*," he says warmly. "Please come with me. Nyina-wa-Njeri is eager to meet you." Wanja makes the introductions, and Wanjohi leads us to a rectangular house with wood siding and a cement floor. We step into the house and find ourselves in a sitting room with two large, comfortable sofas and a corner table between them. Karuana settles on one sofa, and I take the other, while Wanja sinks into an overstuffed chair opposite me. The velveteen sofas have a yellow and green pattern that brightens the otherwise dark room. The only light comes from the doorway. Wanjohi excuses himself to get Lillian, who has been busy dressing their 18-month-old daughter.

Lillian appears, wearing a gray-green dress with a matching jacket and black shoes. Her hair is pulled back into a low ponytail and is tied with a large black bow. She is stylish like her mother, but taller. She greets us as she switches her baby to her left arm, then, so she can bring us tea, hands her little girl to her mother.

I explain the purpose of our visit as we sip tea. "Lillian, do you know you are the very same age as your mother was when I first met her in 1983?"

She looks surprised and eyes her mother, who smiles at her, and says, "That's right. We've been seeing one another for a long time."

"Being able to talk with you, at the same age," I continue, "will give me some idea about how things have changed between two generations of women in the same family. *Ni igua*? Do you understand?"

"*Ii. Ni ndigua.* Yes. I understand." She is standing now in the doorway with her child in her arms again. She looks toward her husband, who has settled into a seat next to her mother, then back at me. "We can talk. There is no problem."

"Do you have any questions about the interview?" Karuana asks. Lillian shakes her head, *"Asha.* No."

"Good," Karuana continues. "How far did you go in school?" I know she is asking the question to assess whether to use English or Kikuyu.

"I completed Form Four and took the exams," Lillian responds in English.

"Where would you like my wife to sit?" Wanjohi interjects.

"She can sit here next to me on the sofa," I reply, patting the cushion beside me.

Lillian moves to the sofa and sits down next to me with the baby on her lap.

"But for our session," I explain, "I will need to talk with Lillian alone as I have with all the other women we have met with." I look toward Wanjohi and Wanja.

Wanjohi looks blank, so Karuana explains my request in Kikuyu. Wanja gets up, nodding her head in understanding and goes outside.

Wanjohi holds back. "Are you sure you will not need me to answer some of the questions?"

"I think we will be okay," I smile to reassure him. "But we will send for you if we do need you for something."

"What will you do with the information you learn from my wife?"

"It will become part of a book, along with the information we have learned from other people, about changes in Mutira over the last two decades."

"I see. As you wish." He gets up slowly and goes outside. Karuana and I exchange knowing looks. He had planned on being present for his wife's interview.

I take a moment to play with Lillian's baby before we begin talking, handing the baby my glasses to explore. After a moment, I take them back. The little girl smiles and rocks back and forth. Her acceptance seems to relax her mother. We are ready to begin.

Lillian Kiangu Wanjohi, Wanja's Younger Daughter

I am 26 years old. When I was growing up, I learned a lot from my mother, like cultivating the shamba, picking tea, fetching firewood, and household chores like cooking, washing the utensils and chopping firewood. I was about four or five years old when I first learned how to collect firewood and water. I didn't learn how to wash clothes until I was about ten. My mother also used to send me to Gatwe to buy things. I never had a list. I kept the things she wanted in my head.

Because my mother was able to read, she used to read me stories. She also told me stories, mainly about giants. I guessed that Wanja had told her daughter the same stories about giants that her mother had told her when she was a child. Wanja had shared one of them with me in 1984.

I started nursery school in Gatwe, where I learned how to read and write and count. By the time I went to primary school, I already knew how to read and write. In primary school I learned English, Swahili, Kikuyu, science/agriculture, mathematics and GHC [Geography/History/Civics]. *I was 15 when I finished.*

I remember I got my first [menstrual] *period before I started secondary school. I already knew what was happening because the primary school teachers had prepared us. But now I have seen that young girls are getting pregnant at a very early age. This is because they are getting to know things about sexuality earlier, even at 10 years, and they are maturing faster than during our times.*

We had Family Life Education beginning in primary school. And we were taught about diseases like tuberculosis, malaria and AIDS in subjects such as home science, biology, social education and ethics in secondary school. The teachers also used to bring visitors to talk to us about these diseases. The visitors helped to get the points across. We had no electricity at Gatwe Primary, so there were no films or videos on these topics.

For secondary school I went to Ngaru Girls Secondary. It's a boarding school. Even though I had to leave home, I was excited and happy. I felt very comfortable at that school and never missed home, even once.

Wanja with her daughter, Lillian, on the right.

I joined several clubs while I was there, like Science Congress, 4-K Club, which stands for Kuungana, Kufonya, Kusaidia Kenya Club [To Unite, To Work, To Help Kenya Social Service Club], *Young Farmers and the Wildlife Club. I was also captain of the dining hall. As captain I had to make sure the girls behaved themselves during meals.*

Going away to school taught me to interact freely with people whom I had never met before—people who came from different places. My favorite subject in secondary school was commerce. I got a C grade on the KCSE exams and went to college, where I did catering, which is about food and beverage production.

I've also taken a training course in pharmacy. It included learning how to prescribe and dispense medicines. But I have not been able to use this knowledge because getting a job in a pharmacy is difficult. There is high competition for every opening because many have done the same course.

If I had a chance to visit President Mwai Kibaki, I would tell him what people in this area need. I would begin with education, telling him we need free education, which I think is possible. And that the schools need to teach subjects that are most useful to people, like commerce and agriculture. I took these courses along with the others, and they have been very helpful to me.

One thing I would change is the behaviors of some teachers in primary school. They should stop making friendships [having relationships, including sex] *with school girls and work harder at their teaching and stop relaxing so much.*

I think the health system here is satisfactory because we have a good clinic at Gatwe now. It is a walking distance of about 30 minutes from here. There have been a lot of changes here over the last ten years, like now we have computers in Kagumo. Also we have more available transport. Most people are educated, not like some people's parents who never went to school. I was very lucky that my mother had been to school because she saw how to assist me with my studies.

The major problem I see in Kenya now is lack of jobs. Also school fees have become very costly. There is a lot of corruption in Gatwe, Kagumo, and even in Kerugoya. Where is it? You find it in tea production, in the KTDA...in transport...in the police, even in schools. You see, the teachers are too busy trying to earn outside money and not performing their teaching duties. They are just relaxing, so they cheat students on their education.

The discipline in schools like Gatwe has fallen. In the primary school there were six girls who became pregnant last year. The teachers seem to have become lenient with the girls. They do not send them away when they get pregnant anymore. Once a girl is pregnant, she should be dropped from school. Girls have to be taught to abstain until they finish school. Some teachers try and talk to these girls, but they have become "hardcore" and are no longer listening. The best thing to do would be to send pregnant girls away so the rest would see the consequences and abstain from sex until they finish school. And it would help them protect themselves if any of the teachers has AIDS. No, I have not heard of any girls getting AIDS from the teachers. But it might be possible.

I hope by the time my daughter is school age, she will continue up to university level. Then she will have more opportunity of getting a job.

Of the problems Lillian cites, lack of jobs in her chosen field, pharmacology, seems to outweigh health issues as her major concern. She is not alone. Both the boys in the Gatwe group and Wanjiku's granddaughters saw lack of jobs as the critical issue among youth their age. Moreover, that Lillian's husband, who has a Master's degree in education and has taught teachers, lost his job when Nyeri Technical College closed last year must be an additional burden for her family.

At the same time that educational achievement among Kenyans has continued to advance, their country's economy has stagnated, with fewer jobs for the increasingly qualified graduates seeking them. As a result, Kenyan employers have steadily set the educational bar higher for entry-level positions in key areas, especially in health care, business and computer technology. Jobs that once required a secondary school certificate now require a bachelor's degree. With the shrinking budget in education and government cutbacks, even people with advanced degrees, such as Wanjohi, have little job security anymore.

Saying good-bye to Lillian and Wanjohi, we hastily leave the compound as the rain, which has held off for most of the morning, begins pelting down on us. We're sopping wet by the time we get back to the car. We drop Wanja off at the tea weighing station and the last we see of her, she is making a dash for the shelter of the building where others are waiting out the sudden downpour. With Karuana driving, we descend carefully down through the ridges on the slippery road and head toward Kerugoya. At a major intersection in town, Karuana asks me to take the wheel; she wants to drop by her secondary school to pick up her mail and class assignments for the year. I continue down the hill, avoiding jaywalkers and scrawny dogs, toward home.

I close myself in my room, glad to have some time to review and file the piles of material I've collected. And I want to re-read the reports Wang'oo did for the boys' discussion groups. As none of the teenagers is around, it's blissfully quiet.

"I'm famished," Karuana says, knocking on my door sometime later.

"Come in," I call.

She opens the door and pokes her head in. I'm sitting on top of the bed, with pages of notes and reports spread out around me.

"How was Wang'oo's report?" Karuana has shed the dress she wore to Gatwe and put on a simple blouse and blue *kanga* cloth wrapped around her waist. It falls to her ankles. Her feet are in generic blue rubber thongs.

"Okay. It could use a bit more organization and detail. I still don't feel like I'm learning much about AIDS education."

"It's pretty basic here."

"Fill me in."

"We usually depend on an outside speaker from a health clinic to cover that topic. It's not something everyone knows about."

"Teachers don't get any training in how to approach it?"

"No. Not really. The district health officers provide speakers. Sometimes we get a video."

I'm sensing a reticence to talk about AIDS on Karuana's part, which surprises me. "Wanjiku and Nge'endo told me that young people don't talk about it openly, that they use a word like *cholera* as a euphemism, as code for AIDS. Is that true?"

Karuana tilts her head, like a robin listening. "It's a mysterious disease to people. They don't know whether somebody has died of AIDS, or malaria, or some other disease. And AIDS testing is not widespread. People are afraid of being tested, for fear of what it might show. Come on. You need something to eat."

"Well, it's frustrating. A girl in the group at the clinic the other day told me afterwards, 'Everyone here knows somebody who has died of AIDS.' But nobody is talking about it."

"If a person gets AIDS, that one tries to hide it. They don't want to admit loose ways. And some families reject a person if they find he has AIDS. Let's go eat now."

Seeing that she wants to drop the topic, I shift gears and agree to join her.

"I wonder if the kids have left any of the spaghetti you made last night?" She asks then answers her own question, "Probably not. They like eating it for breakfast."

"Yuk!" I shout, getting up from the bed. "How were things at school?"

"The usual. I got my assignments and teaching schedule. It's not bad. Mostly biology classes and only one introductory course."

"That's good...I guess I'm a bit hungry, though you know I'm not a big eater."

"Well, I'm starved," she repeats.

"I have some groundnuts if there's nothing left."

"Those won't hold you till dinner."

Karuana disappears into the kitchen. Suddenly I hear her yell, "Those kids! I told them to clean up the kitchen after they finished lunch and look at it. A sink full of dirty dishes! Wamuyu," she calls. "Wa-mu-yu?" Louder now.

No answer.

I grab a bag of peanuts off the small table in the corner where my stuff that's not in a suitcase is piled. I hear running water in the sink, the clatter of dishes.

Karuana and Mugo have been fighting the battle of the dirty dishes with their teenagers ever since I arrived. It seems that at boarding school the kids got used to having someone else do their dishes; they resent having to clean up at home. There are no dishwashers here. With four teenagers, instead of the two each had before they decided to share a home, the work has doubled. Mugo makes breakfast, Karuana dinner. The kids rarely cook, but the teen team is supposed to clean up. Thinking about the situation, I also recognize the tensions that invariably go along with a newly blended family. It doesn't take much to recall the time my widowed mother of three married a widower with two small children when I was 16. It was no serenade.

"Here, let me do the dishes while you get something to eat," I offer, going into the kitchen. "Do you want a groundnut?"

"No. I need something more than that right now," she answers distractedly, moving away from the sink and drying her hands. A stray piece of hair teases her forehead. Her mouth is set. "The spaghetti is gone, but there's some leftover *pilau* [a spicy rice dish]. I'm heating it up for us. Do you want some spinach with it?"

"No. I'll just fix one of the avocados we bought yesterday. I love them and they're not in season at home." I step to the sink and turn on the tap. "Are there any lemons in the fridge?"

"Yes, we have lemons, but will an avocado be enough?" She looks askance.

"Sure. Avocados are filling." I'm rinsing a white plate that I've scrubbed clean under the cold tap—there's no hot water in the kitchen. The shower has a monopoly on all hot water. I set the dish in the plastic drain rack on a stack of shelves next to the sink, and begin washing another plate with the scouring pad dipped in soap.

"I wonder where Wamuyu went to?" Karuana is stirring the *pilau* in a pot on the stove. It smells delicious, a celebration in spices.

"Probably seeing her friends."

"It's hard keeping track of that girl sometimes," Karuana says with frustration. She begins carving up a football-size papaya and putting the slices on a plate with avocado wedges.

Looking out the window over the sink I see Doctari's ancient mother sitting on her stoop in the shade of the eave. She's curled into herself and looks half asleep. I can smell the whiff of a smokey cooking fire coming from her quarters. Karuana told me the old woman was angry with me yesterday. "You didn't greet *Cucu* properly."

She was right. I had failed to stop and shake *Cucu*'s hand, asking the usual litany of questions, when we came home from Kagumo. In Kenya, age makes a difference. That I, a younger woman, did not greet her, asking about her health and her day, was an affront. I slipped up. Seeing her now, I make a mental note to do better when she comes in for tea.

"You haven't seen my *shamba*," Karuana observes as she takes the plate of fruit out to the dining table, then returns. "After we finish our snack, I'll take you out to see it. I planted 50 new banana plants over the Christmas holiday, and I want to see how they're doing." Her mood seems to have shifted. I'm relieved.

"Fifty?" I'm impressed. "I didn't know you were into farming, Karuana."

"We have a couple of avocado trees, and I've planted *skumawiki*, spinach, and cabbages. The *skuma* is nearly finished, but some of the cabbages should be ready. The bananas I planted are down at the bottom of the hill, below the maize. With all the rain we had, I want to make sure they didn't drown." Karuana begins dishing up our *pilau* on separate plates.

"Not so much," I caution.

"They're going to say I don't feed you," she admonishes.

When I dry off my hands and carry out the plates, I find that Karuana has already put out utensils.

I drop down into one of the places at the table and sit for a moment, looking at the hot spicy rice dish, feeling its heat, absorbing its aroma, then help myself to several avocado and papaya slices. Karuana has squeezed the juice of a lemon over them. Its citric essence smells fresh, inviting.

We eat in silence, enjoying the food and tranquility.

Carrying our dishes out to the kitchen afterwards, we put them in the sink to soak.

"You ready to see the *shamba*?" Karuana asks, smiling.

"Yes. Let me get my tennis shoes on." I'm cautious about wearing closed shoes in muddy or dusty areas because of my run in with chiggers in the '80s.

"I'll show you where we plan to build the new house," Karuana says. "That's what the bricks are for—a new house with big windows and wooden floors, and plenty of space, but not too big.

After the kids are gone, Doctari and I will become lost in a maze of rooms if the house is too large."

I laugh and follow her outside. We go through an opening in the hedgerow and out into the gardens and fields beyond. They are a patchwork of greens and yellows against the red hills. Iron-green kale, onions and pale jade cabbages grow in neat rows in the rectangular plot outside the hedge. Two huge mango trees and an avocado stand guard. The avocado tree is hanging with fruit that will soon be ripe, but the mango trees are merely a mass of long, dark leaves. No fruit. Darn.

Further along the hill healthy green maize stalks crowned with translucent white tassels stand like giants waving their short arms, waiting for their ears to ripen. Green beans crowd between them, twisting up their stalks. Sugar cane and Napier grass grow in thick clusters at the bottom of the cultivated hills, threatening to clog the meandering stream that provides water for the crops. Following a path uphill, Karuana shows me the site of their future house at the top. A pile of large rocks that will be used in construction marks the spot.

"This is where we're going to build." She stands in the shade of an enormous fig tree, looking out over the terraced crops. "The house will have lots of louvered windows to let in the breeze. It will be cooler up here. What do you think?"

"It's a great spot. You'll even have a view of your *shamba* in case monkeys come down and try to steal your fruits."

She chuckles. "Next time you come, we'll be living here. And you'll have a bigger room."

"But you have to visit me in America first. It's your turn."

"You mean it?"

"Of course. Next year. I'll send you a ticket."

"Then I'll come. Now let's go see my bananas." We head down through the terracing to the rich bottomland where small leafy banana trees are nestled in muddy dark mounds, a trench surrounding each plant.

"You did all this? You really *are* a farmer. I had no idea."

Getting a tour of Karuana's *shamba* has been a treat for both of us because it's the first time she has ever had room for a real farm. It's also a good break from the work we've been doing.

We make our way back along the uphill side of the stream and take the path back to the compound. When we get there, Karuana steps through the hedgerow. She walks towards the raised metal water tank at the back.

"I think I'll sit outside in front for awhile," I call after her. "I'll come in later."

"Okay. I'm going to fix some tea. It was hot out there."

I backtrack to the front yard and sit down on a log, hoping to catch Jumbe so I can talk to him about my AIDS quandary.

CHAPTER 13

The Elusive Shadow – Confronting AIDS

It's late afternoon, still uncomfortably warm. Sitting on a log under the mango tree, I ponder how best to approach Jumbe about the AIDS gap, the silence that goes with the territory in Kenya. Gazing up into the dark foliage of the tree, I hope for a bolt of inspiration. Instead, I find myself wishing that it were mango season so I could slurp up the messy fruit. The pungent aroma of papaya ripening on nearby trees is not nearly as enticing. A papaya has dropped to the ground and partially broken open, its black seeds nestled in the plump orange flesh, inviting insects and bees.

On a line strung between the papaya and mango trees, men's shirts flutter fretfully, competing for my attention. The breeze brings a moment of respite from the January heat. Its cooling whisper reminds me to breathe. I wiggle my toes crushed in hot tennis shoes, wishing I had on rubber thongs. Looking up, I see Jumbe coming out of the boys' quarters. Dressed in khaki Bermuda shorts and a T-shirt with Star Player on the front, he seems relaxed, approachable. Standing on the small veranda overlooking the garden, he catches sight of me and waves.

"*Jambo* Jumbe. *Uhoro waku?* What's your news?" I call playfully, getting up to greet him.

"Hi, Jean. *Timu uru.* No bad news," he reports, grinning.

"Got a minute?" I approach him. "I need to ask you a couple of questions about the boys' group you led."

"Sure, I can even give you a few minutes," he says with a twinkle.

I laugh. "I saw that the group covered some diseases they learned about in school, but their comments about AIDS were like shooting stars—brief, but no light. Was there any sort of exchange about the specifics of AIDS or its prevention?"

"It's a sensitive topic here," he replies slowly, dropping into a wicker chair. I take another chair, thankful that neither of his 17-year-old brothers is around at the moment.

"I didn't really think to ask about what they learned in those courses," he says. "But teachers stick mostly to what AIDS can do to one's body and that the disease can be fatal. I can remember being told that loose behaviors can open the door to AIDS infection with horrible consequences. The trouble is, most people here identify AIDS with prostitutes. Some people, especially less educated ones in rural areas, think it comes from witchcraft, the kind without a cure."

"Tell me more about the witchcraft."

"You know there are those who still believe in curses, that someone can put a curse on you. It can lead to the death of the victim. So some people believe AIDS is the result of a curse."

"Then someone thinking that might go to a *mundu mugo,* a traditional healer, to be cured?

"Yes. But the cure hardly ever works."

"What about your agemates? Do they fear HIV/AIDS?"

"Not really. Those with more education, who are informed, might use condoms, but some people just ignore precautions, thinking *they* will never get the disease."

"Sort of like they're invincible?"

"Yes, I think so, especially men. There's another thing."

"What's that?"

"Discrimination against people with AIDS here in Kenya is a reality. Some family members and friends avoid the one with AIDS. They won't even sit with him to eat, fearing the disease. Then the person feels bad, like he's shunned. It's a matter of shame." Jumbe says it with a lowered head, his hands fidgeting with a rubber band in his lap. He looks up, without looking at me. "People feel shame to admit that someone in their family got AIDS. They try to hide it. And when someone dies, they can say he died of cholera or some other disease that has similar symptoms."

"No wonder I'm having trouble getting people to talk about AIDS. It's taboo, in a sense."

"Yes, somewhat I'm afraid."

"Do you know of anyone in the group you led who knows someone affected by AIDS? Or someone who has AIDS himself who might be willing to talk with me about it? I know it's a risk, but if someone were willing to meet me, it would help me understand how this gorilla-sized disease attacks people here."

He flashes a brief smile at my analogy and stops to weigh my request, looking out over the front lawn. A bird with a long black and white tail whistles from the papaya tree, then flies down to the broken fruit on the ground and begins pecking at its succulent, soft skin. "Yes," he nods slowly. "I might know someone. But people here don't like talking about it, especially if it involves family."

"*Ni nda menya.* I understand," I say quietly, thinking about the way a Kenyan friend told me that her son had died of typhoid fever, when I knew it was probably AIDS. What Jumbe says fits; it has a familiar ring.

"It sounds like Malawi," I reflect. "When I was there in the early '90s, we began losing so many students to AIDS at the university that the faculty became frightened they might get it, too. And sure enough, some did, but they were afraid to admit it. They'd go to a *sinyanga,* a traditional healer, hoping to find a cure. There was even a rumor going around that a well-known *sinyanga* was advising that if a man got AIDS, he would be cured if he slept with a virgin." I feel a sense of irony, remembering the consequences.

"For girls in secondary schools," I continue with purpose, "there was a real danger. Traveling men would seek them out, offering sweets or to buy them a pair of shoes in exchange for sexual favors. I knew of one girl in a secondary school in Nykosi who slept with a truck driver for money to help pay for her school fees. She died of AIDS. The girl's death shocked the teachers and really upset the other students. It was a crisis they didn't know how to handle. That was in 1991. Come to think of it, I also know a Kenyan teacher who had similar problems with her students in the late '80s. The girls were becoming prey for sugar daddies who offered to buy them things in exchange for a night with them. The guys feared sex with any grown woman, other than their wives, knowing they might get HIV/AIDS. But becoming an ostrich with its head in the dirt won't help."

"The same thing has happened here," Jumbe admits. "I know of a girl who died at Kabari Girls Secondary School for the same reason."

"Kenya is taking a big risk if people refuse to look the disease in the eye and confront it openly, like they finally did in Uganda. They had a serious AIDS crisis there in the 1980s and lost nearly a tenth of their population. When a new government came into power, it launched an aggressive national campaign that reached down to local villages to stop the AIDS plague before it killed all the young people."

"Maybe the new president will begin a campaign here." Jumbe is silent for a moment. "I do know one guy pretty well who might help you. His parents both died of AIDS. Let me see him and ask him if he'd be willing to speak with you. Would you be willing to give him some shilling or something for his trouble?"

"Yes. Of course. Talking with him would be helpful, Jumbe. Having seen the monsoon speed with which AIDS can move on communities, I know its devastation to families. Some villages in Malawi have been left parentless. Rather than sending the children to an orphanage, the mother's relatives take them in to ensure that siblings stay together and are raised in their natal village. I'm part of a support group that is assisting one of these AIDS-decimated villages. And we still have AIDS in the U.S., though you may not hear about it. Anti-retroviral drugs have helped to control the disease, but there isn't a sure cure. Some guys in the U.S. think they don't have to worry either, because there's a cure for AIDS.[*] They're fooling themselves."

"I thought Americans could be cured," Jumbe says.

"I saw an article in *The Standard* about the AIDS problem in Kakamega Provincial Hospital in western Kenya," I continue. "It said over half of the hospital's beds are occupied by AIDS patients. They've got a program planned to give anti-retroviral drugs to the worst-hit patients, but it's been delayed. The superintendent of the hospital says it's because of 'lack of funds and a modern laboratory,'" I gesture, curling my first two fingers on each hand into quotation marks.[32]

Jumbe grins at my fingers then becomes sober. "It couldn't be that bad here."

"I don't know. A girl in one of the groups in Kagumo told me after our meeting that 'Everyone here knows somebody who has died of AIDS.' And I just saw an article about a Kenyan artist, John Solly Savala...I think that was his name. He paints pictures showing the effects of AIDS for rural communities. Have you seen any of his work?"

"No." Jumbe scratches the side of his head.

---

[*] An anthropologist friend in the U.S. reported that male students at the University of Texas have a nonchalant attitude about HIV/AIDS because they think there is a cure if they should get it.

"He belongs to a group that exhibits paintings of promiscuous behaviors that can cause AIDS. They also illustrate how people can take precautions against getting it. Savala's work is really good. I've only seen one poster about AIDS here—at a clinic in Kagumo. I wish I'd had more time to talk with that girl. Maybe I would have learned more about the disease here. It's like tracking a leopard in the grass!"

Jumbe nods sympathetically. "Let me ring my friend; and the next time we meet, I'll ask him if he can speak with you. His sisters suffered very much when their parents died. I'll let you know when I find out the answer."

"Thanks, Jumbe. And thanks for facilitating the group. Did you enjoy it?"

"Yes, once it got started. It was good that Wang'oo was doing the recording. It made it easier for me with him there."

"Being able to facilitate a focus group may come in handy for getting a job someday. Put it on your resume. I'll even write a letter of recommendation."

He lights up, relieved to get off such a depressing topic. "Never thought of that."

The next few days are crammed with work. It keeps me from thinking about Jumbe's offer and what it might elicit. Then, one evening when I've almost forgotten, he hails me in the sitting room.

"Hey, I think I have it worked out. Benjamin said he's willing to meet you. I suggested he come here so you'll have privacy. Wednesday is the day. Is four in the afternoon okay? He thinks he can get off work early."

"Perfect. Thanks, Jumbe. I owe you one. By the way, does he have a surname?"

"Kabuge." Jumbe grins. "Benjamin Kabuge. He wants to know how much you can pay him? He needs the money; he's trying to help his sisters through school."

"Heavens. I'm clueless. What do you think would be fair?"

"About 500 shilling [roughly $7.00]."

"Are you sure?"

Jumbe nods his head. "That's enough. It will help."

"Okay. Should I offer him a beer?"

"No. Tea is fine," Jumbe says, getting up to go.

It's my last week in Kirinyaga. Karuana is in the midst of pre-school meetings and classroom preparations that always accompany a new academic year. Her responsibilities as a seasoned biology and chemistry teacher include the Form One class's orientation to the school's science courses. Transcribing audio tapes for me is being sandwiched between other commitments. She works from her small house on the school's campus. I joined her the first two days because her house is quieter than Doctari's house, where the teenagers have laid claim to the sitting room with its TV. But today, when Karuana left, she warned them that I will be at home in the afternoon for a meeting and will need quiet for working.

When I return from a trip to Kerugoya for sodas and groundnuts, no one is about. The house is wrapped in silence. I go into the kitchen and get a banana to eat while I make tea and sandwiches for my meeting with Jumbe's friend, Benjamin. I pour the milk tea through a strainer and into a large thermos, then put the thermos, two mugs and a bowl of sugar onto a metal tray.

Settled at the far end of the dining table, I go over a batch of transcribed interviews, making notes in the margins. I lose track of time.

A knock on the half-opened French door and a voice calling *"Hodi...Hodi,"* startle me.

"Karibu," I call while hastily stacking my papers into a pile. "Benjamin?" I greet him at the door, offering my hand.

He nods with a half smile. *I'm Benjamin Kabuge, Jumbe's friend.*

"Nice to meet you. Come in."

Benjamin Kabuge is almost as tall as Jumbe, who is close to six feet. With a sparse, athletic frame, he gives the appearance of being a slightly hunched runner. His hair is cropped short. Olive brown eyes betray nothing as he enters and follows me to the dining table. He's dressed in brown slacks and a light blue shirt with a gray wool cardigan over it.

"I thought we'd sit here if you don't mind." I pull out a chair for him next to mine at the end of the table.

This is fine, he says, settling into a chair. *Do you mind if I take off my sweater? It's quite hot outside and I walked from town.*

"Not at all. It *is* hot. I'll get the tea." I disappear to the kitchen and return with the tray, setting it down in the middle of the table, then pour him a mug of tea and offer him a spoon and the sugar.

He helps himself to a couple of heaping spoonfuls, while I fetch a bowl of peanuts and the sandwiches.

Benjamin is looking at a photo poster of an "ideal house" in Thailand that hangs above the sideboard. Colorful posters of other "ideal houses" and gardens from Russia, Yugoslavia, Holland and England grace the walls around the sitting room. Doctari must have collected them at some point in his life.

"Do you like the house in Thailand?" I ask.

Yes. It's very grand. It must belong to a rich politician.

"It probably does." I laugh. "I've been to Thailand and seen a house like it, though not as large. I hired a small boat on a river to get away from tourists. I wanted to see how people live along the banks. It's a famous river because it's where British prisoners of war tried to make a last stand against their Japanese captors who forced them to build a railway bridge across the river Kwai. It happened during World War II. The Japanese wanted to conquer Burma, next door. A lot of European prisoners died during the building of that railroad. Even a few Americans." Why am I going on like this? I wonder. Maybe it's nerves. How will I bring up AIDS?

"Ni'guo? [Is that so?]" Benjamin says, helping himself to a sandwich. *I didn't know the British were held prisoners anywhere.*

"In Thailand they were forced to work on the railway in hot steamy jungles. A lot of them died of exhaustion, cholera or malaria. For some, it was a combination of all three."

That's amazing. I had no idea. Then he's silent for a moment as he bites into his sandwich.

I watch the way he handles the half sandwich. His hands are sensitive and expressive, grasping the sandwich as if it were a butterfly. I like the way his tapered fingers move to hold the soft bread. If his hands are any indication of the soul inside, he's a sensitive person. I must be careful in my questions, patient and alert to his needs.

"Did you and Jumbe go to school together?" I ask, changing the subject.

Yes, we were at St. Martin's Secondary School. He finished one year ahead of me. We were in the same hostel.

"Please have some groundnuts." I push the peanuts toward him.

Thanks. I like eating groundnuts with tea. He takes a handful and holds them in one hand, rubbing his thumb back and forth against his fingers to loosen the nuts from their dry skins. *In western Kenya they serve them together all the time, but here people don't do that.* He shakes the red skins onto a plate, and then empties the nuts cupped in his hand into his mouth, chewing thoughtfully.

I help myself to some nuts, following his example. "How did you happen to go to western Kenya?" I ask.

My father's brother stays out there. He's with the forestry service in Kakamega.

"I know the forestry station out there. I visited it once in the '80s."

Really? Then you know about eating tea with groundnuts.

"Sure. But out there they always serve them hot, fresh from the pan. They're scrumptious that way."

I know…I miss being able to visit there.

"You don't visit your uncle anymore?"

Only on holidays. He was the one who took in my older sister when my mother passed on.

"How long ago was that?"

About two years ago, when I had just completed St. Martin's.

"How did your mother die, if you don't mind my asking?"

It's a long story. My father was diagnosed as having AIDS several years ago, when we lived in Nairobi. We never knew how he got it. The family came here to Kerugoya to be near my father's younger brother and his family after my father lost his job. He planned to help his brother on the farm, but he was getting weaker. Benjamin stops and sighs slightly.

My father was finally admitted to Kerugoya Hospital, then to Nyeri Hospital as his condition got worse. It was difficult for my mother. She and my uncle's wife were taking cooked food to him every day, and my mother was not so well herself.

He pauses and takes a long sip of tea. I remain silent and drink my own tea.

My oldest sister was 16 at the time. She was enrolled at Moi Girls. The lastborn, a girl, was enrolled in a primary school here.

"How old was she then?"

She was eight and in Standard Three. He looks down for a moment. *My father became worse and worse until he began looking almost like a skeleton. We could hardly recognize him. He finally died during Christmas holidays two years ago.* He pauses. *It felt like a big hole was left in the family. As the oldest, I had to get a job to help the others rather than continuing my education. Someone had to pay for Claudia's school fees, and we wanted Phoebe to continue schooling, too.*

"That must have been very hard for you," I offer softly. "I lost my father in an airplane accident when I was 14. It's not easy to lose a parent."

For me it was both my parents. First, my father, then my mother. At the beginning my mother told us my father had died of cholera, but I overheard her talking about his death being related to AIDS with the wife of my father's brother. Then I knew the truth. I told my mother not to be cheating us that way. If my father died of AIDS, we should know. After that my mother began warning Claudia and me about the dangers of AIDS. She'd say things like, "Take care of yourself. Don't take up with anyone with loose ways." When I heard her say these things, it made me sad and angry at my father.

But then I began to see my mother growing thinner and thinner. Benjamin stops and swallows hard, his eyes misting. *And she had trouble doing things she normally did, like cultivating the maize. I suspected then that she might have AIDS, too, but I didn't tell Claudia. She was boarding at Kabari's Girls so that made it easier as we didn't see one another so often.* He stops and looks out through a distant window as if struggling with his emotions.

My urge is to reach out my hand in sympathy, but I'm not sure he'll understand my gesture, so I remain silent, listening.

When my mother died six months after my father, it was a big shock, especially to Claudia. You might say she went crazy. She used to be among the top students in her class, but when our mother died, it was as if she became someone else. Her marks started falling in school, and the headmistress called my uncle. My younger sister came to live with my father's younger brother and his family who had children close to her in age. That way she could continue going to Kerugoya Primary. But my older sister dropped out of Kabari's Girls and ran away to Nairobi to stay with a friend of hers from childhood. We learned that she was smoking and getting into trouble, and the friends' parents sent her back to my uncle here. Benjamin's mouth is turned down at the corners as he studies his mug. His look is one of desolation.

I tried to talk with Claudia, he says, a sense of urgency in his voice, to ask her what was wrong. "What do you think?" she said. "If our father hadn't gotten AIDS, our mother would be alive."

What could I say? She knew our mother had died of AIDS, too. There was no hiding it. She was angry, furious at our father's weakness. And our mother's passing shocked her.

"How terrible for you."

Ii, that was a tough time. I finally found a job clerking at a shop in Kerugoya, where I still work today. But my sister Claudia was becoming worse and worse. She refused to go to school. When my uncle insisted, she ran away again. It was as if she'd turned into a wild animal, someone we didn't know. Finally, my younger uncle consulted with our father's older brother in Kakamega, and they decided that if Claudia were sent to him in Kakamega it might be better because his family is far from Nairobi. And he has teenagers who are my sister's agemates. Benjamin takes another sip of tea and then pushes it away.

"Can I give you some hot tea? There's more."

No. Ni nda hona [I'm satisfied].

It was my mother's death that caused my sister to go crazy. It's as if she doesn't care if she lives or dies. She was such a good student. At the top of her class! And now, it's such a waste! He spits it out with a bitterness that catches my breath.

I recognize his anguish. It takes me back to another time in my life, when I, too, as a teenager felt life was not worth living. But growing up in the shadow of AIDS must be a suffocating burden for any kid whose parents have died of this insidious disease.

"It must be really painful, seeing your sister destroy herself. Is it working out in Kakemega?"

Not really. She's still running away...as if something is threatening her. Tears come to his eyes and he looks away, his hand quickly brushing the rim of one eye.

"Benjamin, I can't tell you how sorry I am to hear what happened to your family. AIDS really is a monster. How is your little sister doing?"

She seems to be okay.   We were lucky that my uncle and his wife took her in. She is being looked after well. She gets sad every once in a while and asks if her mother hasn't just gone away for a time. Then I have to remind her that she saw her at the funeral. She gets quiet then, but in the next minute she's talking about school or what one of her cousins did. I think she'll be okay. It's my older sister who bothers me. I don't want to see her destroy herself.

"Let's hope something happens to pull her out of her hole. Does she go to church?"

She used to when she was here in Kerugoya. But I don't know now. I'll be seeing her over the Easter holiday. I'll look into it then. He's thoughtful for a moment. *Do you know of any schools in America that might take her?*

"Not offhand. But it's very hard to get a student visa anyway these days. I don't think going to America would be the answer. Kenyan students find it very hard adjusting to the realities of our country, especially when they see people living on the streets. The U.S. is not what it seems from here." I feel the need to change the subject. "How did you find the discussion that Jumbe led?"

It was interesting. Some of the things we hadn't thought about before...like that there could be a real change in the school curriculum, that computers are here to assist in changing how we do things.

"Why hasn't the government made more of an effort to educate people about the AIDS crisis?"

I don't know. People resist talking about it, like they'll get it just by mentioning it. Maybe it will change now that Kibaki is president.

"Let's hope so. Now...do you have any questions you want to ask me?"

He stops to think, the turns to face me. *Yes. How do people with AIDS in America get the medicines they need to cure it?*

"Well, first of all, anti-retroviral drugs don't cure anyone. They control the disease, giving an infected person a longer life."

Really? I thought America had a cure.

No. The cost of anti-retroviral drugs is coming down so they are affordable for more people, but they're no cure. Some clinics treat AIDS patients and have medicines that cost very little."

I wish we could get those medicines.

"I do, too. If American drug companies changed their minds and allowed poor countries to buy generic anti-retrovirals, it would help. But these companies carry a lot of weight with our government right now. They even persuaded Bush to veto an international agreement that would have made it possible for countries like Kenya to purchase generic drugs at a low cost."[33]

We hear that it is mostly homosexuals who get AIDS in America. Don't any women and other men get it?

"Of course. But AIDS first spread through homosexual relations. Now people know that anyone can get it unless they take precautions. Even babies can be infected. Are the schools here teaching about precautions?"

You mean like abstinence and not being loose?

"That and using condoms, what we call "safe sex" in America.

Mostly we're taught about abstinence. But some clinics give out condoms.

I look at my watch. It's nearly six. "I can't believe the time! I've kept you talking too long. It has helped me understand how bad AIDS is for a Kenyan family. It would be great if Kibaki took the lead in trying to stop it from spreading."

I take an envelope filled with hundred shilling notes and hand it to Benjamin. "This is just a small token of my thanks, Benjamin. What you've shared today is invaluable. It can't be measured in shilling. *Ni wega muno muno.*"

We get up and he stretches with his hands at the back of his neck. *I hope I will see you again before you leave. And if you see me in Kerugoya, please greet me.*

I smile. "I certainly will. Let me take you to the gate."

Benjamin takes his sweater off the back of the chair and puts it on while I tie my tennis shoes. Then I walk with him to the gate, where we shake hands.

Coming back into the house, I realize I need to write down everything that has transpired in the last two hours while it's fresh. I gather up my notebooks and retreat to my room to work, sitting Indian fashion on the unmade bed. I locate my journal hidden under a pile of papers.

As the sky begins to darken, I hear Karuana and Doctari enter the house. I can hear them removing their shoes. I stay in my room, writing.

"Jean?" Karuana calls through the door. "Are you there?"

"Yes. I'm here. I'm writing. How was the day?"

"Not bad. How was your meeting with Jumbe's friend?"

"It went well. I'll tell you about it later."

"Do you want a cup of tea?"

"No thanks. I've already had one."

"Okay. I'll let you do your work."

Questions crowd my mind. Benjamin said, "We didn't know how my father got AIDS." Would it have helped if he'd been told? Would it have served as a lesson? After nearly 20 years of the disease's appearance in Kenya, are most people still in denial? What would it take to change the culture of reticence that surrounds AIDS?

Moi's government left it largely up to health organizations to educate people about HIV/AIDS. Is that enough? Or like Uganda, does it take a commitment on the part of the government to tackle AIDS on a national scale so that donor resources to combat the epidemic can be used more effectively? Would it be easier for hospitals with limited laboratory and financial resources, like the Kakamega District Hospital, to attract donor funds and AIDS expertise if the new government launched a first-class campaign against the disease?

What about the effect of AIDS on communities and families? Are resources readily available to help AIDS patients and their families in towns such as Kagumo and Kerugoya? With the scarcity of anti-retroviral drugs in African countries like Kenya, Zimbabwe and Malawi, is death the inevitable outcome? What kinds of social services exist to assist extended kin to care for the orphans of HIV/AIDS victims? I ponder the quandary that Benjamin's family faced. After the death of their parents, the children were split up to be cared for in the homes of paternal relatives. Is there an alternative?

Finally, I mull over the problem of Claudia, Benjamin's sister, and the crisis that it provoked in this teenager's life. Do boarding schools have the necessary resources to cope with children in such crises? Are counselors trained to handle the problems of youth whose parents are afflicted with HIV/AIDS or who contract AIDS themselves? Claudia couldn't cope with the crisis, and there was no one at home or school to help her through it, to provide guidance and empathy. Without this support, Claudia is likely to wind up on the streets. That is Benjamin's fear. It's a legitimate one.

Karuana and I are madly transcribing tapes. It's the week she begins teaching. The primary schools have been in session for a week. The "rush to education," as the newpapers are referring to the reintroduction of free primary education, brought a myriad of problems. Schools were overwhelmed by the response, and many were unprepared. It is prompting a running commentary in the daily papers and among talking heads on TV.

A *Daily Nation* editorial advocates involving local district councils in building more schools and providing desks and other equipment to ease overcrowded classrooms. It suggests that these councils might pay a portion of the cost of educating teachers.[34]

The new Minister of Education, Professor Saitoti, has taken a few tentative steps toward solving the crisis. Parents will not be allowed to transfer their children to new, better schools, and children enrolling for the first time must do so at the school nearest their home. Some parents had used the new initiative as an excuse to switch their children to better schools. Double shifts may be initiated as a partial solution to crowded classrooms. Employing more teachers will have to wait. Funds are not available.

With free education the morale of teachers in suddenly overcrowded classrooms is worse. The teacher shortage has reached crisis proportions, exacerbated by a hiring freeze. Saitoti promises that help is on the way (possibly from the World Bank) to pay for hiring trained teachers presently out of work and for training new ones. He has formed a ministerial task force for implementating the new free education program. Every time I hear the term *task force*, especially at the national level, I cringe. A task force tends to operate at a snail's pace and offers recommendations that have no binding power.

The director of Central Province education, which is responsible for schools in Kirinyaga district, announced that nearly all schools in the province have seen Standard One enrollments double since the beginning of the school term. To solve the immediate problem of teacher and classroom shortages, the provincial education department will initiate learning shifts. Some first-graders will come in the morning, others in the afternoon. It's a beginning.

In the U.S. we take education for granted, forgetting that our parents have paid the costs, first through taxes and increasingly through special fund-raising efforts. Education is a given. In Kenya's rural areas it is not. It is a privilege that parents like Nyambura, Wanja and other women in Mutira struggle to secure for their children every day of their lives. And it is through education that these children have the best chance of learning about AIDS and what they need to do to protect themselves against it. Other educational initiatives that reach a broader population also are underway. The Women Fighting AIDS in Kenya organization (WOFAK) is tackling the disease using a bundle of approaches, including less costly treatments that make use of local herbal medicines under research in Kenya.[*]

An initiative that links AIDS education with basic education is crucial. The health of the nation depends on it.

---

[*] WOFAK employees an herbalist, Jacenta Wairimu, who sees drawing on Kenya's botanical roots and the knowledge of traditional healers as a way of providing less costly alternatives to AIDS treatment (Gathanju, Denis Maina, "Kenya's Herbal Rebirth," *The Herb Quarterly*, 103, 2005, pages 46-49 (also www.herbquarterly.com).

CHAPTER 14

Kwa Heri Kirinyaga

"We're leaving. Are you coming?" Karuana's voice is insistent. It's Sunday. She and Mugo are headed for church in Kerugoya. I saw little of them yesterday because I spent the whole day up in Gatwe with my "sister" and her family. The tenor of Karuana's voice makes me feel queasy. I *should* go to church with them this last Sunday, but I'm not.

I've gone twice this month. The service is held in a large hall, like a state fair exhibition venue with windows on both sides. The difference is a dais at one corner of a slightly raised, wooden stage at the front and the Anglican Church's religious symbols carved in contrasting shades of wood on a large plaque. A modern painting of an ebony-skinned Jesus hangs at the back of the stage.

People get dressed up for church here, even the teenagers. I've seen very few women in trousers. Men wear suits and ties. The service is in Kikuyu, and everyone brings their Kikuyu Bibles; the Kikuyu version is at the front of the Bible, the English at the back. Two weeks ago, all the children and youth who were returning to school for the new term were called to the front of the church for a blessing from the pastor. So many came forward that they filled the nave and crowded the aisles. When I looked around, there were large gaps in all the rows of metal chairs, only a few adults here and there. Two-thirds of the congregation was involved in that blessing! It was some ceremony, one that brought tears to my eyes thinking about all those kids eagerly heading back to school. Wamuyu and three of her friends, and Tony and Jumbe were among those blessed. The ceremony was followed by a rousing, pulsating hymn accompanied by tambourines and drums that brought everyone to their feet, swaying and dancing like any rocking African-American church in the U.S.

But today I need to stay home. I crave solitude to get organized for moving on.

"Okay," Karuana says. "It looks like none of the kids are going either. I guess it's just me and Doctari this Sunday."

"Sorry," I offer lamely.

"That's okay." Karuana waves as she goes out the door. "See you later."

The house is blissfully quiet. I take a deep breath and focus on staying calm even though I've been unable to reach Air Madagascar. I've been trying for three days. From Kenya I travel to Madagascar, a large Indian Ocean island that once was part of Africa, to join a World Wildlife Fund group. Air Madagascar flies between Nairobi and Antananarivo, Madagascar's capital, only once a week—on Mondays. I *have* to make that flight tomorrow.

I hear the Peugeot's motor purring, then a sudden commotion as Wamuyu dashes out the front door. The car door slams. I go to the window and pull back one of the heavy curtains. The front yard is deserted. The clotheslines look forlorn this morning without their usual array of shirts flapping like colorful prayer flags in a steady breeze. Unlatching a window, I push it out to let in the fresh morning air, daring a mosquito to enter. Leaving windows open at night here is madness; screens are nonexistent, and mosquitoes, those vectors of malaria, are voracious little beasts.

What I remember of malaria is a wicked high fever, chills, aches and hallucinations. At one point, as I wrestled with the fever, I thought *Maitu* and her women's church group from the Full Gospel Church were shuffle dancing in a circle under a full moon outside, singing incantations to bring me back to life. When I came to several days later, the old lady told me that she and her group from the church had, indeed, come into my room with candles and had sung chants around my bed, praying for my recovery. I guess it worked, along with a locally produced medicine. In ten days I was up again, though moving slowly. My run-in with malaria gave me a renewed respect for what Africans have to contend with every day of their lives. HIV/AIDS is only one of the many disease bullets they have to dodge in order to survive.

Packing up my gear prepares me for making the transition from a country I know and love to one I can barely imagine, Madagascar. This large island off the coast of Africa was originally settled by Indonesians, Arabs and East Coast Africans. It later became a French colony before its independence in 1970. It has lots of lemurs, large and small, chameleons galore and a host of exotic reptiles and birds. I've read that Indonesians dominate the country politically, and that Muslims, both Arab and African, are about 15 percent of the population and growing. I know less about the ethnic Africans. As in many countries, racial mixing, in this case between Africans, Indonesians and the smaller Arab population, has proliferated, adding zest to the island pot. A tiny expatriate French community persists, with its own unique flavor. That's the sum of my knowledge. Madagascar's unique wildlife and its people draw me eastward toward the Indian Ocean.

Once I finish packing, I settle down in the front room to finish a novel, *Cane River*, that I want to pass on to Karuana for its insight into American slavery and the history of race in Louisana. Wang'oo and Jumbe are nowhere around and I suspect they've gone to town. On my last day here, we're celebrating the successful completion of our work together by going to Nyeri for Sunday dinner at the Green Hills Lodge, a favorite venue of local Kenyans.

The yellow Peugeot slides to a stop in the shade of a papaya tree. Jumbe and Wang'oo climb out of the back seat.

"You made it to church after all," I tease Wang'oo.

"Yeah. We missed our ride, so we had to walk."

"And it's getting hot," Jumbe adds, looking for sympathy.

"They surprised me," Karuana says, pleased her two had come.

"But they were very late," Wamuyu adds peevishly.

"Just because you got accepted to Limuru Girls doesn't mean you can be cheeky," Wang'oo chides his sister. Wamuyu learned on Friday that, as the girl who placed first in the district on the Primary School Leaving exam, she had won a place in one of Kenya's top-ranked secondary schools. Limuru Girls Secondary School was her first choice. She and the family were elated.

"Never mind," Karuana smooths the ripple between her kids.

"Are you ready, Jean?" Mugo asks.

"Yes. I'm packed, except for the passionfruit."

He laughs. "You don't think they'll have some in Madagascar?"

"I'm not taking any chances."

"You sit in front with Doctari," Karuana orders me.

"Are you sure? I can sit with in back with the kids."

"No. It will be too crowded. We're used to it. You're not."

I get into the passenger seat and look back at the three lanky teenagers squeezing into the car with their mother. There's hardly enough room for Karuana. She's sandwiched between them, leaning forward on a fraction of the seat. She hands me her purse.

"Don't feel bad. You'll see more from up there."

The first time Wamuyu tries to close her door, it won't shut. She presses against Jumbe and tries again. The door shuts this time, squeezing the four of them into an accordion pleat.

We coast through the gates, then the car stops while Wamuyu, as the youngest, gets out to close the gates after us. It's the watchman's day off.

When she gets back in, the shift towards the center begins again. Poor Karuana. But this time, Wamuyu gets the door closed on the first try. We're off, stopping at the gas station in Kerugoya to fill the tank for Nyeri and the trip down to Nairobi tomorrow. Doctari offered to take me to the airport. "Anyway, Jumbe has to go back to college, and Wang'oo has to drop by his school. It's outside Nairobi," he explained. I know that if I were not around, they'd be crowding into a *matatu*.

We get through the crowded streets of Kerugoya and head north. It's slow-going in Kagumo between the speed bumps and the people and cars on the road. At last, we leave the budding town behind, winding through the tea-carpeted hills toward Karatina. The town has one of the largest outdoor markets in East Africa and is on the main road between Nairobi and Nyeri. Karatina has grown too, with two-story department stores and supermarkets sprouting up like mushrooms after a new rain.

After Karatina, we hit a divided, four-lane highway for a while, then the road narrows again, and we encounter a section with large potholes before getting to the turn-off to Green Hills Lodge. Arriving at the parking lot, the quiet crew in back tumbles out, stretching their cramped muscles.

Doctari gets out his camera and takes a picture to mark the occasion. Wamuyu wears a red-checked bandanna rolled and tied around her head. She came into the sitting room with it on one day last week. "Wamuyu, don't wear that thing," I heard Karuana tell her.

"Why?" Wamuyu asked, her brow crinkling.

"You know why," her mother told her emphatically.

Wamuyu took off the bandanna, said nothing, and walked out.

I was puzzled. When I asked Karuana about it, she said, "Wearing a red bandanna here means that someone is gay. I don't want Wamuyu wearing it."

Astonishment is what I felt, especially over Karuana's attitude toward homosexuality. I guess old attitudes die hard in Kenya just as they do in some parts of the United States. In any case, it seems that 13-year-old Wamuyu has declared her independence today, wearing the red headband regardless of her mother's views.

We walk slowly across the lodge's parking lot, which is edged by date palms, and trickle through the open lobby to the dining area on the terrace. Tables have been set up for lunch. It's 1:30, and only a few tables are occupied. The lodge, a single long building, is shaped like a crescent. It sits on a hill overlooking terraced gardens. Broad cement steps in the middle of the curve lead down to a broad expanse of lawn at the bottom. Flame-red poinsettias, bougainvillea in flamboyant shades of purple, red and pale apricot, and yellow lantanas are everywhere. Lush, dark-green coffee bushes in full bloom with sprays of tiny white flowers bracket the lawn and terracing. We take a table partway round the crescent and stretch out in comfortable lounge chairs. A skin-shrinking thirst leaves us drained, lethargic. We need a drink. "Have anything you want," I offer.

A waiter dressed all in white ambles over with menus to take our drink orders. The adults and Jumbe are the only ones who get menus. Age hierarchies! It nettles me that Wang'oo and Wamuyu don't get menus. "We'll share," I make a gesture to give my menu to Wang'oo.

"Keep it," he says. "I'll look at it later."

He doesn't seem to be perturbed by the slight. Age stratification is taken in stride.

Everyone looks to me to order first. Of course, I'm the oldest! I order a Tusker beer—*baridi* (cold). Karuana orders a Fanta, Mugo a Sprite. Jumbe and Wamuyu want sodas. Wang'oo, whose stomach is slighty off, orders a ginger ale.

"Can we order our main course now?" I ask, knowing how long it can take and judging that it might be even longer with this waiter.

"Let me bring the drinks first," he puts me off.

I resign myself to waiting and look over the menu, deciding on the braised lamb chops with rice and vegetables. Handing my menu to Wang'oo, I lean back in my chair, wishing I had something to fan my face with. Even with a slight breeze, I'm beginning to wilt in the heat.

"What are you having to eat?" Karuana asks Wang'oo across the low table.

"All I want right now is an omelet with chips."

"Is that enough?" she asks.

"Yes. I'm not that hungry."

"Okay." Karuana sighs in resignation. "Jumbe, what are you taking?"

"I'm going to have the same. I ate breakfast late." He gives her a rueful grin.

Karuana raises her eyebrows. "You're thin enough as it is," she says with a playful smile. I can tell Karuana likes Jumbe, as do her children. It's not hard to see why. He's charming and easygoing and has a wry sense of humor.

"What about you, Wamuyu?" Karuana continues.

"I'm having the chicken. It's my favorite."

I know it's my turn next. "I'm having the lamb chops. What about you, Karuana?"

"I think I'll take the chicken."

Karuana turns to Mugo, who, anticipating her question, says, "I'm taking the same thing Jean is having."

"I thought you would," she smiles at him and taps his arm playfully. "You men like your roasted meat."

So true, so true, I'm thinking. Whenever I've been out with Kenyan men, roasted meat is their preferred choice. Forget the vegetables. Bring on the beer and bar-b-qued beef, just like Texans.

After what seems like an eternity, the drinks arrive. "There was no ginger ale, so I brought another Sprite," the waiter says, putting the cold bottles down in the middle of the buffed wood table for us to divvy up. He hands me a canned beer with a glass.

We're all so parched it is all we can do not to gulp the drinks down in one go. I look around the table at these friends who have been my family for the past month. I feel a knot at the back of my throat. Leaving them will mean leaving part of myself behind. I want to remember them just way they are today—the kids relaxed, but slightly bored, their parents serene, enjoying the warm, lazy afternoon. I get out my camera.

"While we're waiting for our food, let me take a photo of you three," I gesture to Wamuyu, Wang'oo and Jumbe, "over there against that healthy-looking coffee tree."

They get up slowly and follow me along the terrace toward the end where two large coffee bushes filled with hanging clusters of white blossoms are planted in a raised bed. I can feel their slight resistance, but they oblige me by standing close together in front of one of the bushes. Wamuyu stands in the middle with her arms around her brothers' backs. She's dressed for the heat in a sleeveless white blouse and short skirt. Wang'oo still wears his white shell jacket, though the day is stifling hot. Jumbe has on a long-sleeved, navy blue and white T-shirt with a red swoosh above his heart. It's hard to get them to smile. They're wearing their *muntu* (serious) masks.

"Come on, guys, you'll make the *Sunday Standard.*" I get some half grins and quickly snap the picture.

The trio wanders off to have a look around the grounds while I'm busy taking a photo of Karuana and Mugo in front of a potted palm. We settle back at the table. With the young people gone, I use the opportunity to query Dr. Mugo about HIV/AIDS. He might have some insights that would shed further light on the disease.

"Mugo, why are people afraid to talk about AIDS here?"

"It's because it's usually caused by promiscuous sexual behavior, and no one wants to admit to that. I tell patients it is in their interest to be tested for AIDS, but few come for fear of finding out they might have it. Men think they are immune to the disease, and when someone has it, he says he has something else. A few who are educated about AIDS use condoms, but not many."

Mugo glances at Karuana, "And women are reluctant to insist men use them. It is usually the man who decides."

"That's true," she confirms. "Women are afraid to raise the issue with their men. There are so many other diseases that can kill our people; they tend to ignore AIDS...until it is too late."

"Even when women know they might be at risk?" I'm troubled by what I hear.

"Yes," Karuana pouts. "Women have been taught to please men, not to question them. At least, that's the way most uneducated women act."

Karuana, like her peers who have completed school, perceives herself to be more liberated than less-educated women. There is some truth in this, but it also creates a form of classism that separates rather than unites rural women around issues like HIV/AIDS or paternal child support. It is a disparity that organizations like Women Fighting AIDS in Kenya are trying to confront and overcome.

At this point, the boys' omelets arrive.

"Let's wash our hands," Karuana gets up. I follow her to a small sink on the back wall, disappointed that the exchange on AIDS was cut short. Mugo goes to hail the trio down on the lawn, letting them know the food has arrived.

The mingled aromas of roasted chicken and spiced lamb smell tantalizing. We savour our food without conversation. While we're eating, an African band with three male musicians and two women comes out onto the lawn below us and begins setting up their instruments and microphones.

When the music begins, it's a mélange of African high life and local ethnic beats. A troupe of five couples emerges from behind a cluster of banana trees and dances onto the lawn, singing a Kikuyu chant interspersed with ululations. The women, mostly in their 20s and 30s, wear modified traditional Gikuyu garb—short grass skirts, colorful tops that show their midriffs (in the past they would have been bare breasted), plenty of beads around their necks, tufts of grass and seed pods that act as rattles around their ankles. The men are bare chested and wear trousers to the knees with leg bells attached below. A few wear skin headdresses.

The couples dance slowly in a pulsating circle to the music, then form single lines with the men in back. The rhythm picks up as their feet move faster, then return to the slower pace in a circle. The steps come from Gikuyu dances laid down long ago. Other dances follow a similar pattern, but with a change of costume.

I notice that most of the female dancers are quite slim, except for one who is comfortably round but firm, as a well-fed Gikuyu woman should look by traditional standards. I glance over at Wang'oo and Jumbe. They seem bored. I am, too. The dances look strangely out of place, and the band is mediocre. Why do Kenyan hotels put on this kind of show? It has its place, I suppose, in hotels that cater to European tourists. But the clientele of Green Hills Lodge is largely African. I wonder what Mugo and Karuana think of the entertainment. They were the ones who suggested coming here. They seem to be enjoying the whole package, and each other.

We finish our meal and decide against ordering tea or dessert. I pay the bill, and we tromp down the steep terrace steps to the lawn and, wandering around the side of the building, find steps leading up to a swimming pool. I hear splashing and laughter. Two brown-skinned boys about ten and eight are diving into the pool and chasing each other around.

Wamuyu is transfixed. She can't take her eyes off the fun in the water. Does she wish she could be swimming, too? Or is she just enjoying the activity vicariously? Few rural Kenyans have ever been in a pool, and most don't know how to swim. If they do, they have learned in a river or lake. Pools are a luxury reserved for safari lodges, elite athletic clubs and the very wealthy. Only the most prestigious secondary schools have them. Watching Kenyan children swimming in one is not an everyday event.

We walk around the end of the pool, careful to avoid getting splashed. The boys' father calls them to get out. One boy hoists himself up on the side, but the other remains in the water, swimming slowly to the steps at the shallow end. We climb the steps to the terrace. The tables are filling up with couples and families.

The sun is beginning its downward journey as we pile back into the car and head for Kirinyaga. Squeezing into the backseat, Wang'oo and Wamuyu fall asleep the minute we hit the road. We clear Nyeri town, but trouble looms ahead. A partial roadblock manned by police has stalled traffic. There's no sawtooth metal barrier laid across the road to warn cars and trucks to stop for a routine inspection. I'm perplexed. A cop motions us to continue. We inch forward in the line of traffic. Then I see it.

A *matutu* lies crumpled on its side in a muddy ditch. Police are everywhere, but it appears that any injured and dead passengers have already been taken to Nyeri Hospital. I feel sadness for Karuana, knowing how this sight must remind her of her brother's death a year ago. Turning to look at her, I see that she has fallen asleep with her head resting against the back of the driver's seat.

It takes nearly an hour to get past this part of the road. Kenya still has too many *matatu* disasters despite the government's efforts to police the trade. I depended on *matatus* to get me between Kagumo and Nairobi in the 1980s. Most of my Kenyan friends still depend on them. I shudder thinking about the risks involved.

"That must have been a terrible accident," I comment softly to Mugo, so as not to wake the sleepers.

"There are still too many road accidents in Kenya, and the police ignore speed limits as much as drivers do." Mugo shifts his position behind the wheel. "Until that changes, we'll continue to see accidents. And some of our roads are in terrible condition. Let's hope Kibaki changes all that. This road to Nairobi is especially bad."

"I know. I used to drive it when I was working at Kenyatta University and rented a car for a while. By the way, thanks for offering to take me to the airport tomorrow, Mugo. With you, I know I'll get there in one piece. Whether the Air Madagascar plane will be there remains a mystery," I add lightly.

"You still haven't reached them?"

"No. They don't answer the phone. I just have to assume the plane will appear. An act of faith." I giggle to reassure him and myself that everything will fall into place.

"It should be there. Maybe there's something wrong with their phone. You know Nairobi."

"Could be. I'll find out tomorrow."

When we get home, it's nearly dark. We hurry into the house, dropping our shoes at the doorway, slipping into rubber thongs. The boys disappear into their quarters and Mugo turns on the TV to get the news. It's my last evening. I sit down and glance over the Sunday papers, then direct my attention to the news. Maybe I'll learn something more about the AIDS issue.[35]

"Do you want anything to eat?" Karuana asks from the dining area.

"No. I'm finished for the day. But I might get a soda. Would you like one, Mugo?" I get up to go into the kitchen as Karuana disappears behind the hall door.

"Sure. See if there's a Sprite."

I get our drinks and settle into the sofa. Karuana comes out with a *kanga* wrapped around her waist and a scarf knotted on her head. "I'm going with you tomorrow," she reveals. "I was able to get my friend to take the introductory science course."

"That's great news, Karuana. I feared you weren't coming, but I didn't want to ask because of school starting."

"I would feel terrible if I had to stay home. We'll take you to the airport first, then take Jumbe to college."

Gray dawn is creeping in when I wake up. I have a moment of panic thinking about what I'll do if the Air Madagascar flight has been cancelled. Still, I have a back-up plan. I lined it up before I left the U.S. My only alternative if I'm to meet the World Wildlife group on Wednesday is to fly down to Johannesburg this afternoon, sleep over and catch the flight from there out to Antananarivo on Tuesday. It would be an added expense, but it's feasible. Remembering this, I lie back against the pillow and do some back stretching exercises since I'll be sitting in a plane all day. I hear somebody in the hall, then the door to the toilet closing. Good. Someone else is up.

Grabbing my towel and some toilet articles, I go into the room with the sink and shower. Leaning over the basin, I splash cold water on my face. It's the way I wake up every morning. Drying my face, I move to a small mirror six by eight inches hanging on the teal-blue cement wall. I can hardly see myself in the mirror, it is mounted so high; it's the only mirror in the house. Standing on my toes, I apply sunscreen to my face and brush my teeth. When I exit, I nearly run into Mugo who is on his way to the kitchen. He makes the tea every morning while Karuana gets a few extra winks. I envy her the luxury.

Mugo has set a thermos of tea with several mugs out on the dining table. Going into the kitchen, I put the last two pieces of wheat bread into the toaster. Mugo turns on the TV, keeping the volume low, to watch the early morning news as he sips his tea. I look out the window at the water tank in back and see two men sitting on the cement ledge that runs around the bottom. One is shining shoes. They look like Mugo's. A rooster struts across the yard, having declared his identity earlier that morning. A few hens are pecking at the muddy dirt for seed. I don't see any sign of Mugo's mother.

Karuana emerges from the hallway with a *kanga* wrapped around her nightgown. She looks groggy. As I rescue my toast from getting too burned and butter it, Karuana asks, "Do you want some fruit salad for breakfast?"

"If it's fixed."

"It's in a bowl in the fridge."

I get a dish for the fruit. Walking over to the fridge, I see a two-inch cockroach scuttling across the red cement floor and step hard on it with my foot. I feel its crunchiness underneath my rubber thong and lift up my foot to see if I've killed it. Its black, shiny body is squashed, white innards seeping out. Putting the dish on the counter, I get the husk of a maize cob from the compost bucket and use it to pick up the remains of the cockroach. It's the first roach I've seen in the house. I forget about the fruit and take my plate of toast out to the dining area.

Karuana sips her tea with a far-away look on her face. I join her at the table but know better than to start a conversation. She isn't fully awake. Pouring myself a mug of tea, I turn my attention to the TV news. A commentator profiles a task force Kibaki has appointed to end the run-away corruption that began under Moi. Accusations are emerging, but it will take some time before investigations can be carried out and justice dispensed.*

After breakfast, I wander out to the front yard. It's 8:15, and the sun, looking like a fried egg against the pale morning sky, is doing its best to heat up the day. I look toward the *kithunu*, expecting to see one of the boys. But all is quiet. A last look around the front yard tells me nothing has changed. The clotheslines between the two papaya trees are empty, except for a skirt. The mango tree stands guard over the piece of ground I have come to treasure for its lush greenness and shade. I will miss this place, it fecundity, its promise. A sadness wells up inside me. I suddenly don't want to leave. It's always the same way...Kirinyaga sticks to my bones like flesh on my soul.

I look at my watch. It's 9:10. Where are Jumbe and Wang'oo? They dash out at the last moment and bolt down a cup of tea, half asleep. Wamuyu comes out to say good-bye. She is staying home. Standing next to the Peugeot, we shake hands and I give her a spontaneous hug. This 13-going-on-16 year old is destined for great things. "Good luck at Limuru Girls, Wamuyu. Study hard, but also have some fun."

She twists a little gold Hebrew symbol-of-life on a chain around her neck. I gave it to her for placing first in the district. "I will," she promises.

Then she shakes Jumbe's hand and gives him an enthusiastic hug. "Stay well," she tells him in Shang' with glistening eyes. She's going to miss this new big brother. She presses Wang'oo's flesh and offers him a hug, too. The boys and Karuana get into the backseat.

I slide into the passenger seat, then wave good-bye to Wamuyu through the window as we pull away from the house.

Heading south, the sun is blinding. I pull down the visor, saying to Karuana, "I'm sorry I couldn't get hold of Mama Njoroge.

---

* In 2003 Kibaki set up the Kenya Anti-Corruption Commission and thereafter parliament passed a series of anti-corruption bills. However, in 2005 the head of the commission, John Githongo, resigned, blaming his commission's inability to weed out graft and corruption on Kibaki's "lack of political will" and inaction. Githongo fled to Britain in early 2006 to escape reprisals. Kibaki reacted by letting go of ministers accused of graft, including the controversial Minister of Energy, Kiraitu Murungi, and Education Minister, George Saitoti, long associated with corruption under Moi's former regime.

We lost contact. She didn't write back after I was here last time, and I don't know if she's even at the same number. I've been trying to reach her all week. I hate not seeing her."

"I haven't seen her for a long time either, not since Mama Mwangi left to go to America. Mama Njoroge may be over there, too. That's what my in-law told me on the phone the other night, that he'd heard she was in America."

"Really? That explains it. I wonder how her son is doing in London?"

"What's he doing there?"

"He became a model."

"I never met him. He was gone before I knew Mama Njoroge."

"He was only five or six when I first met him. When I came with the students from the Branson School—that was in 1989—he was in secondary school. Mama Njoroge brought him up to Kagumo, and he stayed with us at the secondary school for several days, helping us make shelves for the library. He and the Branson students got along famously. When we went back to Nairobi, he came with us. We were staying out at the Jacaranda Hotel in Westlands for a few days before leaving to return home. A couple of the boys snuck him into their room for two nights. One of the maids found out and reported it to the manager. We were practically thrown out!"

Mugo laughs. "I bet they had a good time." The boys in back have fallen asleep.

As we pull up to a major traffic circle coming into Nairobi, Jumbe suddenly snaps to attention. "That's the roundabout," he says excitedly.

"What about it?" his father asks.

"It's the one that had the mountain of garbage in the center that President Kibaki promised to have removed within the first week of taking office."

Wang'oo wakes up and studies the traffic circle. "Looks like he kept his promise. *Takataka* [Swahili for the trash] has disappeared...and it was pretty awful."

"What was it doing there?" I ask, thinking it was a pretty weird place for a mound of garbage.

"People got tired of having no trash pick up and started dumping their garbage in the center of the roundabout."

"How long ago was that?"

"At least five years ago."

"And the city council didn't get the message?"

"No," Jumbe says. "They just ignored the growing pile."

"It's a good sign that Kibaki did something about it," Karuana notes.

"Maybe he'll keep other promises, too." Wang'oo sounds optimistic.

"Let's hope so," Mugo says.

The ostrich people are awakening, shaking off the lethargy and sense of despair I observed a decade earlier when Moi had claimed yet another five-year term. Small steps, like the removal of Nairobi's garbage mound, and larger ones—especially the return of free education and Kibaki's initial moves to end corruption—have made a difference. For the first time in years my friends see hope on the horizon, like the sun emerging after a season of long rains. *Wananchi* proved they could move the nation by voting in droves. There's new vitality in Kenya and Kirinyaga's villagers are part of it.

We cut over to Airport Road at another roundabout, avoiding the city center. When we get to the airport, it's just before noon. We've made good time. My plane leaves at 2:15.

"Why don't you go in and find out if your flight is leaving today while we stay here," Mugo suggests as we pull into a parking space near the international terminal.

My throat tightens and I swallow quickly. "Okay. I'll be right back." I get out of the car, full of foreboding, and head for an entrance. It's locked with chains laced through the handles. A security guard inside motions me to an exit down the hall. I walk to it and find it open but heavily guarded by uniformed security police.

"I need to check on my Air Madagascar flight," I explain.

"Let's see your ticket and passport," one of them says, looking slightly bored.

I get out my travel documents and he looks them over.

He waves me through.

For Nairobi's usually crowded, bustling airport, it is strangely deserted. Only a few travelers are lined up at a Kenya Airways counter and, further down, at an Air Egypt check-in. The place has a too-quiet, eerie feeling. I'm confused for a moment because I don't see an Air Madagascar sign. I approach a serious-looking airport guard and ask him for directions, wondering if the small airline disappeared with the noisy crowds that once filled the terminal.

He points to his right, and I continue down the row until I see the red Air Madagascar sign above a counter. Relief. A few people are in line. I don't see a schedule of flight departures anywhere, so I wait my turn and show my ticket to the airlines representative, who looks Indonesian. "Is the flight to Tana going today?" I ask her, a scared, dry feeling in my mouth.

"Yes. It's leaving on time."

My jaw relaxes. "Halleluiah! I've been trying to reach you for several days and couldn't get through."

"We've been having trouble with the phones. Do you have any luggage to check through?"

"Yes, but it's in my friends' car outside."

"You'll have to bring it in yourself. No visitors are allowed inside the airport terminal."

I look perplexed. "There was another bomb scare last week," she whispers, looking sideways to make sure she hasn't been heard. "But don't worry, we're taking extra precautions." This news doesn't leave me feeling any easier.

I return to the car waiting outside. "My flight is leaving today, and it is on time," I tell everyone. "But only passengers are allowed inside the airport, so we'll have to say our good- byes outside the entrance."

"Why?" Jumbe wants to know.

"Apparently there was another bomb scare last week."

"Oh. I think I saw something about it in the paper," Jumbe confirms as he gets out of the car.

Mugo goes around to the trunk and pops it open. The boys get out my two suitcases. I put on my backpack and balance my tote bag on the black roll-on, the one I will carry on. "Here," Wang'oo offers. "I can at least take it to the entrance."

"I'll take the other one," Jumbe insists.

I give up my bags, touched by their sudden show of chivalry.

Karuana takes my tote bag, and she and Mugo follow me to the guarded entrance.

"Thanks for all you've done for me," I tell them, my eyes glistening. Then turning to Wang'oo and Jumbe, I relieve them of my suitcases, and, shaking their hands, thank them for their help with the focus groups. "Stay well. I'll e-mail you when I get home, Jumbe." He has written down his school e-mail address on a slip of paper. He wants to stay in touch.

Last but not least, I reach for Karuana and pull her aside to give her an envelope full of extra 100-shilling notes I've collected as a bonus in addition to what I've paid her. She pockets the envelope quickly, and we hug while I try to hold back the tears.

"I don't know when I'll be back," I confess.

"But you *will* be back. You'll be coming even when they have to wheel you out of the plane in a wheelchair, and I'll be pushing you up and down the ridges to interview a new group of women."

We laugh, and I wipe the tears away quickly. "What a sight we'd make."

"Safe journey," she smiles, "and give my greetings to Stephen and Barbara, and Rick and his wife, and your daughter—what's her name?"

"Ann," I reply.

"Yes. Greet her for me, too, even though I've never met her."

I take hold of the handles of my roll-ons, one on each side, and approach the entrance. It's difficult to show the security guard my ticket and passport while wheeling both suitcases through. Once inside, I stop to put my travel documents in a small bag that hangs from my neck. I turn around and wave to my Kirinyaga friends, who have waited to see me disappear. Then I pull my suitcases up to the first security checkpoint, suddenly feeling isolated and alone in the ominously silent terminal.

Still, the return to Kirinyaga has spoken to my hopes and dreams. I never imagined the visit could be so rewarding, so filled with love. I came not knowing where I would stay, or who, of the women whose life stories I had gathered like precious beads on a string 20 years ago, I would meet.

I'm going home with a knapsack full of stories from a new generation that has witnessed the aging of their mothers and grandmothers, the global changes in their villages, and the transformation of their country from a one-party state to a multi-party democracy that embraces diverse voices and new ideas. I would not have missed this Kenyan moment for anything.

Indeed, *Kirinyaga* has awakened.

NOTES

Chapter 1

[1] International Coffee Council, <"Prices Paid to Growers in Exporting Countries in U.S. cents per lb. (Arabica): Kenya"> 2002, http:www.ico.org/asp/display7.asp.

Chapter 2

[2] Davison, Jean. *Voices From Mutira: Change in the Lives of Rural Gikuyu Women, 1910-1995,* Boulder: Lynne Rienner Publishers, 1996, p. 169, pp. 174-175, 176.

[3] Ibid. p. 176.

[4] Ibid. p. 177.

[5] Ibid. p. 168

Chapter 3

[6] Ibid. p. 172.

[7] Ibid.

[8] Ibid. p. 141.

[9] Ibid. pp. 86-89.

[10] Walley, Christine. "Searching for "Voices": Feminism, Anthropology, and the Global Debate over Female Genital Operations" in *Cultural Anthropology,* 1997, pp. 409-10.

[11] Anonymous Letter to the Editor, *Daily Nation,* January 4, 2003, p. 9.

[12] Maero, Titus. "NGO: Illiteracy to Blame for High FGM Rate in Pokot," *East African Standard,* January 11, 2003, p. 7.

Chapter 4

[13] Oirere, Shem, "Farmers Earn Less After Drop in Coffee Grade," *Daily Nation,* January 7, 2003, p. 14.

Chapter 5

[14] Nation Team, "It's War on Mungiki as Death Toll Rises to 23," *Daily Nation,* January 8, 2003, p. 1.

Chapter 6
[15] Davison, Jean. *Voices From Mutira,* 1996, p. 97. All other excerpts from Wamutira's earlier life narrative in this chapter come from Davison, 1996, pp. 80-106. I am indebted to Lynne Rienner Publishers for allowing me to use these selected passages.

Chapter 7
[16] "HIV Prevalence in Adults, End 2001," UNICEF Fact Sheet. New York: UNICEF, 2002. The Peace Corps Manual for Kenya, 2003, puts the statistic at 15%, but an accurate rate is difficult to assess as AIDS becomes confounded with other diseases that may take a Kenyan's life, such as tuberculosis or malaria.
[17] "Free School Starts Next Week," *Daily Nation,* January 3, 2003, p. 1.
[18] "Warning on School Fees," *Sunday Standard,* January 5, 2003, p. 1.
[19] "Free School Revived," ibid. p. 3.

Chapter 9
[20] This passage and other excerpts from Wanjiku's life story in this chapter are taken from Davison, Jean, *Voices From Mutira*, 1996, pp. 55-72.

Chapter 11
[21] This excerpt and others from Nyambura's life story are taken from Davison, Jean, *Voices From Mutira*, 1996, Ch. 8, pp. 197-208.
[22] "Big Rush as Children Grab Free School Slots, *Daily Nation,* January 7, 2003, p. 1.
[23] "Admission Chaos Hits Schools," *Daily Nation,* January 8, 2003, n.p.
[24] Ibid.
[25] Ibid.
[26] "Commentary," *East African Standard,* January 11, 2003, p. 11.
[27] Government of Kenya. Compiled from Table 1, Population by Sex, Age Groups and School Attendance, Central Bureau of Statistics, Ministry of Finance & Planning, 2002, pp. 1-5.
[28] "Teachers Warn of Pitfalls," *East African Standard,* January 11, 2003, p. 20.
[29] Muya, Wamahiu, "Councils Should Fund Free Schooling," *Daily Nation,* January 7, 2003, p. 9.

[30] Nation team, "Saitoti Acts to Clear Free Schools Muddle: New Guidelines Issues on Fees and Admissions," *Daily Nation,* January 9, 2003, p. 1.

Chapter 12
[31] Excerpts from Wanja's 1984 life narrative in this chapter are from Davison, Jean, *Voices From Mutira,* 1996, pp. 217, 223, 225-226.

Chapter 13
[32] Lumiti, Dennis, "Hospital Fails to Dispense AIDS Drugs," *East African Standard,* January 10, 2003, p. 4.
[33] In December, 2002, the U.S. trade representative to the World Trade Organization (WTO) had alone vetoed an agreement approved by all the other WTO countries, including Switzerland and the European Union, to allow the world's poorest nations to buy generic drugs to fight AIDS, malaria and tuberculosis. It wasn't until early September, 2003 in advance of global trade talks in Mexico, that a compromise was worked out between the U.S. and a key group of developing countries, including Kenya and South Africa, prompting the Bush administration to reverse its earlier decision.
[34] Muya, Wamahiu. "Councils Should Fund Free Schooling," *Daily Nation,* January 7, 2003, p. 9.
[35] Three years later, I learn that under Kibaki, the Kenya Medical Research Institute (KEMRI) is beginning HIV/AIDS vaccine trials in Kericho district in collaboration with the U.S. Walter Reed Foundation, a medical research unit in the army. The vaccine will be administered to volunteers after eight years of on-going research. (Tanu, Sonu, "AIDS Vaccine Test to Start," *East African Standard,* February 27, 2006, www.allAfrica.com).

GLOSSARY

In Kikuyu, u is often pronounced as a soft "o" and i as soft "a".

Agikuyu	Gikuyu people, pronounced Ah-gay-ko-yo
Mugikuyu	(s. form)
aii (also "ii')	yes
andu akuru	old people
asha	no
Cucu	Grandmother (pronounced "shosho")
cuka (kanga)	piece of cloth worn around lower half of women's bodies
gikabu	large, woven basket used for hauling tea leaves
gutara matu	piercing of earlobes
guthinjiro	animal sacrifice to seal betrothal
guthokia	gift of homemade beer during betrothal
haiya	expression of exclamation, as "wow."
harambee	Swahili, meaning "working together for self-help"
hinya	strength
Hodi	Anybody there?
ii	yes (pronounced "aye")
irio	general term for food, special dish of mashed potatoes and peas
Irua	initiation-circumcision ceremony
kaana	infant
kahii	small boy
kanini	little one
karibu/karibuni	welcome (s.)/welcome (pl.)
kirigu	small girl
kienji	broad-bladed knife used in traditional circumcision ceremony
kiondo	woven basket
kirigu	a big, uncircumcised girl

kirira	secret knowledge
kithunu	bachelor's hut
kiumbi	handsome
kubibo	traditional blood-sucking ritual used by healer
mabati	Swahili word for corrugated iron roofing
mariika (riika)	age-set (adolescents circumcised at the same time)
matu	pierced earlobe
matutu	minivan or station wagon used for transportation
mbuci	pierced upper rim of each ear
mugunda	cultivated garden for vegetables
mugomo	native fig tree (kagumo refers to a small fig tree)
muhiki	bride with a young child
muiritu	adult woman, traditionally circumcised
mukwa	sisal or leather tumpline for basket
mundu mugo	medicine man, traditional healter
muthuri	man
mutumia	woman with several children (grown woman)
mweretho	dance for young people in which young men fling their partners in the air
Ni guo	Isn't that so?
Ni ndigua	I've understood or heard
nduma	arrowroot
nduka	Swahili, meaning shop
Ngai	The Creator, God
ruracio	bridewealth
shamba	Swahili, meaning tilled field
shang'	special language of youth
skumawiki	Swahili, kale/collard greens
sufuria	Swahili, metal pot for cooking
thingira	man's house
thira	reed and bead skirt worn during Irua
tuthii	let's go
twana	children
ugali	Swahili, meaning maize meal porridge cooked to a hard consistancy

uhiki	married one, marriage
unga	maize meal
wamung'ei	traditional term for woman with several children, some of them circumcised
wanachi	Swahili, meaning "the people"
Wimwega	How are you?

ACKNOWLEDGEMENTS

Many people are responsible for assisting the birth of this book. First and foremost, I want to honor Karuana Kimiti and Dr. Mugo for their generosity and unfailing support. They gave me a home and assisted me in every way possible. I'd also like to thank their teenage children who became part of the project, organizing and leading discussion groups with their peers. My long-time friend J. Mithamo, likewise, was helpful. To all the wonderful people who have shared the nubby fabric of their lives over the years and whose children have picked up the threads, *nwega muno, arata akwa.*

At home, without the encouragement of publisher Lynne Rienner, who produced my earlier books on Gikuyu women and suggested I return again to Mutira, I might not have undertaken the journey. I also am indebted to her for giving me permission to use in this book, selected excerpts from the earlier life narratives and graphic materials that I produced with Lesli Brooks for *Voices From Mutira.*

My son, Rick Glascock, forced me to face certain issues connected with writing for a trade market that I'd sidestepped and, in his quiet way, supported the project.

Several reviewers of earlier drafts of the manuscript gave me the critical input I needed to launch the book. Among them were Cindy Brettschneider, Guiliana Lund, Nancy Heizer, Beth Carlson, B.J. Fernea, Patricia Saunders and Kathryn Rogers. In addition, the Deer Isle Writers' group in Maine listened critically to parts of the manuscript and gave me discerning feedback. Their affirmation is appreciated.

Many Kenyans in this country have given me support by making sure that this book gets out to all those who love Kenya and those who yearn to learn more about Africa.

ABOUT THE AUTHOR

Jean Davison is the author of four books. She is an anthropologist and international consultant who has worked in Africa for over 25 years. She was a prose co-editor of the Eggemoggin Reach Review, an anthology of short stories and poetry by Maine writers most recently. She founded a non-profit group, the International Development and Education Association (IDEA) in 1986. The organization has linked small communities in Africa, Asia and Latin America needing seed funds for self-help projects with sponsoring groups in the United States and Canada. Dr. Davison has been a consultant to a variety of international organizations, from the United Nations World Food Program in Sudan and the Kellogg Foundation in South Africa to Project Hope in Malawi. She also directed research projects for the U.S. Agency for International Development in Egypt, Ethiopia and Malawi. More recently, she has worked on the effects of the North American Free Trade Agreement on Mexico's workers and on peace issues in Northern Ireland.